F·R·O·M

ROSE BUDD'S

•KITCHEN•

A MUSCADINE BOOK

F·R·O·M
ROSE BUDD'S
KITCHEN

ROSE BUDD STEVENS

Foreword by Jerry Clower

University Press of Mississippi
Jackson and London

EDITOR'S NOTE: *From Rose Budd's Kitchen* is a collection of traditional recipes reflecting the way Southerners have eaten for generations. Many of the recipes have a higher fat, sugar, and salt content than generally recommended by physicians and nutritionists today. If these ingredients are of concern to you, you may wish to reduce the sugar, fat, and salt when preparing some of these foods.

Copyright © 1988 by the University Press of Mississippi
All rights reserved

Printed in the United States

92 91 90 89 88   5 4 3 2 1

Designed by Williams & Williams, Inc., Jackson, Mississippi

Illustrations by Sam Beibers

Library of Congress Cataloging-in-Publication Data

Stevens, Rose Budd.
  From Rose Budd's Kitchen.

  "A Muscadine Book."
  Includes index.
  1. Cookery, American—Southern Style. I. Title.
TX715.2.S68S84 1988   641.5975   88-27854
ISBN 0-87805-370-0 (pbk.)

Contents

Foreword

Rose Budd Stevens is a national treasure. Education and country and goodness and compassion and style and class were all homogenized in that process which formed Rose Budd Stevens. One reason she is so well liked and has entertained millions in writing her newspaper column "Along the RFD" is that from her childhood until now she has been blessed by living in the most fantastic period in the history of the United States or the world. If you will just review, you will see that just about everything that has ever been invented was invented during her lifetime. I share the period in which she has lived, and it is just wonderful to have seen so many of those things which make life comfortable and enjoyable being invented in our lifetime.

Rose Budd has seen it all. She has gone from making biscuits using flour and hog lard in a dough tray, squashing them with her fingers, and choking them off to TV ads bragging on who's got the best "homemade" biscuits at the fast food stores. She's gone from scalding and scraping and butchering hogs to walking up to a long counter and picking out any cut of hog meat she wants. She's gone from running down a frying size chicken, wringing its neck, scalding it, picking it and cutting it up, to just reaching over the counter and picking up the size broiler she wants.

She has gone from walking to riding in the horse and buggy, from the car to the jet airplane. She has gone from the old battery radio to the ultimate in stereo sound. When she was a little girl she heard folks arguing about "the world ain't round," and as an adult she has actually seen folks fly all the way around the world.

She has gone from striking a match and lighting a coal oil lamp (city folks call coal oil "kerosene") to flipping a switch and there is light. She came "along the RFD" before we had all the modern conveniences, so when she tells you how to cook something she has seen her folks or her own hands make it the hard way. She did not have any oven temperature to set, nothing to come on or go off automatically.

One of life's pleasures is eating. If Rose Budd tells you a rooster can shoulder a bale of cotton, you had better find a place to put the bale of cotton. If Rose Budd tells you how to whip up some vittles, you pay close attention and whip them up just like she says, and you will bite into a taste that will make a puppy pull a freight train. Anybody that wants to cook something fit couldn't do better than to cook something contained in Rose Budd's cookbook.

I love Rose Budd Stevens. I would trust her with my life. She has been and is a daughter, a wife, and a mother. She has seen rural life in Amite County as well as modern life in Amite County, and nobody can describe it like she can.

Another nice thing about Rose Budd is that she married a "good ole boy." That good ole boy knew how to catch them fish, hunt them rabbits, and set the proper example for them younguns.

I love Rose Budd because they did not have to get the Supreme Court to make her abide by the law on how to treat people. She has always believed in the rights of every individual, regardless of race, color or creed, and that folks ought to be treated like you would want them to treat you.

As I write this my heart is beating real fast, because at this minute nails are being driven in my new house and I'm moving back "along the RFD," where I'll once more be a neighbor to Rose Budd. Oh, just think, I won't have to do much cooking, because when I want a real fine piece prepared I know I can drop by Rose Budd's house and she'll help old Jerry fix it.

Jerry Clower

Preface

Many of the recipes in this book were sent to me over the past forty-one years by readers of my columns, to be used if found worthy. Very few of the senders said the recipes were original; most claimed only that their family had enjoyed eating these sure-to-please dishes, handed down from aunts, mamas, grandmothers and mothers-in-law. Even a few grandfathers who enjoyed cooking sent in their family standbys. Some of the recipes date back to the 1800s; cornstarch pudding is an early recipe we still enjoy here in 1988 when farm fresh fruits and berries are in season.

Recipes have been sent to me on torn paper bags, and I have been entrusted with the only copy of a recipe that had belonged to the sender's great-great grandmother. Thank goodness I took care of the recipes for Grandma's Winter Special Hash and for Boneless Pig Feet. The sender's granddaughter wrote for them a few years ago. And there they were, tucked away in the safe place I had left them—behind the kitchen clock.

The comments shown alongside the recipes are also mostly from my columns, and they are usually written in present tense. When you read the comments, you must realize that the present tense does not necessarily refer to the time this book was published, but to the time during the past years when the original column was written. If you're one who is interested in historical accuracy, you can get a general idea of the date by knowing the ages of the children who appear frequently in them. My own children—Ben, Will, and Celeste Willoughby—are the Joe, Tim, and Rose, Jr., of the columns. Today Ben is 48, Will 44, and Celeste 41.

The beginning cook who uses this book may notice that some recipes do not give exact quantities. A greens recipe, for instance, will call for, "a piece of pork the size of three fingers." Most cooks who have grown up around Southern cooking will know to cut the meat to fit the greens. Those new to

Southern cooking may have to experiment a little when the quantities of seasonings are not given in exact measurements.

I grew up cooking. When I was a little girl, I stayed under Mama's feet in the kitchen; so she started early teaching me to "help" her. I learned a lot also from Grandmother Budd and my maiden aunt Phleta, who lived with her just across the road. Both were good cooks. In their kitchen I had my special box to stand on before I was able to reach the cooking table. My own apron hung on a low hook behind the pantry door.

One thing they taught me was never to flood vegetables with water when cooking. I remember an iron dipper holding a scant half cup of hot water from the iron kettle. Grandmother never added more than one dipperful to any vegetable pot. The pot liquor from the vegetables was so rich and tasty; corn bread served in dessert dishes with pot liquor and chili sauce was a treat! She also let her greens make their own broth: after first searing a piece of meat (pork) in the pot, greens were washed and put directly into the pot, and watched very carefully with water being added as needed by the cooking spoonful.

My mother saw that Brother and I had our own split oak baskets to help gather garden sass, fruits in season from the woods, fields and gardens, and oak chips for making fires. We also helped to shell, snap, peel, pare, and chop the various foods we ate at mealtime.

Of course, I was brought up cooking on an iron stove using wood for fuel. Oven temperatures were "slow," "middling," and "hot." A cook opened the oven door, stuck a hand in the oven, and by feel knew when to put the biscuits in. Too hot for a cake? Just leave the oven door open a few minutes. Every kitchen had a huge wood box for stove wood. Children were expected to keep this box filled not only with wood, but with cobs from the corn crib, splinters from fat pine stumps, and oak chips from the post pile.

Rural households in my salad days were often run by a firm rule: "use it up, wear it out, make it do, or do without." There were no electric lines—therefore, no pumps to bring water from wells to kitchen and no lights in the house. Mama had a huge barrel mounted outside on a platform by the kitchen door. Rain water from house eaves drained into the barrel, and a pipe ran from it to the kitchen. Such a time saver this water was!

Our Southern meals were always rich with vegetables—fresh in season,

canned or dried for winter meals—all cooked with side meat from hogs raised, killed, and processed on the farm. In the springtime we would have mutton roast, steak, stews, or ground patties from the flock of sheep my father
kept for wool and food. A typical summer meal would be fried chicken, cut
corn, sliced tomatoes, field peas (stewed in their own juice), new Irish
potatoes, hot biscuit, corn bread, and a stack cake, cobbler, or two-crusted
fruit pie—with pouring cream, of course! If the ice truck came by, iced tea
was a special treat.

These meals I grew up with have remained the favorites in my own and
many other Southern households. Another practice from the old days I still
follow: after a heavy meal or a very spicy one, I always have a dish of
canned-in-its-own-juice pineapple to "clean your tongue"—the better to enjoy a
slice of lemon pie with mile high meringue!

When I married I took along with me the knowledge and practices I had
learned from growing up on a farm. Of course my husband Bennett (Dale in
the columns) and I did have a couple of modern conveniences: a small four-
eye iron stove (It cost $13.89—no tax!) and the heavy wood box filled with
sawdust that my father had placed in our backyard under an oak tree—our
ice box for almost ten years until electricity came over hill and dale to Shady
Rest. How we looked forward to Mr. Brosky coming in his Ford truck with
blocks of ice. For fifty cents he placed a large block of ice in the box. How
grateful we were to be able to dress chicken on Saturday for Sunday cooking!

Often in hot weather I cooked outdoors. We had holes dug in the ground
away from the house and fires made in each hole. When the fire had burned
down, black iron pots with food were put directly in the hole; iron lids were
on and hot coals heaped on top. Today people accomplish the same purpose
with the outdoor barbeque grill, but I was following my grandmother's example. For baking corn bread a side fire would be made—a slow one; I used my
three-legged black iron "spider" (cast iron skillet) with deep lid. After the
bread was poured in and coals heaped on the lid, the whole thing would be
covered with an old wash tub. Even gingerbread was baked this way. My husband and the children welcomed a cool kitchen to eat our night meal in.
And how firm the butter, cool the buttermilk, and crisp the cabbage slaw—
thanks to our sawdust ice box.

The changes in lifestyle from yesteryear till now are so obvious and so many they hardly need mentioning. Now many homes have one or more electric ice boxes, freezers in several sizes, and enough electric appliances to open a small shop. Today we have learned to eat light, mamas are in and out of the kitchen, and dishes are put in the dishwasher until later. But one thing hasn't changed: a true Southerner's taste for good country cooking.

Sweetly be,
Rose Budd Stevens

LIGHT COUNTRY FARE

Appetizers, Snacks, & Comforting Foods

Our Uncle Ben lived with his wife Mae a few hops and skips from our house on Shady Rest. They lived down the road toward the Primitive Baptist Church called Plymouth. Aunt Mae never drove their Model A Ford, never voted, never worked a day away from home, and never set foot in their gardens or in the fields. Uncle Ben saw to it that she had help with the housework at least one day each week. She did not milk the fine Jersey cow, nor slop the pig in the pen. Neither did she gather the eggs, feed the chickens, nor do the weekly wash.

Aunt Mae was a plump woman who enjoyed cooking, churning butter, doing fancy work, and having company. She was an excellent cook when it came to sweets. Her pineapple cheese pie was famous, as was her apple-cheese pie. She boasted that her buttermilk pound cake had no rival. And Aunt Mae sold her butter to many appreciative families.

A wood stove stood on a platform in the kitchen just off the house where she did summer baking and canning. Beside the kitchen was a long shelf where she worked up her butter after it had been lifted from the tall stone churn and washed in fresh well water. She expertly pressed every last drop of water from the big lump of butter, using a whittled paddle.

Then the art of making molds of butter came into play. The wooden mold had been scalded and chilled in cold spring or well water. Lightly salted butter would be pressed into a round half-pound mold with a sheaf-of-wheat picture carved into the bottom of the mold. When turn-ed out on a square of butter paper, the picture would be on top. Aunt Mae had molds with the following pictures: a lumbering-looking cow with a knocked-down horn, the wheat sheaf, a pineapple, a flower with five petals and leaves entirely different, and one with a pine bough carved on one side and the other side boasting dainty frilled leaves. Some of the molds had split over the years and were bound together with tightly twisted wire or heavy fishing cord. Families who wanted butter in pound prints were sent square blocks of butter with no fancy pictures on top.

Each Saturday Uncle Ben loaded up the Model A with farm produce, in season, and butter the year-round, which he took to Gloster to his "regular customers." Cousin Prentiss Lusk had a store in Gloster, and after the sausages, eggs, melons, and butter had been delivered, Uncle Ben went to the Lusk store for weekly treats to take home to Aunt Mae and to the hired man who lived just up the road: two pounds of hoop cheese, a box of crackers, stick candy, chocolate drops, a tall can of pink salmon, three cans of flat sardines, oranges, and bananas—three dozen of them when they were five cents a dozen.

Very often he bought delicious ginger stage planks, iced with a wash of vivid pink icing. The two stage planks were scalloped on all sides and slipped into a waxed paper envelope. If we happened to be at Uncle Ben's when he came from Gloster, we were treated to a single stage plank, a sardine or two, a stick of candy, plus banana for dessert—with lemonade made with ice so cold our teeth ached!

Boiled peanuts always smack of fall to me. We can hardly wait for them to fill out properly. We dig buckets of them by the little branch that runs swiftly over sharp clean rocks and wash them in the cold water. We pick off the stems that have escaped our dirt-caked fingers and throw out the ones that are clearly pops.

Always I boil the first batch in the black pot, and never do we end up with as many as we started boiling, so peanut hungry are we. The whole family keeps dipping the wooden spoon into the swiftly boiling water to get a few nuts to see if they are ready. It doesn't matter that they're only half

Shrimp Appetizer

3 cans shrimp, drained
2 T. parsley
1 stalk celery
Mayonnaise to mix
Lemon juice
Cayenne pepper

Mash shrimp to fine paste; cut celery into very small pieces; chop parsley fine. Mix well with mayonnaise; season to taste with a little lemon juice and cayenne pepper. Serve in pretty dish surrounded by assorted salty crackers. Tiny sweet pickles add extra crunch served on the side.

Smoky Olive Dip

1 cup sieved cottage cheese
1 3-ounce pkg. cream cheese
2 T. sweet cream
¼ tsp. Accent
½ T. onion, minced
½ to ¾ tsp. Liquid Smoke
A bit of garlic or garlic juice
½ cup minced ripe olives

Beat cottage cheese, cream cheese, and cream until fluffy. Add seasonings, fold in olives, and chill.

Serve with celery curls, carrot sticks, and cauliflowerets as dunkers. For a spread, use less cream and serve with Wheat Thins.

Roll-ups

1 2-ounce tub softened cream cheese
2 green onions, chopped fine
1 tsp. Nature's Seasons (seasoning salt)
1 4½-ounce jar mushrooms, chopped
2 cans crescent rolls
Beaten egg
Poppy seeds

Stir cream cheese, onions, seasoning salt, and mushrooms together. Separate crescent rolls into 8 rectangles. Divide cream cheese mixture into 8 parts and spread evenly on dough rectangles. Re-roll. Brush with egg and sprinkle liberally with poppy seeds. Slice in ¼-inch thick rounds. Bake on cookie sheet at 375 degrees for 8 to 10 minutes or until golden.

Hot Cheese Balls

1 cup grated cheese
1 tsp. flour
1 egg white, stiffly beaten
½ tsp. salt
Dash black pepper
Cracker meal or cracker crumbs

Mix seasonings and flour with grated cheese. Beat in stiffly beaten egg whites. Form into balls and roll in cracker crumbs. Fry in deep hot fat, serve hot. Chili sauce goes well with these goodies.

done. The boys throw them from hand to hand to cool them, and Rose Jr. goes on the porch and pours a dipper of water on hers to cool them. I squish a few between a clean dish cloth and eat them very hot.

When they do get done, I drain them and sit the pan on the porch to cool. All comers help themselves and soon there is a row of shells to the barn, to the pear tree and around the house.

Store popcorn in the refrigerator and the moisture that the corn draws will help make each kernel pop up fluffy.

This is especially good when served with crisp cheese thins. You can also serve it with beef roast, vegetable dinner, or as a topping for hamburgers.

Stuffed Dill Pickles

12 large dill pickles, cored
3 cups brown sugar
2 cloves garlic, cut up

Mix together, place in casserole container and store in refrigerator for three days.

Mix together: 8-ounce package cream cheese, 2 cans potted meat, and ¾ cup chopped pecans; chill. Use this to stuff pickles. Slice across pickles to serve. Arrange on party platter.

Poor Man's Appetizer

16 ounces bean sprouts
1 cup chopped white onions
½ cup chopped celery
Crushed red pepper
Freshly ground black pepper
4 ounces vinegar and oil dressing

Chill bean sprouts. Rinse in cool water. Place in large mixing bowl; add chopped celery and onions. Sprinkle with peppers, using a liberal supply of each. Pour in vinegar and oil dressing and add 1 teaspoon salt. Turn (do not stir) ingredients with a gentle hand, being careful not to crush the sprouts.

Cheese Cookies or Straws

2 sticks margarine
1 tsp. salt
½ pound sharp cheese (grated)

2 cups plain flour
½ tsp. cayenne pepper

Mix together until every particle of flour and cheese is blended with margarine. Shape out in two long rolls, wrap in waxed paper. Chill well. Slice as for ice-box cookies. Place on lightly greased cookie sheet (with pecan half if desired) on each slice. Bake at 300 degrees for a few minutes. Take from oven before they start browning. Let cool in pan. Store in air-tight container—not plastic, please, for these seem to take on an odor if kept any time in a plastic container. Plastic wrap doesn't impart this odd (imagined, I am told) odor.

Lucille Dupont's Cheese Straws

1 pound sharp cheese
¼ pound butter, melted and cooled
6 dashes Tabasco
2 cups flour
¼ tsp. red pepper

Mix grated cheese, butter, and Tabasco. Add flour, salt, and pepper. Press through cookie press or roll thin and cut into strips. Bake 15 or 20 minutes at 350 degrees. Watch carefully.

Cheese Strata

Use 2 slices of bread for each person to be served. Cover the bottom of a casserole dish with a layer of buttered bread slices. Next place a layer of thinly sliced cheddar cheese over the buttered bread. Repeat the bread, butter, and cheese layers

A cheese straw does to a meal what a brushing of rouge does to the tired housewife—perks her up, adds interest, and, above all, color appeal. NOTE: When making your straws, do add a dash of red pepper for that tongue tingle and paprika for that reddish yellow that sparks the eye.

I like a boiled egg sandwich as well as the next one, but right now I am tired of the things. Easter always catches me tired of eggs and we must use up the many boiled ones. I serve them in white sauce, mashed with sardines and lemon juice, baked in tomato juice, added to mashed potatoes and covered with a yummy cheese sauce. Easter always leaves an eggy taste in my mouth.

until all the bread is used. For 6 slices of bread, beat an egg in a cup of milk, season with salt and pepper. Pour this over the bread, butter, and cheese layers. Place the covered casserole in the refrigerator for several hours to give the bread time to absorb the milk. Bake for 45 minutes at 325 degrees and serve immediately.

Bologna Eggs

(from Jim South)

Dozen or more cold-storage, or water
   glassed, eggs (can use regular eggs)
Bologna, chopped (one slice per person)
1 medium onion, shredded
1 can 10 oz. vegetable soup

Handle eggs carefully and break the 7 you have left into a bowl. Stir in bologna, onion, and soup. Cook on a slow blaze and serve in double portions. Tain't fancy, but mighty tasty.

Deviled Eggs Delmonico

2 T. grated onion
½ cup grated sharp cheese
1½ cups thin white sauce
2 cups cooked macaroni
10 deviled (stuffed) egg halves
Paprika or parsley garnish

Blend onion, cheese, white sauce, and macaroni. Put in buttered 1-quart shallow casserole. Season deviled (stuffed) eggs generously with steak sauce and press into mixture. Cover casserole. Heat in 400-degree oven for about 20 minutes. Garnish with paprika or parsley.

Back in the olden days town folks used cold storage eggs. Country folks put down eggs for winter use in water glass—sodium silicate dissolved in water to form a syrupy liquid. When my grandmother was ready to water glass her eggs, her roosters were shut away from the hens. The eggs to be put down were infertile, as fertile eggs would not keep. Five-gallon stone churns would be filled with eggs. Water glass was poured over the eggs to preserve them. The water glass sealed the pores in the egg shells.

Cakes, cookies, and scrambled eggs were tasty using these eggs—pies just didn't turn out tasty.

Pickled Eggs

Boil several dozen eggs, cool and shell. Place in a gallon jar, add a few peppercorns or pickling spices, fill with cold vinegar. If you like, add red cake coloring to the vinegar. A few tablespoons of crab boil seasoning does fine in place of pickling spices.

Crisp crackers and a glass of iced tea with a couple of pickled eggs make a great quick snack.

Vegetable Sandwich

1 large tomato
1 long cucumber
1 large carrot
1 medium green pepper
½ tsp. onion (optional)
1 cup mayonnaise
1 tsp. mustard
1 tsp. Worcestershire sauce
½ tsp. salt
1 pkg. unflavored gelatin softened in
¼ cup cold water

Mix vegetables in food processor until fine but not mushy. Put gelatin in double boiler over ¼ cup hot water; stir until dissolved. Mix gelatin with vegetables and seasonings. Chill overnight. Spread on whole wheat bread. Makes about 18 sandwiches, 36 halves. It's great for making sandwiches for a group.

I well remember the sweet little tin lunch box I had when I went to a one-teacher school: pink enamel outside, tin color inside, and there were two handles. My father had punched my initials in the lid with a nail and hammer to let air in so the food would not sweat and my lunch taste funny.

Our lunches were always good and filling, for mama was a past master at fixing up good things for us to eat. She used boiled dressing in place of oil mayonnaise that came to be so popular in later years. With strips of lean bacon and a garden lettuce leaf we had delicious sandwiches in early spring. We had jelly biscuits, fruit of some kind, baked sweet potatoes, custards in pottery *pots, ham biscuits, cookies, and layer cakes. Often we had cracked (but not picked out) pecans or parched peanuts. We had homemade peanut butter for crackers, which were bought by the tin. The crackers came in a large square metal tin with a hinged lid that could be bought for $1.35. When empty, the tin would be swapped for a full one.*

Of course not all of the food was put in the box at one time; however, the list of good things we found in our lunch boxes seemed endless and mama never seemed ruffled and worried over fixing our boxes.

Sweet milk was a must. In warm weather we would put our bottles or jars of milk in the little spring that furnished our drinking water at school. The spring was in a deep hollow below the school, and it was deemed an honor to be the one selected to take all the milk bottles to the spring. In cold weather we would put the milk outside on a window ledge; it would often be frozen solid at noon.

Back then the Postum people sent darling little sample cans of their

Sandwich Spread

Tomatoes (ripe), ground enough to make 1 pint
    after juice has been drained off
2 large green peppers
2 red sweet peppers
Salt
½ cup water
6 medium size cucumbers
Sweet pickles to suit your family's taste

Grind tomatoes, green peppers, and red peppers; mix. Add salt to taste, then drain. Put in kettle with water and boil until tender. Grind the cucumbers and pickles; add to tomato mixture. Keep mixture hot while you make the dressing.

Dressing: Mix ½ cup sugar, 2 T. prepared mustard, 2 T. flour, ½ cup vinegar, 3 eggs, and ½ cup sour cream. (The sour cream we used was the kind skimmed from clabbered milk. You can substitute the commercial kind, but it will not be as tasty!) Let come to a good boil, pour over hot vegetables and stir well. Put in ½ pint jars, seal, and process 10 minutes at a simmering temperature. Mustard seed or celery seed or both can be added to suit your taste.

Pink Pig Filling

8 ounces cooked ham, coarsely ground
¼ cup pickle relish
2 tsp. prepared mustard
2 T. mayonnaise
2 tsp. finely chopped green pepper
¼ tsp. Worcestershire sauce
Dash pepper

Combine ingredients and mix well. Spread a generous amount of filling on whole wheat bread. Wrap in waxed paper until eating time. This freezes well, but you should butter the bread slices and wrap in foil before freezing.

Brown Sugar Spread

1 pound brown sugar
½ pound butter
Cinnamon to taste

Mix well, store in covered jar in ice box for toast. I also use this spread on cake, placing between layers while cake is hot. For a different flavor, add raisins, coconut or pecans.

Mustard Butter

½ pound fresh butter
4 T. prepared mustard

Mix together and keep in the ice box to use in place of mayonnaise. It will not soak in bread and is wonderful with meat sandwiches. It is also good on bread when you are using hard-boiled eggs for a filling.

Pimento Spread

(from Depression days)

1 5-cent can evaporated milk
(smallest on market, 5 oz.)
1 jar 10-cent sandwich spread (8-ounce size)
Pinch of salt

product, and our teacher would give us a Postum treat about once every three weeks. On Postum day the teacher would pour all the bottles of milk into a great big granite boiler, then add the Postum and heat to simmer. The wood stove would be chucked full of lidered knots. We pulled the long benches close to the stove, ate our lunch, and sipped hot Postum from our tin drinking cups.

I remember those days with pleasure and pride.

Today—September 1, 1988—Dale and I canned 24 half pints of red peppers. If you'd like to have this pleasure, here's what to do: Remove the seeds, wash, cover peppers with cold water, and let come to a boil. Boil for twenty minutes or until skin will peel off. (Use a tablespoon to "scout" meat from peel.) Pack in half-pint jars, cover with hot water, leaving one-half inch head space. Seal, put in water bath and boil for twenty minutes. Cool and store in a dark place.

Eleven months to the week, Betty Lou brought us another calf. A fine little heifer with a white face, and already little horns are sprouting. A fine little girl calf that runs about the lot, kicking up her heels with joy at being alive. Betty Lou is giving right smack on five gallons per day with a calf. We are feeding the calf on a bottle three times a day, and if some dairymen are right the calf will thrive better on a bottle than sucking her mama.

I milk until I stagger to the house with a bucket in each hand, then discover there is nothing to strain the milk in. Every pot, bowl, and crock is full of yesterday morning's milk and the milk from last night. Mama sends over her

½ tsp. sugar
Large can red pimentoes, 10- or 12-ounce size
1 pound hoop cheese

Shred cheese. Put milk in top of double boiler and gently simmer. When milk is heated, add cheese, stir until melted. Remove from water, let cool; add sandwich spread and mashed pimentoes that have been drained. If too thick, add pimento juice to thin. Spread will "set up" so be generous with the saved juice. Store in refrigerator.

Comforting Foods From My Childhood

My mother, Grandmother Budd, and our Maiden Aunt Phleta made any illness special. Children were allowed to use a fat pillow to prop up in bed when tray meals were served. Bibs were worn, and how we felt grown-up when using a starched white napkin. I remember oatmeal cooked all night in the fireless cooker—soft, creamy, flooded with whole milk, sweetened with sugar from a gallon of molasses gone to sugar.

Children with sore throats were pampered with thin gruel. Grandmother Budd always was ready to wash sifted meal, pouring off the water into a heavy enamel pot, then washing the meal again. Sometimes she used fresh sweet milk to wash the meal. When she had at least a pint of meal water or milk, she would cook this until thick. Seasoned with salted butter and black pepper, this delicious gruel felt comforting to sore throats. It was always served in a pretty soup plate.

A tummy filled with goodness, a sear cloth

on the chest, feet bottoms rubbed with camphor salve, and a hot chunk from the fireplace. (A "hot chunk" was the end of an oak log from the fireplace, dampened down until steaming and wrapped in newspaper, then in a piece of an old wool blanket. Then it was snuggled beside the ill child.) Who wouldn't be comfortable when tucked in bed?

An extra special treat was milk toast: two slices of white "light" bread well buttered, sugar and cinnamon sprinkled over with a generous hand, toasted until bubbly. Sweet milk heated to the almost boiling point would be poured over, then let "set up" a few minutes. We ate this goodie with a real silver spoon, creamy bits of luscious goodness served in "the blue bowl."

Ah! Toad in a Hole! All children—cranky sick, fussy about breakfast—perked up when this was served. Butter a slice of white bread. Cut a round hole in the center and reserve cut-out piece. Place bread, buttered side down, in heated skillet. Break fresh egg in hole. Let cook until bread is lightly fried. Using a wide turner, flip egg and bread slice over, taking care not to break yolk. Cook about half a minute. Remove to warm plate. Top egg with slice of bacon and the reserved center you cut from bread that has been toasted in skillet. Stewed apples and hot cocoa go well with a Toad in a Hole. Be sure to have plate warm for this special breakfast dish.

We had yellow grits from yellow corn served with red-eye gravy and wee hot biscuits with watermelon preserves. The "said-to-be-sick child" relished this supper. My mother cooked her yellow grits for several hours before serving. Nothing to my mind is so comforting to a sick child than a bowl of hot

dishpan but that only holds milk for one time and I skim cream, fill the chicken pans full, give the hog a bucket of skimmed milk and send some down the road to a family with lots of children, and get a few pots and things ready for tonight's milk.

Blessings on a cow that produces milk and plenty of it. Butter for biscuits, hot cakes, pies, cookies, and butter cakes; cream for cobblers, fruit pies, whipped for desserts, and hot coffee and cocoa; smearcase for breakfast eating and sour milk for making lots of good cooking. Then there is the joy of ice cold sweet milk, a quart and to spare for each person in the family. Don't forget the buttermilk flecked with drops of gold for drinking, giving away and selling to town friends.

A good cow is a treasure and a pleasure.

Truly Mississippi is a "land of milk and honey" now that late July is with us. All the lush floods of spring, except for huckleberries, are with us in addition to peaches that are bigger, more flavorful and eye appealing than ever I have seen. Watermelons that have no peer can be bought for as little as eight for the dollar—not great whopping fellows but 15 pounders that are sweet, red and ripe.

Fig trees hang loaded with sweetness and for a treat out of this world, take a sharp knife to the fig tree, climb to a good sitting limb and feast like the often talked about king, knowing full well that you are eating food fit for the gods. Early morning the figs are cool and just right. Mid-morning they are sun warm and nothing can beat a fully, soft ripe fig that has been kissed by the sun. The scent of the leaves is a heady smell.

Then for dessert after an early supper, walk to the old burnt house to eat figs. The great purple kind puts the stamp of "this is a wonderful world" to the end of a perfect day.

buttered grits. Whenever my own boys were a bit sick and didn't care for hot gruel, I always cooked grits on the back of the stove for an hour. Then I would break a fine leghorn egg right into the boiling grits and stir like mad so the grits would cook the egg. Salt and serve on your best china, with your good silver and a company napkin. If the child had no fever, a tall cold glass of sweet milk was welcomed along with the grits.

I especially remember flapjacks served with hot molasses and melted butter. We would sit around the stove. Mama had two griddles going, pouring the batter from a pitcher. How round her flapjacks turned out. We ate this common food for a night meal on cold winter nights. There would be a pitcher of ice cold milk to wash down the fried-to-a-turn flapjacks. Here in 1988 it seems strange to remember we used soup dishes and teaspoons to eat our flapjacks, holding the dish on our laps.

Do you remember the refreshing taste of a molasses milk shake? After school we used a pint jar each to shake up these shakes, and we saw nothing odd about having pecan cookies to go with this drink.

Stewed apples, pears, quince or mince meat had their place on our table in the form of fried tarts. In my childhood there were always fried tarts in the warming oven, no matter whose house I visited. These special goodies can now be made using rolled-out biscuit dough —a few spoons of filling placed to one side, the other folded over, edges dampened and crimped well. Hot fat in a heavy skillet worked magic on these tarts. Golden brown with flecks of darker gold made tarts special, no matter how often these were served—hot, cold, fresh from the stove or in lunches the next day.

Chocolate puddings were extra special. Aunt Mamie used cold biscuits in hers. She would muse aloud, saying, "Now, if I had fresh eggs from the hen house, I'd make a chocolate pudding for dinner." Of course, we rushed to bring in eggs, often getting pecked by fussy hens for our wanting to be helpful. Aunt Mamie never used a recipe—just cocoa, butter, eggs, whole milk and cream plus the crumbled cold biscuits. Stirred in a big yellow crock, the mixture would be poured in a black baking pan and baked until a hand stuck in the oven felt just right. When done, the four corners had puffed, then fallen. The center was a lovely custardy pudding. Dipped into blue dessert dishes, sweet cream was passed, never refused. I was grown before I realized chocolate biscuit pudding could be enjoyed without cream.

A very special treat in the dead of winter: canned boiled peanuts. Our Grandmother Budd always made sure to have at least ten to fifteen quarts of shelled boiled peanuts—boiled when the peanuts were green and in the hull. This boiling took place outside in the iron pot where clothes were washed. After the peanuts were boiled in salted water, they were cooled, shelled, and canned in glass jars processed in boiling water. The jars were put in a dark place. We always felt special just knowing the sweet secret of boiled peanuts to be eaten in January.

Hot chocolate made from scratch was our favorite winter drink. Mama made it in a white granite pitcher every day of the week. Served with her famous toasted biscuits, scrambled eggs, tart jelly, and bacon, hot chocolate got our day off to a good start, and the mile walk to our one-room school didn't seem hard. Sometimes we carried a jar of chocolate to warm at noon to go with our sandwiches and cookies.

If you keep a small crock of butter on the table the children will bless you. Soft butter is easier to spread— no torn bread or biscuits when making jam and bread treats.

To our way of thinking, sweet cream that is heavy and thick is almost a must with blackberry jam and sour biscuits. I make it a point to strain all the night milk into a dishpan, then put it into the refrigerator to let the cream rise. A big dish of sweet cream will appeal to old and young. Some of my children love nothing but biscuits and cream, topped off with a fruit juice and a cup of cocoa.

Don't forget to put your extra butter in the home freezer, or if you don't have a freezer, fry down the butter in a hot skillet and seal in clean hot jars. It's fine for making stews, gumbo and pies in the wintertime.

Scrambled Eggs

1 T. butter
½ T. onion, chopped fine
⅛ tsp. pepper
3 eggs
⅛ tsp. salt
3 T. water

Melt butter in skillet, add onions and when heated well add eggs that have been beaten with seasonings and water. When eggs begin to thicken, lift with a fork and allow uncooked eggs to run under. Keep heat low, and do not tear the eggs to pieces. In this way you have large flakes of scrambled eggs that are a joy to serve and a tasty treat to eat.

If you have never eaten hominy grits, you can't imagine how good it is. Of course, it takes long cooking, plenty of attention and much stirring. But when you put red ham gravy on hominy grits, take a couple of hot biscuits, a slice of pink ham, a serving of scrambled eggs, a spoon of wild plum jelly, pull your coffee cup a bit nearer your plate, say, "Daughter, pass the butter," then, dear reader, you are about to have the best breakfast you ever tasted.

Baked Grits

1 cup regular grits
¼ cup butter
⅓ cup milk
3 eggs
½ pound sharp cheese, grated
Salt to taste

Cook grits as directed on box. Add ingredients as listed. Beat hard after each addition. Bake in 325-degree oven until firm and slightly brown on top. This is very good served with fried or barbecued chicken.

Homemade Cottage Cheese

In June, dairy month, many milk pails overflow. Why not make a batch of whole milk cottage cheese? This delicious product, known for years to country folk as smearcase or dripped cheese, is a treat for breakfast. Serve it in small bowls, sprinkle with sugar and then make it fattening with a pouring of sweet cream. Town relatives enjoy a side dish of fresh picked strawberries, blackberries, or huckleberries, along with hot buttered biscuits.

To begin with, you must make clabber. After the milk has clabbered, turn the clabber along with the cream into a colander that has been lined with a wet cheesecloth. Place over a deep pan or boiler to drip overnight. Back in the first days of our married life I made this drip cheese by putting skimmed clabber in a clean flour sack and hung the sack from a pecan tree limb in the back. A bucket was put under the dripping sack to catch the whey, which was given to the hogs. Even if I hadn't been in a saving mood, the whey would have drawn flies once daylight had come.

Homemade Sweetened Condensed Milk

2 cups non-fat dry milk
2 cups sugar (white)
1 cup boiling water
½ cup (half stick) margarine or butter

Add margarine or butter to boiling water; add sugar and milk, mix well. Put in top of double boiler and cook about 30 minutes over hot water stirring often. When finished, stir again and keep

To make clabber milk, place a cup of clabber in a crock; strain sweet milk, fresh from the cow, over the clabber. Let set in a warm place overnight or longer. Skim cream off to be used in recipes calling for sour cream. You will have nice firm clabber for making devil's food cake, hot cakes, corn bread, biscuits, cottage cheese or just for "spoon eating" with a piece of hot buttered corn bread.

During the war between the North and South, Borden's Condensed Milk proved to be helpful in caring for sick and wounded soldiers. Today, condensed milk is used all over the world. History records that Gail Borden was granted a patent for the first successful milk condensing process in 1856. But how many know that he began developing the process when he lived in Liberty, Missisippi?

Gail Borden had a small house in Liberty, and he often visited Shady Rest to see his friends. He also enjoyed fishing in Waggoner Creek. My great-great Aunt

Sallie kept a book with the following information about Gail Borden:

"My father was a man of strong character, one that believed in the right; honest in every way and died without owing man anything. He came to Buffalo, New York, when only 18 years old and learned the cooper's trade. After learning he came to Madison, Indiana, and worked for Gail Borden's father for quite a number of years. There he met my mother, Elizabeth Saunders Walden, who had been adopted by the elder Bordens as her mother had died before she was grown.

My mother was married to my father in the Borden home, then lived right near them on the Ohio River. Cyrenus, Lorena, and William were born there. Gail Borden and my folks came to Amite County where they lived for several years, then Gail and two of our relatives went to Texas where they lived and worked some years."

Aunt Eula was known for her baked macaroni. She had no regular recipe. She always said she "broke the

stirring while it cools to keep mixture together. Place in refrigerator after the mixture has cooled completely. This makes 1⅓ cups or the equivalent of 1 15-ounce can of bought milk.

Modern Day Yogurt

2 T. plain bought yogurt
¾ cup powdered milk
3½ cups warm water
¼ cup evaporated milk

Put bought yogurt in a container that is slightly larger than a quart. Mix powdered milk with warm water, evaporated milk and salt, add to yogurt. Make sure there is not one lump in the water-milk mixture before pouring it in the container with the yogurt. Shake well to mix; put it in a warm place for 5 hours, then in your refrigerator to chill.

When you are ready to make another batch of homemade yogurt, save 2 tablespoons of the first batch to add to the new making.

"Quickie" Macaroni And Cheese

While the macaroni is boiling, shred your cheese into the sweet milk, add salt and pepper and, if you like, hard-boiled eggs. Place over hot water and allow the milk to become heated and the cheese to melt. When macaroni is done, drain and mix with milk and cheese mixture; serve at once.

Poor Man's Butter

1 pound margarine
1 cup buttermilk
1 cup cooking oil
Pinch of salt

Have margarine at room temperature. Chop the margarine in pieces and put along with the buttermilk and oil in a blender. Whirl until blended; add salt and give it another spin. If you like a more golden color, add a drop or two of food coloring. Pour into a wide-mouthed container and store in refrigerator. Keeps well for two weeks or more.

Note: Do not bake or cook with this spread. However, if you cook vegetables without salt and fat seasoning, add a spoon of Poor Man's Butter to them on your plate.

macaroni to fit the crowd." Once boiled and drained, it was put in the macaroni pan (a lovely sky blue and white granite pan). Fresh egg, beaten with sweet cream, plenty of shredded cheese, salt and pepper mixed, and fresh whole milk were then poured on top. Baked in a wood stove for about an hour, this macaroni was food fit for company and homefolks.

Perhaps you'd like to shake milk and cream to make butter. Put clabber milk and cream in a gallon jar. I like to use my beautiful blue glass Ball jars with screw zinc tops and a red rubber ring. I take this make-shift churn to the front porch and shake away.

Farm women sometimes rode to town with their husbands just for fun. Not wanting to waste a minute from work, they would take their jar of cream and milk along to shake. They saw the countryside, enjoyed a ride, and had butter and buttermilk ready for the noon meal.

Soups & Salads

Snow over the past week was a real experience for Dale and me. We are of the school that a cold bedroom is better for sleeping than a heated room. During the night of the snow, I got out of bed to let the cat in. As I passed the sewing machine before an open window, I felt for my glasses only to find snow had blown in through the screen, covering the top of the machine and frosting my glasses as well.

Outside was too beautiful not to share with Dale—my opinion only, I soon found out. When I suggested he get up, he did, but not with too much grace. A cup of coffee and hot chocolate mended matters. By that time it was too late to go back to bed, so we got an early start with making a fire and having a hearty breakfast—not cooked in the fireplace, for that fun was left for the night meal. For supper I made hoecake on a shovel, fried sweet potatoes in the three-legged "spider"—the one with the sunken lid, so hot coals can be heaped atop, the better to cook what's inside. Soup had been slow cooking all day in the crock pot, with a nice chuck of meat on the soup bone. We feasted as in the days when the children were small and the whole family enjoyed fireplace cooking when the weather was bitter cold.

Chicken Corn Soup

1 whole fryer, cut up
1 large onion, diced
1 stalk celery, diced
3 hard-cooked eggs
2 cups whole kernel corn
30 tiny dumplings

Cover fryer with water and cook until well done. Remove chicken from the broth, take the meat from the bones, cut it up fine and return the meat to the broth. Add onion, celery (Grandmother used dried celery leaves as celery was a vegetable we had only at Christmas), and eggs. Add corn. Cook until corn, onions, and celery are done. Add dumplings, a few at a time. Simmer about 10 minutes more. Serve in deep soup bowls with homemade pie crust crackers.

Roasting ears in the lower field and spring fryers in the coop under the pecan tree seemed to trigger among the folk on Shady Rest a longing for Chicken Corn Soup. Grandmother Budd was a master at stewing, simmering, and boiling homegrown goods to turn out something fit for kings and queens if they happened to stop by for a meal. The recipe she used was a standard one in the Shady Rest Community. But she added a little something extra to her soup—tiny dumplings no bigger than a fingernail, very tender and thin as tissue paper.

We could eat a pot of soup every day, and often do. I cook my soup over the lowest fire I can manage. When I have coals in the fireplace, I bring the black iron pot into the living room and let it simmer all day, as did my grandmother in the very same pot. Every bone we have from beef killed for the freezer is saved for soup stock.

Dumplings for Chicken Corn Soup

1 cup plain flour
1 small egg, beaten
Milk, sweet
½ tsp. salt

Sift flour and salt. Beat egg, add small amount of milk (⅛ cup). Make well in flour; add milk and egg; stir (dough should be stiff). May need to add more milk. Roll out thin on floured board or wax paper. Cut in postage size (or larger) squares—drop in hot soup. Cook at simmer until dumplings are transparent and tender.

Serve the chicken corn soup with dumpling in center of bowl before dipping soup. This is a hearty soup for crisp fall days; fruit salad on the side served with retoasted crackers. Dessert: Seven Layer Lemon Filling Cake. Iced tea goes well as a drink.

Creamed Tomato Soup

2 large cans or 1 quart home-canned tomatoes
½ tsp. soda
⅓ cup flour
⅓ cup butter
1 tsp. salt
½ tsp. pepper
1 quart milk

Cook tomatoes about 30 minutes, then run through colander to juice. Add ½ tsp. soda while hot. Stir well. Make white sauce from ⅓ cup flour, ⅓ cup butter, 1 tsp. salt, ½ tsp. pepper, and 1 quart milk. While sauce is hot, add tomato pulp. Serve hot with buttered, then toasted crackers, or if your family leans toward very thin buttered hot biscuits, cater to their whims.

Victoria Soup

1 carrot, chopped
2½ cups chicken stock
1½ T. flour
Salt
Pepper
1 small onion, chopped
1 T. fat
1 cup milk
2 T. grated American cheese
1 T. parsley, chopped

Cook carrot and onion in chicken stock. Strain through a sieve; press vegetables through. Make sauce of fat, flour, and milk. Season to taste. Add chicken stock, cheese, and parsley. Serves 6.

Marrow Balls

¼ cup fresh marrow
2 T. fresh butter
2 eggs
Salt
Nutmeg
Chopped parsley
Cracker crumbs

Beat marrow and butter until creamy. Add remaining ingredients, using just enough cracker crumbs to make mixture right to roll into balls. Cook in simmering soup for 15 minutes.

Make Chicken Soup out of the liquor your hen for chicken salad was boiled in. Add rice and pimento for flavor. Thicken with a little flour and serve with toasted cheese sandwiches, sponge cake and orange sauce. Makes the old hen go lots farther.

I remember one time Mary Cain of Summit had a meeting at her home and served Peanut Butter Soup with homemade crackers made rich with sharp grated cheese. For dessert we had bunches of green grapes and ginger cookies. Each person had a pair of small scissors to cut off grapes from a bunch; I had never seen grape scissors before!

Country cooks always put the washed lettuce in a cloth bag or pillowcase. Then the lettuce was slung around and around—outside of course—to get the water off.

Cream of Peanut Butter Soup

(from Ellen Orr)

¼ cup butter or margarine
1 cup sliced celery
1 medium onion, finely minced
2 T. plain flour
2 quarts fresh chicken broth
1 cup creamy peanut butter
1 tsp. salt
⅛ tsp. fresh pepper
1 cup light sweet cream

In a large heavy skillet, saute celery and onion in butter on low heat. Add flour and stir until mixture is smooth. (Do not let flour brown.) Stir in broth and bring to a boil. Blend in peanut butter and simmer about 15 minutes. Add cream, salt, and pepper and stir until thoroughly blended and soup is very hot.

Wilted Lettuce Salad

Wash about 2 pounds of garden-fresh lettuce. Pat dry, store in cool place until just before the noon meal. Fry 2 slices of bacon for each person and crumble; reserve grease. Boil 1 egg each. Tear lettuce in pieces and put in large heated bowl. (Do not cut with scissors or knife.) Heat bacon grease blazing hot. Add 1½ tablespoons sugar, dash of pepper sauce and 2 tablespoons of vinegar, turning skillet this way and that to mix well. Add bacon to lettuce. Pour skillet mixture over bacon and lettuce, using 2 forks to mix. Add sliced eggs and serve at once.

Cucumbers in Sour Cream

8 cucumbers
1 medium onion, thinly sliced
1¼ tsp. salt
1 cup sour cream
2 T. vinegar
¼ tsp. sugar
⅛ tsp. paprika
1 T. parsley (optional)

Peel and draw tines of fork lengthwise down cucumbers, then cut in thin slices (rounds). Add onion slices and sprinkle with 1 teaspoon salt; let stand 10 minutes. Press out liquid. Mix sour cream, remaining salt and other ingredients. Add to cucumbers, mixing thoroughly but lightly with fork. Chill. After cucumber slices have been eaten, use same sour cream mixture to chill more cucumbers in.

7-Day Cole Slaw

½ head cabbage (medium size) chopped fine
1 carrot, grated
1 medium onion, chopped fine
½ sweet red pepper, chopped
½ sweet green pepper, chopped
1 teaspoon celery seed

Pack in layers in a small crock or a glass container; sprinkle thin layer of sugar over top. Mix together and bring to a boil: ¼ cup vegetable oil, sugar and salt. The amount of sugar and salt depends on how much your family likes. Try a little bit: you will be surprised how good this is without lots of salt.

Let mixture cool a bit. While still hot, pour

Right now, life is wonderful. My most serious question every day is which dressing to use on the garden lettuce salad. Shall it be sweet cream with a dash of chili powder, or shall I use sour cream and chopped onion? Will Dale like the chopped bacon and hot grease dressing best, or should I cook up a batch of French dressing over the kettle?

The garden is lavish in her giving at this time— greens with roots, peas to make with dumplings, lettuce that needs to be pulled twice a day, baby carrots that are extra special cooked in butter and served on crisp toast. The strawberries show promise of enough berries in time for a shortcake or two. The Irish potatoes have golf ball-sized potatoes, and I gathered enough for potatoes in sweet cream. The anticipation of a huge bowl full is something looked forward to by the whole family.

I believe the corn bread bakes to better perfection when the spring days are just right. I know two eggs added instead of one makes a texture almost like cake.

over layered vegetables. This amount makes about a quart, will keep on and on, not just seven days.

Aunt Sadie Bob's New Potato Salad

Freshly dug Irish potatoes, about 4 cups when cooked and cubed
6 hard-cooked eggs, chopped
2 T. chopped onion (green tops, also)
1 cup chopped pickle
¼ cup chopped dill pickle
¼ cup chopped green pepper
¼ cup chopped celery
Salt and pepper to taste
Mustard as needed
Mayonnaise
Paprika for garnish

Have potatoes cold. Mix all ingredients together, being careful not to mash the potatoes (new potatoes stand up better than old potatoes) and eggs. Add enough mayonnaise and mustard to blend well. Salt and pepper to taste. Chill. Sprinkle with paprika just before serving for a bit of zip for the eyes.

In case you are hankering for a green salad but aren't up to cutting a mess of poke greens, try Garden Slaw, which I believe you will put on your "try again" list.

Garden Slaw

8 cups shredded cabbage (use knife)
2 carrots, shredded
1 green pepper cut in thin strips
½ cup chopped onion
¾ cup cold water
1 envelope unflavored gelatin
⅔ cup sugar
⅔ cup vinegar

2 tsp. celery seeds
1½ tsp. salt
¼ tsp. black pepper
⅔ cup salad oil

Mix cabbage, carrots, green pepper, and onion; sprinkle with ½ cup cold water; chill. Soften gelatin in ¼ cup cold water. Mix sugar, vinegar, celery seeds, salt, and pepper in sauce pan; bring to a boil. Stir in softened gelatin. Cook until slightly thick, stirring well. Gradually beat in salad oil. Drain vegetables, pour dressing over, mix well. Serve at once or refrigerate overnight. Will not wilt. Stir just before serving to separate pieces.

Whole Tomatoes (Salad-Style)

1 pint jar whole salad tomatoes plus juice
¼ to ⅓ cup thinly sliced red onion
¼ cup vinaigrette French dressing
1 tsp. Worcestershire sauce
¼ tsp. dried basil or oregano

Combine all ingredients in glass or china bowl; turn gently to mix. Cover tightly and refrigerate for several hours or overnight. Serve chilled as a side dish.

Canned Tomato Salad

1 can tomatoes, well-drained
3 hard-boiled eggs
3 cups coarse cracker crumbs
1 cup chopped celery
1 tsp. grated onion
Mayonnaise and salt to taste

Country people often had Canned Tomato Salad with a roast mutton dinner.

Mix all ingredients except cracker crumbs, adding these just before serving.

Corn Bread Salad

12 oz. self rising corn meal
8 slices bacon, cooked and crumbled
1 onion, chopped
2 tomatoes, chopped
1 green pepper, chopped
2 boiled eggs, chopped
1 cup of mayonnaise

Cook your corn bread; let it cool, then crumble. Add the crumbled bacon, then add the vegetables and eggs. Put tomatoes last and stir in mayonnaise. Chill until served. Yields about 10 servings. It gets better each day. If you like it hot, you can add a small amount of hot pepper.

Tomato-Cheese Salad

1 10 oz. can condensed tomato soup
1 T. gelatin
¼ cup cold water
1 cup smooth cottage cheese
½ cup mayonnaise
¼ tsp. salt
¼ to ½ cup chopped celery, olives, sweet pickle, and sweet peppers

Soak plain gelatin in water for 5 minutes. Heat soup to boiling, taking care not to let it scorch (do not dilute it). Dissolve gelatin mix in soup. Cool and stir in cottage cheese and mayonnaise. When mixture begins to thicken, add chopped relishes. Lightly oil shallow pan or rinse in cold water. Pour

Pear halves for dessert and salads are canned exactly the same way: both cooked until tender in a very lightly sweetened water. The pears for salad have their cores hollowed out a bit more, the better to hold cottage cheese, sharp rat cheese, chopped pecans mixed with peanut butter and honey, or shredded cheese topped with mayonnaise and a red cherry.

mixture into pan and chill in refrigerator to firm. Serve on shredded lettuce and pass mayonnaise mixed with a little curry powder.

Chicken Salad

1 hen
1 bay leaf
1 large onion
1 small "smarty" (hot) pepper
6 hard-cooked eggs
1 cup chopped celery
½ cup crisp tart apple cubes
¼ cup chopped sweet pickle
Juice of ½ lemon
½ cup fresh homemade mayonnaise (if you can make it)
Salt and pepper to taste

Boil the hen whole. Add bay leaf, onion, and pepper to the water. When hen is tender, remove from liquor, allow to cool, and take meat from bones. Cut chicken very fine with a sharp knife. Mix with remaining ingredients. Allow to stand for at least an hour before serving. Serve on crisp lettuce leaves, with a few drops of lemon juice on top.

Hot Chicken Salad

4 cups cooked chicken, cut in small cubes (use scissors to cut)
2 T. lemon juice
¾ cup mayonnaise or cooked salad dressing
4 hard-cooked eggs, sliced
1 tsp. minced onion

Chicken salad! How long has it been since you made a big bowl of homemade chicken salad? Made with fresh mayonnaise and seasoned just right, nothing could be better with hot buttered biscuits, iced tea, strawberry shortcake and good company.

This is a meal for Sunday night supper or for dinner when there is no heavy work to be done. I do not advise using a frozen hen for this salad, and surely not a young frying size chicken. Shop at the stores for a live hen, or if none is to be had buy a fresh hen, plump and fat, one that has not been dressed for more than four days at the longest.

¾ cup cream of chicken soup

1 tsp. salt

2 tsp. lemon juice

2 pimentoes, minced

1 can water chestnuts, chopped

1 cup grated cheddar cheese

½ cup crushed potato chips

⅔ cup finely chopped toasted almonds

1 cup diced celery

Combine all ingredients except cheese, potato chips, and almonds. Pour into 13-by-9-by-2 baking dish. Top with cheese, potato chips and almonds. Let stand few hours in refrigerator Bake for 25 minutes in 400-degree oven.

Sager's Oyster Salad

4 egg yolks

1 cup vinegar

2 T. all purpose flour

1 T. butter or margarine

2 12-ounce containers fresh oysters, undrained

1 cup water

2 cups fine cracker crumbs

1 tsp. pepper

1 tsp. celery seeds

Lettuce leaves

Combine egg yolks, vinegar, flour, and butter in a medium sauce pan. Stir until well mixed. Cook over medium heat, stirring constantly for 10 minutes or until sauce is thickened. Cool completely. Chill. Place water and oysters in medium sauce pan; cover and cook over medium heat 5

When I was a small girl, our New Orleans Aunt Dele sent barrels of oysters to Shady Rest. Packed in ice, the oysters (in their shells) came to Gloster, Mississippi. Then more ice was added, assuring fresh oysters for Grandmother, Aunt Phleta, and my family. Nothing was wasted. We ate the oysters, and the shells were pounded to bits for the hens to make their egg shells stronger.

minutes. Drain and chop oysters. Combine cracker crumbs, pepper, and celery seeds; mix well and add to chopped oysters. Add half of chilled dressing to oyster mixture; toss gently until all ingredients are moistened. Spoon oysters onto a bed of lettuce leaves and pour remaining dressing on top.

Tomato-Cheese-Shrimp Salad

1 10 oz. can tomato soup
2 3-ounce pkgs. cream cheese
2 T. gelatin
1 cup chopped celery
¼ cup chopped pepper
1 cup cooked shrimp
½ cup mayonnaise
¼ tsp. salt
1 tsp. pepper

Heat the soup and add gelatin that has been soaked in ¼ cup cold water. Add cream cheese, cool, then add other ingredients. Pour into two molds that have been rinsed with cold water. Chill well and serve on lettuce.

Grapefruit and Shrimp Salad

1 cup grapefruit segments
1 cup shrimp, flaked
⅓ cup cucumber, diced
¾ cup celery, cut fine
½ cup fresh mayonnaise

Lightly toss ingredients together with a fork. Salt

Everybody but mother loves Sunday dinner. Several months ago I put a vote before my family about having our big meal at night on Sunday or even some other day of the week. They agreed, and now we have a salad, hot rolls, dessert, and drink after church—all of which can be prepared the day before. When I come home from church, I turn the oven on to bake the tiny crusty rolls my family likes with all salads with meat in them.

The recipe for Tomato-Cheese-Shrimp Salad is especially tasty, and I know your family will like it, too. For a party during the Valentine month, the pretty pink will go beautifully with your heart-shaped cookies and sandwiches.

to taste. Serve on crisp lettuce with additional mayonnaise if desired. Oranges may be substituted for grapefruit and crab meat for shrimp. Makes 6 servings. Toasted crackers, olives, and hot coffee make this a party plate.

A good salad recipe is always welcome; Cranberry Salad is delicious, very easy to prepare, keeps well, and is lovely on a salad plate.

Cranberry Salad

1 pound fresh cranberries
1 No. 2 can crushed pineapple, drained
2 cups sugar
1 cup chopped pecans
2 cups grapes (optional)
2 envelopes plain gelatin

Cook berries in pineapple juice until they quit popping. Remove from heat, add sugar, drained pineapple, pecans, and gelatin that has been softened in cold water and then dissolved in ½ cup hot water. If you want to be real fancy, pour in cone-shaped paper cups. When congealed turn out on lettuce leaf and decorate like a Christmas tree, using cream cheese tinted pale green, mixed with a little mayonnaise. Otherwise, pour into a pan or dish rinsed with cold water. When set and chilled, cut in squares, serve with a sweet, tart dressing. Be sure to have plenty of tasty little crackers; cheese ones are nice, and remember that you can leave the grapes out if you like.

Schrock is a grand dish to take to family reunions. This recipe was sent to me by a reader many years ago.

Schrock Salad

1 pkg. lime Jell-O
1 pkg. lemon Jell-O
2 cups hot water
1 cup cottage cheese
1 cup mayonnaise

½ cup broken pecans
2 T. horseradish
2 T. pimento, sliced thin
1 cup crushed pineapple

Dissolve both packages of Jell-O in hot water; cool, then add remaining ingredients. Turn into pan rinsed in cold water or slightly oiled with salad oil. Chill until firm.

Fruit Salad

1 pkg. vanilla pudding mix
1 pkg. orange or lemon tapioca pudding mix
1 can mandarin oranges
1 can unsweetened pineapple chunks
1 banana, sliced

Cook puddings together with 3 cups liquid. (Use liquids from canned fruits and add water to make 3 cups.) Cool slightly, then add fruits. Refrigerate. Serve in lettuce cups and decorate with red cherries. Better still, serve salad in a pretty glass bowl and let each person serve his plate.

(You may substitute vanilla tapioca pudding and 1 heaping tablespoon of frozen concentrate orange juice in place of the orange tapioca pudding.)

Pink Applesauce Mold

1 can applesauce
Dash salt
⅓ cup Red Hots
1 pkg. lemon gelatin
1 small bottle lemon-lime soft drink

Rose Budd's Recipes for Country Living

It seems to be the fad or rage these days to keep busy every minute of the day. If your work gets done, then hire yourself out and go help out the woman or mother who has her hands full with children or some other doings.

Not too long ago I had gotten to the point where I thought I could sit in the sun and do nothing but read, push the swing with my toe just enough to keep myself swaying, and stop often to gaze over the pine trees and think—let my mind wander to the heavens or to the oil

*well being drilled three miles
deep just up the road from
our house.*

*I felt no guilt in my idle
ways when one of my do-
good friends came by and
chided me for not helping out
with something or other in
the county seat. Supper was
ready—a fine roast, potatoes
in a casserole ready for the
oven, greens already cooked
tasty with pieces of ham fat,
a luscious lemon pie piled
high with meringue, and a
pitcher of iced tea ready to
be poured. Rolls were rising
higher and higher in a tall
tin pan. Yes, I was at peace
with the world; the unfolded
and unironed clothes
bothered me not at all.*

*For many years I have
strained at the bit every day
of my life, doing my work
and then rushing away to
help someone. I have planned
things that were never
carried out and many that
were. I have baked cakes for
cake sales that didn't sell for
enough to pay for the
ingredients, sent sandwiches
to sell at football games that
sold for 15 cents, when the
bread and filling cost 22
cents each. I have taken
clothes off the backs of my*

Add salt and Red Hots to applesauce. Heat slowly until red hots are melted. Add dissolved gelatin, then add soft drink. Pour in mold that has been rinsed in cold water. Decorate with cherries or red crab apples and a few sprigs of parsley after mold has chilled.

Black Cherry Salad

1 pkg. lemon Jell-O
1 pkg. cherry Jell-O
1 small can crushed pineapple
1 can black cherries (pitted)
2 bananas
1 cup hot water

Dissolve both packages of Jell-O in hot water then add juice from pineapple and cherries to make 2 cups of liquid. If it doesn't equal two 8-ounce cups of liquid, add water as needed. Let Jell-O and fruit mixture cool. Mash bananas well; add to fruit mixture along with cherries and pineapple. Pour into oiled pan; congeal. Cut in squares and serve on crisp lettuce with Whipped Cream Fruit Dressing.

Whipped Cream Fruit Dressing

1 dozen marshmallows
4 T. water
4 T. white vinegar
4 egg yolks
2 cups whipped cream

Mix and dissolve all ingredients except whipped cream in double boiler until melted. Let cool and fold in whipped cream.

Festive Fruit Salad

1 large tub non-dairy whipped topping
1 medium tub cottage cheese (small curd)
1 medium can fruit cocktail (drained)
1 small can crushed pineapple
1 pkg. strawberry gelatin

Mix first four ingredients thoroughly. Blend in the package of gelatin. Turn into a serving dish; refrigerate. Just before serving, cut into squares.

Congealed Carrot and Pineapple Salad

1 envelope unflavored gelatin
½ cup hot water
⅓ cup sugar
⅛ tsp. salt
¼ cup lemon juice
1 small can crushed pineapple
3 medium-sized carrots, grated

Strain pineapple and use juice to help make up the ½ cup water to soften the gelatin in. Add sugar, salt, and hot water and stir until dissolved. Add lemon juice, mix thoroughly. Add crushed pineapple and grated carrots; pour into mold that has been rinsed in cold water. Chill in refrigerator. Serve with crisp lettuce and tiny biscuits that have grated cheese in them.

children to give to those who had none, and regretted it not one whit.

But by gosh, I am tired of being tired all the time, and one day each week is going to be mine to do as I like, to store strength for the other six.

Tomorrow for instance is my day and the minute the family leaves, I intend to take off for the woods to squander the sunlit hours on myself.

Cranberry Cream Squares

1 pound can whole cranberry sauce
1 9-ounce can crushed pineapple, drained
1 cup sour cream

Fold fruit into sour cream. Pour into freezing tray and freeze until firm. Just before serving cut into squares or wedges. Serve on lettuce or watercress. Makes 6 servings.

Waldorf Salad

2 cups unpeeled chopped red apples
1 cup chopped celery (add a few leaves)
½ cup broken French walnuts
½ cup raisins
1 tsp. sugar
Mayonnaise or salad dressing as needed

Put all ingredients in a bowl and mix with enough mayonnaise to hold together.

We often forget the simple salads of the past. Apple salad, as we called Waldorf Salad, was always made during Thanksgiving and Christmas holidays. Walnuts (bought ones) tasted extra special when Aunt Phleta made this salad, serving it in a lovely pressed glass square dish, called the salad dish.

Cooked Salad Dressing 1

1 cup vinegar
6 or 8 egg yolks, or 4 whole eggs
¾ cup sugar
1 tsp. salt
2 T. flour
1 tsp. mustard, dissolved in 1 tsp. hot water
½ cup sweet or sour cream
1 T. butter

Place vinegar in sauce pan and heat to boiling. Place egg yolks with sugar, salt, mustard, and flour in small mixing bowl. Beat until thick and lemon-colored, about 3 or 4 minutes. Add cream and beat until well-blended with other ingredients. Add egg mixture to boiling vinegar, stirring constantly, and cook over medium-low heat until thick, continuing to stir constantly all the while. Add butter. Return to mixer bowl and beat at medium speed for 2 minutes. Cool. Store in refrigerator in air tight container.

Cooked Salad Dressing 2

4 eggs
6 T. cider vinegar
1 cup milk
2 T. melted butter
1 tsp. salt
2 T. sugar
1 tsp. dry mustard
1 tsp. celery seed
½ tsp. paprika

Using a wooden spoon, mix all ingredients in the top of a double boiler. Set over simmering water (not boiling), stirring constantly until thick and smooth. This will take about 10 minutes. Pour dressing into a pint jar, cap tightly, and store in refrigerator until you are ready to use it.

Cooked Salad Dressing 3

½ tsp. salt
1 tsp. mustard
1½ tsp. sugar
2½ tsp. flour

Cooked salad dressing— does that bring back memories of bygone days when your mother opened the top of the kettle, placed a bowl of dressing makings inside and had you stir until thick? We used this dressing on sandwiches and in salads, and Mama sometimes varied the taste, according to what she was dressing with it. There are many variations to this recipe, as you will see from the three in this book. Experiment to find the one that suits you best.

2 eggs
1½ T. butter
¾ cup milk
¼ cup white vinegar
Cayenne pepper

Combine dry ingredients. Gradually add milk and vinegar. Add butter and cook until thick, stirring constantly. Store in covered container in refrigerator.

Homemade Mayonnaise

1 egg yolk
½ tsp. dry mustard
½ tsp. salt
½ tsp. white sugar
¾ to 1 cup Wesson Oil
2 T. lemon juice (or in a pinch, same of white vinegar)

Beat egg yolk in jar. Mix dry ingredients in beaten egg yolk. Slowly blend in 1 tablespoon of lemon juice or vinegar, then beat constantly while adding the oil drip by drop, gradually increasing amount as mixture thickens. Add other tablespoon of lemon juice or vinegar at last, mixing gently. The following hint was passed around on how to save the curdled, runny, or separated mayonnaise: gradually add the mayonnaise to either 1 beaten egg yolk or 1 teaspoon very cold water, beating well until blended.

This mayonnaise recipe came to my mother well before sliced bread appeared in grocery stores. Mama's only sister, Hallie Christine, gave Mama a pint tin can of Wesson Oil plus a mayonnaise maker—a tall glass jar with a screw-top sunken lid with two holes. One was a very small hole for allowing one drop of oil at a time as the housewife (in fear and trembling) made a batch of mayonnaise. The other hole in the center of the lid allowed a metal plunger to go up and down to bring the ingredients to perfection. The recipe shown here was written in raised letters on the outside of the jar.

Women of that time were warned not to breathe in the mayonnaise while they were making it or the mayonnaise would curdle. I

Mrs. Temple's Salad Dressing

4 T. unsweetened evaporated milk
⅛ tsp. dry mustard
¼ tsp. salt
1 T. vinegar
1 T. lemon juice
2 T. tomato juice

Have milk well-chilled. Combine mustard and salt in custard cup; add vinegar and stir until free from lumps. Add lemon juice to vinegar mixture. Stir tomato juice into well chilled milk. Gradually add lemon vinegar mixture, stirring constantly until well-blended and slightly thickened. Serve with any type salad, vegetable, fruit, egg, meat or fish dish. It is delicious and keeps well in the refrigerator for a few days.

Thousand Island Dressing

¼ cup chili sauce
1 dill pickle, finely chopped
¼ cup chopped green olives or green pepper
¼ cup chopped stuffed olives
4 sweet pickles, chopped fine
1 chopped pimento
1½ cups mayonnaise

Fold all ingredients into the mayonnaise, blending well. This makes about 2½ cups of dressing.

have an idea that the warning may have been the brainchild of a busy mother who wanted to "shoo" the curious children from the kitchen, so she could work. Or perhaps this belief was tossed around first by the men because making mayonnaise was a heart-stopping job—a new-fangled something compared (by husbands) to bobbed hair, jelly-rolled hose, and a touch of rouge to the cheeks.

Prior to the "invention" of mayonnaise, cooks had actually to cook to make salad dressing. In those early mayonnaise days, the women met in neighbors' homes to make mayonnaise. County Extension workers were asked to help perfect the recipes, as many failures were being made. These meetings were held much to the dismay of farm husbands, my father among the many! It was said that women were getting out of hand: they had been allowed to pay poll tax and vote, next came twin beds. And now mayonnaise. Why, next women would be running for office!

Ruby French Dressing

1 8-ounce can tomato sauce
1 tsp. salt
1 tsp. Worcestershire sauce
1 cup salad oil
¼ cup finely chopped onion
2 T. sugar
1 tsp. dry mustard
Dash pepper
½ cup vinegar
Dash celery salt

Combine ingredients; beat or shake until well-blended; chill. Shake before serving. This is good for leafy salads and cold meat dishes.

Pear Salad Dressing

4 egg yolks
1 T. melted butter
1 cup whipped cream
4 T. white vinegar
18 large marshmallows
1 cup chopped pecans

Combine beaten egg yolks, vinegar, and melted butter in top of double boiler. Stir while cooking. Add marshmallows when mixture begins to thicken. Remove from heat, allow to cool; add whipped cream and nuts, fold gently. Serve over chilled pear halves.

Dressing for Grapefruit Salad

4 egg yolks, beaten
1 T. vinegar
1 T. sugar
½ tsp. salt
1 tsp. mustard
⅛ tsp. red pepper
1 dozen marshmallows, cut find
½ pint cream, whipped
½ cup pecans, cut fine

Cook all ingredients until real thick. While still hot, add marshmallows, cream, and pecans. Do not crush the pecans or grind them: the crunch of the pecan pieces is part of the goodness of this salad dressing.

Tartar Sauce

1 cup mayonnaise
1 T. vinegar
⅓ cup chopped green olives
Salt to taste
¼ cup grated white onion
⅓ cup sweet pickle relish
1 T. chopped capers
1 tsp. chopped parsley

Blend mayonnaise, onion, and vinegar. Add remaining ingredients and mix well. Makes about 1½ cups.

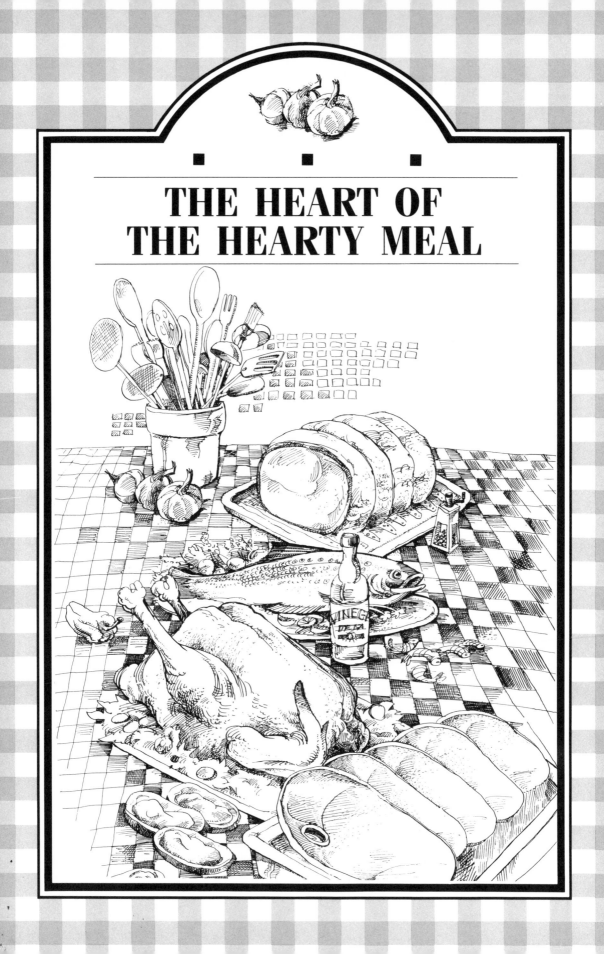

THE HEART OF
THE HEARTY MEAL

Pork, Chicken, Beef, Fish, & Wild Game

Hog-killing time is a busy one, I grant you; however, is there any so richly rewarding? To my way of thinking there isn't. A family works like mad for two days, cleans up the third, sits back viewing the efforts with pride and a sense of knowing nowhere for any amount of money could better sausage, head cheese, bacon, ham, spare ribs, stuffed heart, liver hash, and pickled pig feet be bought.

As a woman forgets her pain of having to bring a child into the world, so do a farmer and wife forget the endless trips to the hog pen to slop and water the ever-hungry and thirsty hog. They forget the vow, "Never to raise a hog again, to buy all the meat we need for half the cost of raising one hog." Forgotten is the splashed-over souring rice polish on clean clothes; the constant reminder to the children to bring a dozen ears of shucked corn (the shucks were saved for the milking cows) for Ole Buddy. Forgotten the tears over a very badly cut finger when a sharp knife slipped while cutting sausage meat. Also not remembered are smarting eyes as red pepper and sage are parched and ground for seasonings.

Remembered is the year no hog was raised, the fact that fresh hog meat was too high. Sausage bought in a weak moment reminded me that I was a gump not to have jars and jars of patty sausage fried down in jars for quick meals. Remembered is the fact that no red-eye gravy courted fresh cooked grits and hot biscuits, and no plate-sized slices of pink smoked ham, no crocks of cheese and souse.

Sure, killing a hog is lots of work. Have you ever seen anything truly worth something, giving pleasure and delight as well as bringing a sense of well being, that wasn't hard work?

Tomorrow Dale and I will rise at four exactly and have water jumping in the black iron pot well before daylight. By the time the sun is sparkling on frosted grass, the hog will be hung ready for pulling out long strips of tenderloin.

Several women will come spend the day, bringing their own aprons. The thoughtful ones will bring a few clean rags. Who has enough clean rags at hog killing time? Liver, lights, and the heart will be put to cooking. Dinner will be liver hash, rice, cabbage slaw, backbone stew, baked sweet potatoes, plenty of coffee, lemon pies using leftover Christmas lemons, and of course, bakers of catfaced biscuits to sop stew juice. I am expecting a day of hard work, some fun, lots of fellowship, sausage ground and seasoned against stuffing on the morrow, lard cooked out with cracklings packaged for freezing.

The men folk will pack the pieces—to be smoked at a later date—down in salt. Chitterlings will be cleaned, put to soaking in salt water. (Indeed these lovely beauties will not be stuffed with sausage meat; we used bought casings or made patties stacked in corn shucks.) The chitterlings will be boiled until tender, cut in pieces, rolled in seasoned flour or meal, deep fat fried and served with baked beans, cole slaw, fresh lemons for squeezing juice over for those who like their annual meal of chitterlings this way, and lots of coffee.

Another hog killing day will be over when the last person takes his package of fresh meat, goes home and tends his night work. Dale and I will be expecting a call soon, "Come help us kill our hog tomorrow, if you can."

No matter what the weather in mid-December, I am sure the woodpile will be getting smaller come the New Year, and surely we will have days that are cold enough to freeze the horns off a billy goat and the comb off a rooster. We will scald two hogs and live off the fat of the land, so to speak, until the spareribs are gone, and the head cheese and sausage have lost their fresh appeal. Then we turn to turnip greens, green onions, and other winter garden sass.

Sausage Scrapple

1 pint corn meal
½ pound seasoned sausage
2 tsp. salt
2 quarts water (boiling)

Add meal gradually to boiling salted water. Stir constantly for 10 minutes. Cook in double boiler for 30 minutes. Add sausage and beat well. Pour in greased baking pan. When cold, slice, dip in flour, and fry in bacon fat (just a little bit) until golden brown. For breakfast serve with syrup; for the noon meal, serve with applesauce.

Baked Spareribs with Dressing

4 pounds spareribs
Water
1 T. salt
½ tsp. pepper
1 "smarty" (hot) pepper
1 stalk celery
1 bay leaf

Cut ribs in pieces, about 3 to a serving. Be sure the ribs are meaty and streaked with a little fat. Put in pressure cooker or sauce pan and add enough boiling water to nearly cover. Add salt, black pepper, smarty pepper, celery, and bay leaf. Cook at 15 pounds pressure for 15 minutes. Cool cooker to reduce pressure, remove the ribs to a dripping pan and take 1 cupful or slightly more of the broth out of the cooker for the dressing.

Dressing for Spareribs

6 cups broken stale bread
½ pint fresh oysters
Broth to moisten
1 tsp. sage
1 tsp. finely chopped onion

Mix bread with sage; add oysters and onion. Barely moisten with the broth. Put in a baking pan with the ribs; brown together. Make gravy with remaining broth by thickening with flour and ½ cup milk. Season with salt and pepper to taste.

Hog's Feet and Chitterlings

Hog killing time is lots of work, but the eating afterwards is worth every tired bone in your body. Just think how good the hog feet are after they have been singed in the fire and scraped good. Cover with cold water in a heavy iron pot and boil gently for two hours. Add a little salt, and when done, take out of liquor and place in a cool dry place to dry out for at least 24 hours. Get out the pepper sauce, the horseradish, a pone of corn bread, green onions, and hot coffee. Fix the

Back in the olden days my grandmother and her maiden daughter Phleta didn't care for stuffed smoked sausage after the "fresh" had worn off. They would send brother and me to the corn crib to shuck 30 ears of corn, making sure we didn't pull the shucks off, and to snap the ear of corn off with a quick turn of our wrist, so there would be no cob left in the shuck cup. Remember that this corn was stored properly and the shucks were pale yellow and clean. Once at the house our aunt would brush the shucks to remove silks from the inside.

On the table would be piles of hand-patted sausage ready to be stacked in the shucks, using the bottom of the shuck where the ear had been removed to begin stacking the patties. Between each patty would be a piece of shuck (cut from other shucks), and so on until at least five or six patties were stacked. The tops of the shucks were brought up and tied with strong cord string.

A long twisted piece of shuck would be threaded through the top, and this in

turn would be placed over a green gum pole resting on hanging wires from the rafters in the smokehouse. The sausage-filled shucks would take their place among hanging-to-smoke stuffed sausage (later to be put down in pure lard) and sides of meat to be used for cooking vegetables. All of this must be done and out of the way when the barrels of brined-down meat were ready for washing and then smoking for days over a low-burning fire of cobs and hickory wood.

children some sausage and eggs and send them in the house. These hog's feet are for Mama and Daddy only. I'll share anything else with my children but hog's feet!

While the hog's feet have been getting ready to eat, the chitterlings have been soaking for a couple of days in cold water that has been changed every day. I boil them slowly in a heavy pot for two or three hours and let them cool. Then they are cut in eating-size pieces, dipped in salted and peppered flour, and fried in hot lard. When nice and brown, I drain them on a brown paper sack. Serve hot biscuits, plenty of homemade ketchup, and onions. With plenty of hot coffee, brother, are we eating!

Oven-Baked Pig Feet

6 pig feet
1 large onion, sliced
1 clove garlic
1 tsp. vinegar
3 or 4 whole black peppers
1 tsp. salt
6 whole cloves
Bread crumbs or corn meal
Melted butter or bacon fat

Wash pig feet. Cover with water, hurry to boil. Simmer covered for 3 hours. Add onion, garlic, and seasonings; simmer 30 minutes longer. Let cool in the cooking water. Remove, let drain and dry or pat dry with folded clean dish towel or paper towels. Split each foot in two lengthwise. Roll in melted butter or bacon fat, then in bread crumbs or corn meal. Lay them on a shallow baking pan and bake in 450-degree oven for about 15 minutes or until nicely brown.

Serve with wilted lettuce salad, green beans, pickled beets, and hot corn bread. For dessert, any kind
of lemon dessert. No lemons? Make a vinegar pie.
Hot coffee is a must with the dessert of your
choice.

Boned Pig Feet

The recipe below for Boned Pig Feet is from the
old days. I daresay nowadays not one person reading this will take time to bone pig or hog feet.
The recipe may bring back memories of the olden
days to many, especially those reared on a farm
where hog killing was part and parcel of winter
life. Farm wives wanted to do something special
with what they had, hence the following recipe
on how to bone the sure-to-be-favorite eating for
the families who had a mama who cared enough
or had time to follow the directions below.

Use the forefeet only, small and select ones.
Before putting them on to boil they should be
wrapped separately in strips of cloth, with the ends
left open. Place the pig feet in enough water to
cover and boil them gently until they are very
thoroughly cooked. Remove from water, and as
soon as feet are cold enough to handle, fish out
all of the bones with a small oyster fork or pickle
spear. Then unwrap, lay on a platter and place in
ice box until thoroughly cooled. When the cook
is ready to broil, fry or serve cold she will have
a delicious meat dish ready at hand. If served hot,
deviled sauce is preferable; if cold a vinaigrette
sauce is very nice.

Back in my pre-salad days a cold boiled hog or
pig foot, a piece of green garden onion (several
whole ones to be exact), a wedge of cold crusty
corn bread, and a small baked sweet potato was
a filling, delicious after-school snack. The amount
of meat in the boiled foot was almost nothing;

*A task that Dale and I
enjoy is slicing down our
smoked hams and packing
away the smoked sausage in
lard. During the day I wash
and sun the stone churns we
pack the ham and sausage
in. After the children are in
bed, the kitchen spotless, we
get out the sausage and cut
it in serving pieces. A layer
of fresh lard goes in the
churn, and a layer of
sausage followed by lard
and sausage until the churn
is full. Over the top of the
churn goes several
thicknesses of clean cloth.
This is tied down with
strong string and the churn
is put in the coolest and
darkest place we can find.
The ham is skinned, and
Dale slices it, ready to serve.
I usually put the hams
into crocks for easy getting
to. A layer of lard, one of
ham, and so on until the
crock is full. A clean cloth
goes over the top and I
have a huge cake plate that
is too cracked and crazed to
be used, so this is used for
the cover. The ham skins are
put into the little wooden
bucket in the safe and used
to season peas, beans, and
greens. Nothing like having*

ham and sausage packed down in lard for winter eating and for summer suppers and quick dinners. Nothing can take the place of ham and sausage.

The ball sausage has been fried down and canned, lo these several weeks, and stands in proud rows in the pantry, for company or home folks. Cracklins in pint jars are a must for summer bread when onions are tender and radishes just a hint of good things to come. English peas must have tiny dumplings, and of course, thin, thin cracklin' bread.

When baking a ham in the oven, place ham on oven rack and slip a pan of water under the ham. The steam will help the ham bake better and the drippings will make good seasonings for other foods.

however, it took such a long time to eat around the bones (mama had no truck with boned feet for her family—just when company came) we thought we were getting plenty of meat.

Grandma's Winter Special Hash

3 pounds pork liver
2 pounds pork lights
2 pounds pork ribs tenderloin or back bones
2 pods red pepper
Water to cover
Salt and pepper to taste

Salt and pepper meat; cut into small pieces. Boil 2 or 3 hours in water seasoned with a little more salt, pepper, and red pepper pods. It will cook down and have a tasty broth gravy. If desired, you can mix flour with water and make a thicker gravy. Serve with collard greens, baked sweet potatoes, corn bread or biscuits. A skillet of ginger bread for dessert with cold buttermilk is tasty.

Creole Ham

(from Mrs. Rauhman Browning)

1 ham steak, about 1-inch thick
1 T. cooking oil
1 large can tomatoes
½ cup chopped celery
1 green pepper, chopped
½ cup brown sugar
1 large onion, sliced
1 bay leaf
1 tsp. salt
⅛ tsp. pepper

Sear ham on both sides in oil in a skillet. Remove to a baking dish. To the skillet add tomatoes, celery, pepper, bay leaf, salt, and pepper and cook together for 10 minutes. Sprinkle the top of the ham with brown sugar and lay the onions on top. Pour the tomato sauce around the ham, with just enough sauce over the top to moisten the sugar cover, and bake at 350 degrees for 1 hour, basting it once during the baking. Remove ham and boil the sauce down until the desired consistency. Pour sauce over ham to serve.

Vicksburg Stuffed Baked Ham

(from Mrs. Bill Poe)

10 to 12-pound ham
1 T. vinegar
2 T. brown sugar
Steaming water

Cut off ham hock. Add vinegar and brown sugar to water and steam ham until meat is tender enough to feel loose at the bone. Remove bone and all fat. Reserve 1 cup of the fat. Fill bone cavity with dressing. Cover outside of ham about 2½ inches thick with remaining dressing. Wrap securely in cheese cloth, then tie tightly with cord. Bake at 300 degrees for ½ hour. Chill 24 hours and slice thinly.

Dressing For Ham

1 cup ham fat, ground
1 pound toasted crackers, ground
1 small loaf toasted bread, ground

I am always in favor of bacon in some form at least once a day. Too many people reserve bacon for breakfast. Some fix bacon and tomato sandwiches for lunch, but there is another meal that takes to bacon like the proverbial duck to water: namely, supper when the dinner leftovers are skimpy. About the middle of the aftenoon, slice medium-thick slices of either home-cured or slab bacon (don't try this recipe with already sliced bought bacon) and soak in sweet milk. Just before supper heat a skillet, add a tablespoon of bacon fat, then dip your slices of bacon in flour or meal. Fry real slow until crispy brown. Be sure to cut the skin so the slices won't curl. Pour off most of the fat, reserving the crumbs and little crisp pieces in the skillet. To this add two tablespoons of flour and a generous sprinkle of pepper and let brown to golden. Add sweet milk to make a gravy of the right thickness for your family. Simmer for a few minutes.

2 T. sugar
1 tsp. mustard seed
1 tsp. dry mustard
1 stalk celery, ground
2 medium-size onions, ground
½ cup pickle relish
1 T. chopped parsley
4 eggs, beaten
1 cup sherry wine
4 dashes Tabasco sauce
Vinegar to make a paste-like consistency, not too soft

Thoroughly combine all ingredients. Stuff ham as directed.

Ham-Peanut Butter Bake

(from Mrs. Sidney Teller)

1 center cut slice of ham, 1-inch thick
Peanut butter (enough to spread at least ¼-inch thick on ham)
1 cup whole milk

Place ham in baking dish, spread with peanut butter and pour the milk over the top. Bake in 350-degree oven for about 1 hour, basting the ham with the sauce several times during baking, being careful not to break the peanut butter topping.

Ham Stock

Ham shank with meat on it, about 4 pounds
9 cups water

Place ham shank in a covered 4-quart kettle. Add water; bring to boil. Cover and simmer for 2½ to 3 hours. When meat is tender and pulls away from the bone, remove from heat. Take meat from bone, cutting in medium-sized pieces and return to cooking liquid. Chill. Skim off fat after chilling, then add water to make 10 cups. Divide and freeze.

Sweet Pineapple Relish

1 No. 2 can crushed pineapple (1 pound, 4 ounces)
¼ cup firmly packed dark brown sugar
¼ cup cider vinegar
¼ cup seedless raisins
½ cup finely diced onion
½ tsp. salt
¼ tsp. ginger
¼ tsp. allspice

Put pineapple, including syrup, in saucepan. Add sugar and vinegar. Rinse raisins in hot water; drain. Add to pineapple mixture with onions, salt, ginger, and allspice. Bring quickly to a boil; boil gently until there is little liquid left—about 15 minutes. Makes about 2 cups. Store in covered container in refrigerator.

Sweet Pineapple Relish is what people used to call a "dainty"—a little extra. This is especially good with baked ham.

Ham with Apple Rice

1½ cups converted rice
3-or 4-pound canned ham
1½ cups apple cider or juice
1 can (1 pound, 4 ounce) apples
1 tsp. salt ½ tsp. pepper

A truly American one-dish meal is something many of us are looking for—one that can be served within a matter of twenty minutes after church on Sunday. I attended a cooking school several weeks ago, and the recipe for Ham With Apple Rice won first prize. I tried it the following weekend and our family sopped the casserole with pieces of French bread.

1 8-ounce pkg. cheddar cheese
½ tsp. ground cinnamon
½ cup dark brown sugar, firmly packed

Remove the ham from the can and save all the ham jelly. Cut 8 evenly spaced slits, about 2 inches deep, across the ham. Place ham with the reserved ham jelly in a 2 or 2½ quart shallow casserole with cover. Add the rice, cider, apples, salt and pepper around the ham, mixing well before adding. Cover tightly (to steam rice) and bake in a 350 degree oven for 1 hour and 15 minutes.

Hog's Head Cheese

To my way of thinking there is no part of the hog so tenderly delicious as the hog head used for making souse, or head cheese. Once in the dim long ago an old woman was asked how she made such delicious rabbit stew and she answered, "First off you must catch your rabbit." The making of head cheese starts somewhere in the middle of late spring or the early beginning of first summer when a wee little pig is brought home from a neighbors and made a plaything for a few weeks. Nothing that gives more pleasure than having a wee little twinkle-toed pig running around behind, as you go about your outside chores—a little fellow who sticks his nose into everything, no matter if it is chicken feed or a put-down bucket of fireplace oak ashes.

Suddenly the wee pig is a thirty-pound shoat and must be put in a pen—a fresh pen that slants from front to back. Across the front end is a trough kept filled with goodies dear to a pig's taste. Several times during the summer there have been minutes of misgivings about having a hog pen within 500 yards of the house, especially on a hot humid day when the wind blows direct from pen to house. A complaint about the smell brought remarks from Dale: "Smells like sausage and ham to me."

A clear crisp day in February is just right for making head cheese. The grown hog was killed yesterday; everything was done in one day—lard rendered, sausage ground, and some of it stuffed and hung to smoke and air dry, hams and other pieces salted down for smoking once it is ready. Of course, the head was cleaned yesterday when the hog was scraped of all hair. The head was split in half, the brains removed, to be added to scrambled eggs for breakfast one morning real soon. In the smokehouse is the hog's head waiting to be made ready for the black wash pot and boiling.

This is a job that needs to be done outside. No matter how careful a cook is, it is impossible to keep greasy steam from ruining the kitchen. Little drops of greasy water will settle on the counters and floors, unnoticed until one day in spring, when everything will begin to look dingy. Once the water in the wash pot is boiling and jumping, take a few dippers full, and pour carefully in and around the ears and eyes. Remove the eyes, and begin scraping the ears well, paying close attention to the inside of the ears.

Some head cheese makers now wash the whole head with soda and hot water, giving the teeth a special brushing. Here on Shady Rest I like to have the snout removed well beyond the teeth, thereby getting the tongue out and saved for a special day when we will have mustard and tongue sandwiches. Place head and feet in the pot, making sure water covers. As scum rises to surface, skim it off. Boil until meat leaves bone. Remove from water using a skimmer and put it in a large wooden bowl or deep dishpan.

When meat is cool remove every particle of bone and gristle, then chop the meat fine. You will

Remember when hog killing time was always a time when the baby in the family was sure to have a new rattle within a few days after the hog had gone to "hog heaven"? The bladder would be washed and carefully scraped to remove fat and membrane, and a few small rocks were inserted in bladder; a piece of cane (the kind used for fishing poles and stems for clay smoking pipes) was then inserted. Fishing cord would be tightly wound and tied around the inserted cane (which later became the handle) and the soon-to-be-welcome toy would be hung in the smoke house to dry, not too fast—about a week would be just right.

Farm folk always put down at least two smoked hams in lard each winter for spring and summer meals. When the hams had been smoked to a deep dark brown, the housewife would remove the skin from the ham, then slice the whole ham. Slices of ham were placed in stone crocks. Over the ham slices she would pour melted lard, taking care to cover the ham.

After the lard had hardened, brown wrapping paper would be placed over crocks, with plenty to hang down. The paper would then be tied down around the sides of the crock. The crocks would be placed on a shelf in the smokehouse until springtime or until all other smoked meat had been used. Mama always said she felt rich just knowing this special treat was on hand.

also chop the ears very fine and, of course, the tender skin will be used if you and yours like. Season with salt and pepper. A little finely ground red pepper can be added, too, if your family enjoys this taste. The above work—as well as the chopping—must be done with your hands, making sure not to mash the meat as you want the meat cut in pieces and not a paste. Season the meat with chopped hot peppers, spices, and hand rubbed sage. Line a colander with cheese cloth, put meat in, fold cloth closely over top, lay weight on it to press whole surface equally.

Allow meat to set until cold—at least 18 hours. When it is cold, take off weight, remove head-cheese from colander, and place in stone crock. Vinegar may be added, one pint to a gallon crock. Clarify fat from cloth, colander and from liquor in pot where head was boiled. The fat squeezed from the souse is prized for frying doughnuts and for making spice cookies—a few tablespoons of this fat is a little extra flip to the molasses and cinnamon used to flavor the cookies. Biscuits for eating with boiled meats had generous smears of this fat in the baking pan as well as on tops. To my remembrance nothing was wasted on Shady Rest.

Here's another way to press head cheese: put seasoned meat in small crock, allow to get almost cold, place wooden board the size of crock directly on meat, then place heavy stone or several bricks on the board, and turn crock, board, and brick (or stone) upside down in a large dishpan. This way there is no cloth to wash—only the board and stone. Most headcheese makers store the board and stone in the smokehouse year after year and these articles are handed from one generation to another. One young homemaker who never heard of head cheese used the cheese board to make a lazy susan for a kitchen cabinet. Many years ago I used two bricks. I was wasteful for I never washed the bricks and salvaged the grease from them—

they were tossed back on the brick pile where they were rained on and the hot summer sun rendered out any fat in them. The board was always boiled in clean water and stored against another winter's head cheese making.

Many homemakers back in what some call the "good old days," would cut their head cheese in squares, boil a dozen or so eggs, then after the eggs were cooled and peeled, the cheese would be put in a gallon jar or stone crock—a thick layer of cheese, a few eggs, and so on until the jar or crock was filled. To keep this delicious goodness from spoiling, boiled vinegar and water would be poured over to cover. A crock of head cheese with vinegar poured over and well covered would last all during cold weather if kept in the smokehouse where it was very cold on a shelf away from the smoking fire.

For an afternoon snack, school children would take the kitchen fork, spear a square of head cheese, an egg, then go by the kitchen safe for a cold biscuit. The kitchen steps, if the afternoon was warm, made a good place to eat. If the weather was cold, the kitchen fire would be chunked up and we would gather close to keep mama company as she began cooking supper. Today, a delicious snack: strips of head cheese, several kinds of crisp crackers, rat cheese from the grocery store, bottled cola drinks or coffee—a good fire to warm your body, friends gathered around to share ideas and chatter.

The head cheese bought in stores is such a poor copy of real head cheese—just a few pieces of meat bound together with gelatin and lots of broth to make something to slice. This store head cheese can't stand heat—the broth and gelatin will melt and spread, leaving the pitiful pieces of meat behind. Homemade head cheese can be sliced, rolled in flour, and pan-fried to make a meat to serve with grits, wild plum jelly, hot biscuits, lots of iced tea, and for dessert my favorite—lemon pie.

A reader once asked if corn flour and corn starch are the same thing. Indeed not! Corn starch is made from corn especially for use in making foods slightly thick. It's often used in making clear gravies or sauces.

Speaking of corn flour, our great-great Aunt Sallie told us how her mother carefully shook the meal sacks and brushed the seams to get bits of finely ground corn meal, sort of a flour, to thicken gravy during the days of the Civil War. Real corn flour is used by those who can't tolerate wheat flour.

She told of the most delicious food she remembered after the war was over and flour could be bought in Natchez. It was a raised flour cake, sweetened with syrup and made greasy with bits of rendered pork fat. It was baked in a black iron spider over a bed of glowing coals. She said it was food fit for war-weary people.

Rose Budd's Recipes for Country Living

*A*t one time I used my vacuum cleaner for chores never dreamed about by the company. For picking chickens it has no peer. You scald them in the usual way, remove any end attachment, and suck the feathers right off. When the refrigerator needs defrosting, turn the blowing end of the vacuum on the freezing unit. In just a matter of minutes the frost is melted off.

Pork Chops, Greens, and Dumplings

2 pkgs. frozen turnip greens
4 thick pork chops
1 cup self-rising meal
1 egg
1 quart water

Place pork chops in water and let boil for 20 minutes. Be sure the chops are thick and have a nice bit of fat on them—do not trim fat off. Place unthawed greens in pot with pork chops. Allow to come to a good boil and boil 15 minutes, or until greens are tender. Remove pork chops to a large platter. Drain greens, being sure to save liquor, and place greens at other end of platter. Return liquor to boiler and immediately drop in small balls or dodgers made by mixing meal, egg, and enough water to a consistency to form small balls. Boil gently for 10 minutes, remove, and pile in center of platter.

Pork Chops and Sausage Stuffing

8 pork chops
½ pound sausage
2 cups cooked rice
1 T. celery leaves, chopped
1 T. sausage drippings
1 T. parsley, chopped
1 small onion, grated
1 tsp. poultry seasoning
½ tsp. salt
⅛ tsp. black pepper

Have butcher cut pockets in pork chops. Mix rest of ingredients and stuff in pork chop pockets. Bake 1½ to 2 hours, covered, at 350 degrees. Brown before serving by removing top or cover.

Pork Chops and Rice

4 pork chops
4 T. quick-cooking rice
4 onion slices
Salt and pepper
4 tomato slices
4 green pepper rings
2½ cups broth or bouillon cubes dissolved in same amount of hot water.

Season chops and brown in 2 tablespoons of hot fat. Put in covered casserole or baking pan. Put slice of each vegetable on chops. Add broth and bake 50 minutes to 1 hours uncoverd in 350 degree oven.

Pork Chops for Two

2 thick pork chops
2 T. margarine
1 large sweet potato
2 slices pineapple
½ cup pineapple juice
1 tsp. salt
¼ tsp black pepper

Brown pork chops in margarine, sprinkle with salt and pepper. Peel sweet potato, cut in half, and place a half over each chop; add pineapple and juice. Cover with tight-fitting lid; simmer 40 to 50 minutes.

Back in the early days of my marriage, our children wanted nothing for Sunday dinner but fried chicken or steak, brown gravy made with drippings from the fried meat or fowl, a salad of some kind—just so it was potato with lots of boiled eggs, pickles and onions—hot cheese biscuits, green beans, iced tea, and lemon pie.

Fifty-two times a year I fixed this same meal. If I dared to try to slip in another kind of meat, they raised their brows, muttered under their breath and announced that when they married and set up housekeeping, it would be a sure thing that no meat reached their table on Sunday except steak or chicken fried just right and served hot, hot.

Back in my salad days, my father would have nothing to do with farm wives putting six-week-old chickens in a coop high off the ground and raising them to selling size. Mama had customers who did not want a fryer to be too long-legged and battle-scarred from fighting with old roosters set in their ways and defending their home turf.

Daddy had hens he could depend on to hide their nests in the most unlikely places. Once a special pet hen hid her nest in a keg half-filled-with-nails. Even though we needed the nails, we put off that bit of work until the hen finished laying and hoveling her eggs. One fine day she brought off her brood of ten chicks, every one different. A special wee one turned out to be akin to the old frizzle rooster which roamed the briars and the small thicketed woods below the hog pens. There were dominickers, Rhode Islands, two half-bantams—ten chicks in all with different fathers, according to colorings and feathers. Other hens stole their nests and brought their straggling babies to the

Operatic Frankfurters

3 T. butter
1 onion, chopped
1 apple, diced
1 large can sauerkraut
1⅓ cup dry white wine
½ cup water
2 T. brown sugar
Salt
Pepper
6 or 8 frankfurters

Melt butter in heavy skillet and saute onions and apples until onions are golden. Mix in the sauerkraut, which has been well-drained, and add water, sugar, salt, pepper, and 1 cup of the wine. Stir well and cover tightly; simmer for 1 hour. Then put frankfurters on top, add remaining ⅓ cup wine and simmer another 15 minutes.

Soft Fried Chicken

Chicken
Flour
Hot fat
1 tsp. flour
2 cups cold water

Roll chicken in flour only and fry in hot fat very slowly in a skillet with a tight fitting lid. Turn often and when done remove chicken and pour off nearly all the grease. Add 1 tsp. flour, brown well, then add 2 cups cold water. Put chicken in water and fit lid over skillet. Turn fire very low and steam 20 to 30 minutes. You may need to add more water, even though you aren't trying to make gravy.

Baked Fryer

1 fryer, 2 or 2½ pounds
½ stick margarine or butter
2 or 3 tsp. Worcestershire sauce
Salt and pepper to taste

Disjoint fryer and sprinkle pieces with salt and pepper on both sides. Melt margarine in shallow baking pan with Worcestershire sauce added. Roll pieces of chicken over so that they are well-coated with margarine and sauce. Bake at 350 degrees for about 50 minutes, turning once.

Chicken Pie

Cut up one 3- to 4-pound frying chicken. Cook in salted water until tender. Remove chicken from broth and cool. Remove skin, bones and pieces of fat and then cut into bite-sized pieces.

Make dumplings using 1 cup plain flour, 2 tablespoons shortening (no oil), and cold water. Mix dough as for pie pastry. Chill for about 20 minutes. Roll dough very thin on floured surface. Cut in 1½-inch wide strips; allow to dry on waxed paper until broth is ready. Using a large boiler, bring broth to gentle boil; add ½ stick butter or margarine. Add dumplings a few at a time. Don't allow boiling to stop.

When dumplings are transparent, use slotted spoon to remove to baking dish where you have put ½ cup of the broth and a handful of the cut-up chicken. Continue cooking dumplings and layering with chicken and broth; pepper as desired. When all dumplings are cooked and pie

mule barn where they scratched for scattered corn, ate drained clabber and had fresh well water twice daily, courtesy of my brother, who hated this chore.

With company coming, Daddy would have six of his almost grown chickens penned for four days "to clean them out," as they said back in the old days. They would have clabber, corn, and cropped collards for their fare along with fresh water drawn twice a day from the deep well on the side of our front stomp.

Late Saturday afternoon these chickens would be killed, scalded, and picked. Mama never trusted others to scrape and cut up her chickens as she wanted the bony pieces to make chicken pie. A block of ice had been brought from Liberty for keeping the chicken chilled until frying time Sunday morning. Gallon jars would have the best pieces tucked inside, and the jars placed beside the ice in the sawdust box under a pecan tree. Mama boiled the chicken pie pieces, and this rich golden broth went in jars beside the ice.

We went to church, company or not, and Mama was up early to fry the chicken and make her pie, before cooking breakfast for our family. Two black iron skillets would be half filled with hog lard, the chicken dipped in sweet milk and rolled in peppered flour. When the lard was smoking just right, in would go the meaty pieces of chicken in the middle of the skillets. Heavy domed lids would be put in place and the skillets moved to the back eyes of the woodstove. Mama could tell by the way the grease was popping or purring when it was time to turn the chicken. Once the lid was lifted from the first skillet, the chicken quickly was turned, taking care not to let all the heat escape. The second skillet was done in the same way. When the frying sounds were just right, lids were removed to give the chicken time to crisp up. Next the chicken pieces were removed to brown paper to drain a bit.

There it was: crisp, brown pieces with crumbs clinging—and still enough crumbs in the skillet to make delicious brown gravy,

is built, thicken rest of broth with a paste of 2 tablespoons flour mixed with ½ cup cold broth.

Pour into small bowl, add ½ can cream of chicken soup, stir well (you may need to add more broth). Pour over contents of baking dish. There should be plenty of juice to cover.

Make measure of regular pie crust dough, using ¾ cup plain flour, ¼ teaspoon salt, ¼ cup vegetable shortening and enough cold water to form ball. Roll out on waxed paper and cut in wide strips; place over baking dish. Bake in 350 degree oven until contents are bubbly and top crust is brown.

Chicken Croquettes
(from Virginia Snow)

1 hen, boiled and chopped
2½ T. butter
2 T. flour
Enough milk to make thick white sauce
Dash salt
Grated onion (optional)
1 egg, beaten
Crushed corn flakes
2 T. butter
2 cups chicken stock
1 cup chopped mushrooms
2 T. flour

Cook 2½ tablespoons butter, 2 tablespoons flour, and milk together until thick. Mix with chopped chicken, dash salt, and grated onion. Shape into croquettes. Roll in beaten egg, then in crushed corn flakes. Bake at 350 degrees for an hour. Melt 2 tablespoons butter in pan, add flour, then blend in stock and mushrooms. Pour over baked croquettes.

Chicken Almond Casserole

1 can cream of chicken soup
1 cup cooked chicken breasts, chopped
2 hard-cooked eggs, chopped
1 cup diced celery
½ cup slivered almonds
1 tsp. minced onions
½ cup mayonnaise
Small bag potato chips

Mix all ingredients, except potato chips, gently. Turn mixture into shallow casserole dish and top generously with potato chips. Bake in 350 degree oven for 20 minutes. Serves four easily for a main dish.

Chicken Webster

(from Mrs. Evelyn Bain and Mrs. Amanda Jones)

1½ quarts chicken, cut into medium-size pieces
1 cup cold cooked rice
4 T. parsley, chopped
1 cup evaporated milk
1 button garlic
2 cups Rice Krispies
4 T. pimento, chopped fine
2 cups strong stock
4 eggs, beaten
1 medium-size onion, grated
Salt
Pepper

Mix all ingredients. Bake in individual molds at 375 degrees. Makes 20 molds. Serve with Almond Sauce or Mushroom Sauce.

peppered and salted just right. None of this milk or broth sort of gravy, but plain browned flour with all the crumbs bubbling in the dark brown fat, to which boiling water from the steaming tea kettle would be added. The cook had to stand back so the rolling and upward bound steam didn't steam her stirring hand nor hit under her chin. (That happened once, and Mama never could make those asking what had happened understand she was in the way of rising steam from brown chicken gravy.)

There is nothing more delicious over rice than this almost burned brown gravy, heavy with crisp bits of crumb from chicken fried in hog lard.

I, for one, like to have a baked or roasted hen around. Sandwiches made from cold chicken can fill any bill if you have boiled potatoes to slice and fry in a little bacon fat, frozen fruit to smother in cream, and a cookie jar filled with cookies of your choice.

To my way of thinking, a Chicken Pie dinner can't be beat! Especially if the mother or keeper of the home has other plans and must have a complete meal ready to serve noon or night.

There are some who flatly and frankly say, "Well, I like the dumplings or crust, can't get enough of the gravy or juice, but that wet chicken isn't for me." The happy solution to this problem is to buy two chickens; one a stewing hen and one a fryer. Cut the fryer up, reserving the meaty pieces to fry crisp and golden for those who don't like "wet" chicken, and use the less choice parts in the stewing pot.

The pie can be made early in the morning and reheated for the night meal. If it is to be served at the noon meal, please do not put it in the refrigerator. Put it in a cool place and allow it to come to room temperature.

Green beans, whole grain corn, a congealed salad, iced tea, hot rolls, and a dessert makes this meal good enough for any family.

Almond Sauce: Mix equal parts stock with evaporated milk and ½ cup sliced toasted almonds.

Chicken Little

1 broiling or frying chicken, cut into
  serving pieces
1 T. oil
1 tsp. salt
⅛ tsp. pepper
½ tsp. paprika
Juice of ½ lemon
½ cup water
¼ tsp. dried savory
¼ tsp. dried thyme
1 clove garlic (optional)
1 medium onion, sliced
1 medium green pepper, cut into strips
¼ pound mushrooms

Sprinkle chicken with salt, pepper, and paprika. Brown in skillet in 1 tablespoon oil for 20 minutes, starting with skin side down. Add lemon juice, water, herbs, and garlic. Cover and cook 10 minutes. Add vegetables, cover and cook 10 minutes longer, or until chicken is tender.

Chicken Spaghetti

1 large hen
2 pounds round steak
6 large green peppers
6 large onions
1 can mushrooms
2 cups chopped celery and leaves
2 large cans tomatoes

1 can tomato paste
Red pepper to taste
1 or 2 buttons garlic
2 to 5 bay leaves
Salt

Boil hen. Debone, return meat to broth. Add beef cut into chunks (do not grind). Add all other ingredients, adding mushrooms last. Boil slowly for 1 to 1½ hours being careful not to burn. Turn low and cook until all is a thick sauce, about 4 hours. Serve over spaghetti. Sprinkle a few buttered, browned bread crumbs on top and serve with Parmesan cheese. This will serve 12 to 16 people.

For a meal quick to fix, Chicken Spaghetti with lots of sauce is the answer. Serve with hot French bread or tiny crisp biscuits, a green salad with lots of vegetables in it, iced tea, and lemon pie.

A tablespoon of butter or oil will keep spaghetti from boiling over and sticking together.

Plantation Chicken

1 bunch broccoli
4 T. butter
4 T. flour
½ cup cream, whipped
2 cups chicken stock
3 T. sherry
½ cup parmesan cheese
Parsley
Toasted almonds
Sliced chicken or turkey

Cook broccoli. Drain on paper towels and keep hot. Melt butter, add flour, and stir. Slowly add stock and mix well. Cook in double boiler over low heat until mixture has thickened, stirring constantly. Cook 10 minutes longer, stirring occasionally. Remove from heat. Fold in whipped cream and sherry. Season with salt and pepper. Place broccoli in baking dish in individual servings. On each serving of broccoli, spoon sauce and sprinkle with ¼ cup cheese. Arrange 3 slices

Here's a cooking hint from the spice shelf that gives beautiful results. Sometimes, does your chicken get done before it is well browned? I have found this true with very young fryers. If you start on them when they are broilers, they need only to get hot through and through to be delicious. Try adding two tablespoons of paprika to the flour and see the wonderful brown it gives fried chicken. It isn't hot at all and makes a lovely red-brown gravy.

Let's get this chicken stew, dumplings, and chicken pie business straight right now.

Chicken Stew: Roll thin dough, cut into strips, drop into boiling chicken broth, and cook uncovered.

Chicken Dumplings: Drop spoonful of dough on top of boiling chicken and broth, cook with tight-fitting lid on, and don't peek.

Chicken Pie: Put layer of chicken and broth in large pan. Dot with butter and black pepper, then layer of rich dough. Bake until light brown; add another layer of chicken, broth and dough, bake. Do this until pan is nearly full. Some hold with a cup of sweet milk added, then bake 30 minutes. I like hard-boiled eggs and sweet cream in my pie.

Last would be cups of cooked-down broth, tasty with floating eyes of chicken fat, all melded together, food fit for the gods, company or family. Remember, this was before it was known you could eat yourself to death!

of chicken or turkey on each serving. Spoon remaining sauce over chicken and sprinkle with remaining cheese. Bake at 400 degrees until brown. Sprinkle with paprika and garnish with parsley and a few toasted almonds. Serves 4 to 6.

Chicken Broth

3 pounds meaty chicken bones, such as neck
½ cup coarsely chopped onion
½ cup coarsely chopped carrots
1 clove garlic, left whole
6 crushed peppercorns
1 bay leaf
½ tsp. dried thyme
Water to cover

Put the bones in a kettle and add cold water to cover. Bring to a full rolling boil and drain. Rinse the bones under cold running water until chilled. Drain. Return the bones to a clean kettle and add the remaining ingredients. Cover with cold water.

Bring to a boil and simmer, uncovered, for 2 hours. Strain and chill the broth. Skim and discard the fat from the surface and use the broth as required. Makes 7 ½-cup servings. Some cooks pick meat from necks and make salad.

Rich Brown Stew

2 pounds beef chuck
4 cups water
1 tsp. lemon juice
1 tsp. Worcestershire sauce
1 clove garlic, minced
2 bay leaves
½ pound small white onions
1 cup celery, cut in 1-inch lengths
1 T. salt
1 tsp. sugar
½ tsp. pepper
½ tsp. paprika
Dash allspice or cloves
6 small carrots, cut in thirds
4 medium Irish potatoes, cut in half

Cut meat into ½-inch cubes. Thoroughly brown meat on all sides in hot fat; add water, lemon juice, Worcestershire, garlic, bay leaves, and seasonings. Cover and cook slowly for 2 hours, stirring to keep from sticking. Remove bay leaves, add carrots, potatoes, onions, and celery. Continue cooking 20 to 30 minutes or until vegetables are done. Remove meat and vegetables, thicken liquid for gravy. Add more water if needed.

When I was a little girl, my daddy and mother would take my brother and me to box suppers. I was always so excited, I could hardly wait to get to the school house where they were always held. Mother would work on her box for hours, and never let Daddy see it. However, he was always expected to know which one was hers and buy it when the bidding got to five dollars. Always there was fried chicken, sandwiches, fruit, nuts, homemade cake and candy. I always planned on going to one and having the prettiest box. However, by the time I got old enough to have a beau, they had consolidated the country schools and box suppers were out of style. I wish I could go to one and take my boys.

Busy mothers are always on the lookout for filling, yet nourishing dishes. Brown Stew is one that will keep in the refrigerator or even freeze if the potatoes are left out and added just before serving.

When our sons became nimrods, fresh game was on our table several times a week, in season. Duck, quail, dove, rabbit, and squirrel cooked many ways pleased our family—also guests who were invited or dropped in at mealtime. Joe and Tim were noted for their method of hunting squirrels: Using a rifle, they would shoot the squirrels through the eyes, thereby keeping the head intact for a super stew. Of course, we used the whole squirrel to make squirrel fried, baked, or in dumplings; but the heads were used for a different stew.

Twenty heads, cleaned well, would be boiled in a black iron pot. A smarty pepper added to the water took care of seasoning. When done, the pepper pod was discarded, a half cup of butter was added to simmering water (salted to taste), and the broth and heads were allowed to rest until a measure of flour dumplings was mixed.

Heads and broth were then poured in a large dutch oven. When the broth was at simmer, teaspoons of the dumpling mixture would

Beef Stew

2 pounds stew meat (no bones)
1 pound Irish potatoes
1 bunch carrots
2 onions
2 fresh tomatoes or 2 cups canned
5 cups beef broth
3 sprigs parsley
3 stalks celery
½ tsp. black pepper
1 T. flour
1 bay leaf

Brown meat; add enough water to cover and simmer until meat is tender. Add vegetables, with bay leaf, parsley, and celery tied in cheese cloth bag. Season with salt and pepper, simmer until vegetables are tender, then remove bag. Pour off broth into heavy sauce pan, thicken with flour. Add thickened broth to meat and vegetables. Serve with wide noodles or hot rice.

Beef Stew with Dumplings

1½ pounds beef short ribs, shank, neck, rump or brisket
¼ cup flour
1½ tsp. salt
¼ tsp. black pepper
1 small onion
⅓ cup cubed carrots
⅓ cup cubed turnips
4 cups Irish potatoes, cut in quarters

Wipe meat, remove from bone, cut in 1½-inch cubes. Mix flour with salt and pepper and dredge cubes of meat in it. Heat some fat in a heavy frying pan, add meat and brown. Put meat with browned fat into heavy stew kettle. Add boiling water to cover, or a pint of tomatoes stewed and strained. Simmer until tender about 2 hours. Add carrots and turnips last hour of cooking. Add potatoes last 20 minutes and dumplings 15 minutes before serving.

Dumplings for Beef Stew

1 cup plain flour
4 tsp. baking powder
¼ tsp. salt
1 egg, beaten
½ cup milk

Sift flour with baking powder and salt. Mix egg with milk, adding all at once. Stir only until mixed. Drop by spoonfuls into boiling stew mixture. Cover and steam 15 minutes. Serve at once.

Meatballs

2 pounds finely ground beef
2 cloves garlic, chopped fine
1 egg
1 small can spinach
Pinch marjoram
Salt
Pepper
Onion juice
6 slices (fresh) bread
Milk
4 T. grated Parmesan cheese

be dropped into the broth. As each dumpling rose to the top, it would be pushed to the side and more would be added. When all the dumpling mixture was used, the heavy lid was put on and the stew set aside to thicken.

Soup plates were used to serve the stew. After the dumplings had been eaten and the gravy sopped with flour biscuits, the heads were enjoyed. Using a spoon the brains were scooped out, spread on soda crackers, then heavily peppered and doused with vinegar.

I haven't cooked such a stew in 30 or more years. Nowadays, my folks lean toward quail and oyster pie.

Meatballs are a surefire pleaser for vegetable soup. They're also good for adding to tomato sauce to serve over spaghetti. For football suppers, these bits of goodness are delicious when a bowl of highly seasoned tomato dunking sauce is nearby. Cheese biscuits go nicely with these snacks, and if you aren't up to making biscuits, serve a rich cheese cracker heated piping hot.

Drain, chop, and fry spinach in oil until dry. Soak bread in enough milk to be absorbed and combine with meat, cheese, spinach, seasonings, and beaten egg. Make into tiny balls and let stand on waxed paper several hours or all day in the refrigerator. Drop in rapidly boiling salted water and cook for 10 minutes, no longer. Cool and freeze in plastic bags.

Make a Meat Loaf, bake a chocolate cake, make oatmeal cookies, bake about two dozen hand-size sweet potatoes, and two apple pies and boil a dozen eggs. Your Sunday dinner will be child's play when you come home from church. Add iced tea, bought rolls, and cabbage slaw. Eat outside picnic style.

Meat Loaf and Vegetable Dinner

1½ pounds ground beef
1 can (15 ounces) tomato sauce
1¼ tsp. salt
¼ tsp. pepper
1 egg
1 slice bread soaked in ¼ cup milk
5 large potatoes, peeled and diced
3 or 4 carrots, cut in about 3 pieces each
1 large onion, cut in 6 pieces
1 can (16 ounce) tomatoes

In a large bowl mix beef, ½ can tomato sauce, salt, pepper, egg, and bread soaked in milk. Tear off heavy-duty foil and put into shallow pan. Place meat mixture in center and shape in loaf about 2 inches high. Surround with potatoes, carrots, and onions. Cover with tomatoes. Some juice can be added if tomatoes aren't very juicy. Seal securely, allowing some slack for cooking expansion. Bake in 400 degree oven for 1¼ to 1½ hours.

Crock Pot Roast

(from Yvonne Rice)

1 4-pound or 5-pound roast
Salt
Pepper
Flour
1 can cream of mushroom soup
½ soup can water
1 envelope Lipton's dry onion soup

Brown roast in shortening. Season with salt and pepper. Put in crock pot, add mushroom soup, water, and dry onion soup. Cook on high for 4 hours. Serve with rice or mashed potatoes.

Plain Chili

1½ pounds steak, ground
1 T. shortening
2 large cloves garlic, chopped
4 T. chili powder
Salt to taste
Pinch of sugar
1 can tomatoes or 5 or 6 ripe tomatoes,
    or can of tomato paste
2 T. flour
Lea and Perrin Sauce

Brown meat in shortening. Add garlic, chili powder, flour, tomatoes, and seasonings. Stir constantly while adding ingredients. Add as much water as desired; cover and cook slowly for an hour or so. In place of red beans or rice, have a bowl of mashed Irish potatoes. Make batch of biscuits to serve with wild plum jelly. Have lots of iced tea.

Do housewives bake bones today? Of course not! Oh, one or two who are getting ready to make a big pot of soup and have a great knuckle bone to be used just might put the whole thing in the oven to help thaw it out, but those doers are few and far between.

Back in my pre-salad days, Grandmother Budd often baked a pan of bones, cracked them, scooped the marrow, and seasoned it with lots of black pepper and salt. This mixture was used as a delicate spread for crackers or home baked fritters (those delicious bits of leftover pie crust rolled paper thin, cut in small squares, and baked, then served with the marrow, hot tea and a dab of plum preserves on the side).

Whenever round steak was cooked at our house, Mama always got the marrow from the round bones. (This would be removed after the meat had been fried.) The marrow would be mashed a bit and spread over the bottom crust of a biscuit, crisp and crusty. This goodie was supposed to be healthy for the growing baby, so it was reserved for babies in most farm families.

Somewhere in our family is a long slender, very-small-bowl spoon, which was used to get marrow from long leg bones. This was done at the table if the father had time for such.

Corned Beef Casserole

1 pkg. seashell macaroni
1 large can corned beef
1 can tomato paste plus 2 cans cold water
1 medium onion, chopped fine
1 medium green bell pepper, chopped fine
¼ cup chili sauce
¾ stick margarine
2 T. ketchup
1 tsp. prepared mustard
Dash chili powder to taste
Salt and pepper, if needed
Cheddar cheese

Saute onion and bell pepper in margarine until transparent, but not brown. Flake corned beef and add to mixture; add tomato paste, water, and seasonings. Cook until slightly thick, not dry. Boil macaroni according to package directions; drain and add to sauce, mixing well. Turn into serving dish and top with cheddar cheese. Bake at 350 degrees until cheese melts.

Two-in-One Casserole

1 pound ground beef
½ pound ground pork
1 medium onion, chopped
¼ cup butter
2 cans condensed tomato soup
1 cup cottage cheese
2 tsp. Worcestershire sauce
2 tsp. salt
¼ tsp. pepper ½ of 12-ounce pkg. medium noodles, cooked and drained
1 cup buttered crumbs

Brown meats and onion lightly in butter in frying pan. Add soup, cottage cheese, and seasonings; simmer for 15 minutes. Arrange layers of cooked noodles and meat mixture in buttered baking dish. Top with buttered crumbs. Bake in 350-degree oven for 25 minutes. Makes 8 to 10 servings.

Salt Mackerel

There is one delicious dish that is never out of season—salt mackerel. Back in the fifities, we ordered little wooden tubs of mackerel from Frank Davis in Maine and enjoyed this delicious different dish several mornings each week during cold weather. Of course, now you can buy mackerel in the supermarkets.

Soak the dried fish overnight in a tub full of water. When morning comes, lift out tenderly and place in a skillet of hot water. Boil gently for 10 minutes and pour off water. Have about a quart of whole milk ready, a big cup of thin sweet cream, fresh pepper, and a dust of nutmeg. Pour this over fish and bake about 40 minutes or until it browns on top. Plenty of hot biscuits and muscadine jelly are a must with this dish.

Oyster Stew

Chicken broth
Oysters
Butter
½ cup green onion snippets
½ cup thinly sliced celery
Generous amount inner celery leaves
Pepper

For those who enjoy snipping green onion tops to perk up salads or to add to dressing for stuffing turkey or chicken during the winter months, remember that it isn't too late to put out a few onion sets. Dale, the steady gardener, always plants three old washing machine tubs with sets. What a good time I have snipping away at the tops until the roots are large enough to use. Recently, I gave the onion tops a good snipping, and we indulged ourselves with oyster stew for supper.

Add chicken broth to 12-ounce can of oysters and their juice. Simmer until the edges of the oysters curl. Melt butter in skillet with green onions, celery and celery leaves. Add extra hard shake of pepper and cook over low heat to wilt. Heat fresh whole milk until piping hot (do not boil) and combine with oysters and wilted onion mixture. You must be the judge of how much milk you will use. Some folks like a lot of milk to absorb crackers, while others use only 2 cups of milk with the other ingredients. To gild the lily, I butter crisp crackers and toast for extra crunch.

One year I gave you my recipe for oyster stew, and the next year we enjoyed oyster scallop. This is a good way to stretch oysters, for they are as high as a cat's back.

Scalloped Oysters

1½ quarts oysters
3 cups dry bread crumbs
¼ cup melted butter
Salt
Pepper
Milk

Drain the oysters from their liquor and pick out any pieces of shell. Mix the crumbs and the melted butter; spread a thin layer of the crumbs in the bottom of a greased baking dish, cover with oysters, season with salt and pepper, add another layer of crumbs, and continue until all the oysters are used. Pour on the oyster liquor and, if needed, milk to moisten thoroughly. Cover the top with the remaining crumbs; bake in a 350-degree oven for 25 to 30 minutes and serve from the baking dish.

Salmon Muffins

(Ann Sturdivant's original recipe)

1 small bunch green onions, chopped
1 clove garlic, chopped
1½ cup seasoned bread crumbs
½ pound cheddar cheese, shredded
¼ tsp. salt
½ tsp. black pepper
1 tsp. Tabasco
3 T. parsley flakes
4 eggs
2 tsp. Worcestershire sauce
1 No. 303 can pink salmon

Saute onions and garlic in small amount of oil, just until tender. In large bowl, mix all other ingredients, except eggs. Beat eggs until frothy, add to salmon mixture and mix thoroughly. Pour into well-greased mini-muffin pans and bake in preheated 350 degree oven 20 minutes or until slightly brown. Can be baked in 9-by-13 metal pan at 325 degrees for 30 minutes. Cut in squares and cool. Serve with plenty of lemon slices.

Cream Gravy and Salmon

3 T. butter
1 large onion, chopped or handful of
    green onions
2 T. flour
1 cup sweet cream
Milk
1 small can salmon

Melt butter in heavy skillet; when melted add onion, cook until soft but not brown. Remove and

A country thing I love is fishing for mud cats. When I have a pan cleaned and ready for the grease, the children get the syrup pitcher, the butter, and the pepper sauce. They don't eat the syrup and pepper sauce together; some like mud cats one way and the rest another way. With hot corn bread and lots of coffee for the grownups and milk for the children, what could be better than about 20 mud cats, rolled in sifted meal, and fried real brown in bacon fat, served with cookies and fresh figs for dessert. Let the dishes stay piled in the sink until morning!

add flour, brown well, and add sweet cream and milk to desired consistency. Cook for 5 minutes and add salmon. Put hot biscuits in a bowl, pour salmon and gravy over them.

At my house we have two little boys and a little girl. Our meals must be meals that we can all eat. I simply do not have the time to prepare grown-up meals, meals for growing boys, and a meal for a redheaded little girl.

I am always on the lookout for a meal the whole family can eat and digest with no trouble on the part of the baby as well as the daddy. Baked Tuna is just such a fish dish. Dip out a bit of the dressing and tuna for the baby, and give the boys a slice of onion to go along with it.

Baked Tuna

1 can tuna (salmon may be used)
6 small onions
2 cups stuffing as prepared for chicken:
    About 2 T. butter, softened
    ⅛ tsp. salt
    Sage, a pinch
    Pepper to taste
    2 cups bread crumbs
    2 or 3 T. milk
    Butter

Butter a small baking dish. Put the tuna fish into the center, keeping it compact. Parboil onions until nearly done; arrange around the tuna fish. Place stuffing made of butter, salt, sage, pepper, bread crumbs, and milk around and over the tuna and onions, filling the dish. Put a sprinkling of bread crumbs moistened with milk over the top; dot with butter and bake at 350 until top is golden brown.

Tuna Onion Bake

4 large onions, cut into thick slices
1½ tsp. salt
2 cups milk
3 T. flour
¼ cup cold water
1 cup grated processed American cheese

½ tsp. Worcestershire sauce
1 egg, well-beaten
6 slices buttered toast
2 7-ounce cans solid packed tuna, drained

Put onions, salt and milk in saucepan; cover and cook over low heat until onions are tender, do not boil. Remove onions and reserve liquid. Mix flour and water together until smooth; add to liquid. Cook over low heat, stirring constantly until thickened and smooth. Add ½ cup cheese and Worcestershire sauce. Stir over very low heat until cheese is melted; remove from heat. Gradually add a little of hot mixture to egg, stirring constantly; stir into rest of sauce. Place toast in bottom of greased, shallow baking dish; break tuna into pieces with fork and place on top. Cover tuna with cooked onion slices and pour cheese sauce over all. Top with remaining cheese and bake at 350 degrees for 40 minutes.

Fish Fillets in Sauce

6 fillets of halibut or flounder
2 T. butter
2 T. flour
½ cup cream
½ cup sherry wine
½ tsp. salt
⅛ tsp. pepper
1 tsp. curry powder
½ cup white grapes
½ cup white raisins

Melt butter over low heat, stir in flour; add milk gradually. While stirring constantly, add wine, salt, and pepper. Stir until the sauce is thicken-

Fish for breakfast—how many of you have tried serving a platter of crispy brown, hand-sized perch for Sunday breakfast, a plate of tender biscuits, and, as a side dish, a deep bowl of brown fish gravy?

Dale is the trout catcher in our family and sometimes we enjoy a nice mess of eel. Dale and the boys think nothing of skinning and cooking four or five of the big fellows. Any left over are carefully saved to warm for another meal.

Fish freezes beautifully. If you are freezing a whole fish, dip in water and freeze until a nice coating of ice is formed over the fish. Wrap in the usual way.

A teaspoonful of mustard in hot dish water will remove fish and garlic odor.

Salty breezes fresh off the ocean do wonders to flagging spirits and appetites. Just the scent of the sea seems to make most of us ravenous. But even if you live far from the shining strands, you can get something of the same effect by cooking with the fruits of the sea. Clams—even the canned variety—carry with them the unmistakable salty tang of the ocean. Combine these delectable morsels with rice, vegetables, and seasonings and you have a clam pilaf that makes a hearty, satisfying supper dish. It's simple to make— in one pan—on top of the stove. Add a tossed green salad, some crusty rolls, and dinner's done.

Time was when men went dove hunting, they left word with their wives to "keep the grease hot." My mother would see to it that a good fire was in the range. She would have biscuits on the rise and a big pot of coffee on slow heat at the very back of the stove. If there was a can of new syrup on hand, the big syrup pitcher would be filled and a dish

ed and cook about 3 minutes, with frequent stirrings to prevent scorching. Cover tightly and remove from heat while preparing fish. Arrange fillets in a greased shallow baking dish. Sprinkle with parsley and curry powder, then with grapes and raisins. Spoon the sauce over the fish and bake about 30 minutes in a 350 degree oven.

Clam Pilaf

4 T. butter
2 T. minced onion
2 cups diagonally sliced celery
½ clove garlic, minced
½ tsp. tarragon leaves
½ tsp. basil leaves
1 tsp. parsley flakes
½ tsp. salt
¼ tsp. pepper
1 cup uncooked long grain rice
2 cups chicken stock
2 (10½-ounce) cans whole baby clams
1 (10-ounce) pkg. frozen peas, thawed

Melt butter in heavy skillet. Add onion, celery, garlic, and seasonings. Cook a few minutes, stirring often. Reduce heat. Stir in rice and cook 3 minutes more. Add chicken stock and bring to a boil. Stir well with a fork. Cover and simmer gently for 15 minutes. Drain and mince clams, add with peas to broth mixture. Cover and cook 10 minutes or until rice is tender and liquid absorbed. If desired, garnish with toasted slivered almonds.

Doves In Gravy

10 doves
1 T. butter to each dove
Water, about 2 cups

Cook the birds in butter in a covered iron vessel, pot, skillet, dutch oven or such. When tender, add cold water. Cook over low heat until liquid is reduced by half. Grind a little fresh pepper over doves and serve each person 2 doves on a slice of toast with gravy poured over all. Have extra toast on the side.

Fricassee Rabbit

Cut rabbit in pieces; dredge in flour seasoned with salt and pepper. Brown in 3 tablespoons hot fat. Cover with 1 large onion, thinly sliced and sprinkled with salt. Pour over this 1 cup sour milk, cream, or water; cover closely and simmer for an hour, or put pan in 325-degree oven and bake for 1 hour or until rabbit is very tender. Pan liquid may be thickened by mixing 2 tablespoons plain flour with ¼ cup cold water and seasoning to taste. Stir into pan liquid. Serve with hot biscuits, green beans, potato salad, and buttermilk. Lemon pie will be a treat for dessert.

of sweet butter was put on the table, which would be set with plates and ready for hungry hunters and families to "pull up and fill up."

Once the hunters crossed Waggoner Creek, they would send loud yells so those of us left back at the house could be ready to skin the doves for the feast. By the time the hunters had ridden their horses into the barnyard, we were on hand with plenty of newspapers, dish pans, and sharp knives. Only the breasts were skinned out and sent to the kitchen for washing, salting, and frying. Within minutes, good smells came from the two huge black iron skillets sputtering with half bacon fat, half ham fat. Back at the barn willing hands made the legs, heart and gizzards of the dove into a heaping pile of meat that would be used to cook up a delicious dish the next day, using rice and finger-sized dumplings. Cream gravy was the last thing to be made while the family found their places to enjoy the first doves of the season.

FROM THE GARDEN

Vegetables

The Gods sent not corn for the rich men only . . .

William Shakespeare

Mama tried her best to teach me everything a farm wife should know. However, Mama didn't reckon on my not paying attention to her instruction when it came to pulling roasting ears. No, indeedy, after one corn-pulling spree when I laid waste to 20 acres (to hear her tell it 50 years afterward), that job was never mine again. Mama decided I could play hob with my husband's corn patch—that is, if I ever got a husband—but not hers.

I take a firm stand and say: "There is no set rule for pulling corn for eating and freezing." I have searched many books, and questioned old folks for surefire ways to tell when sweet and field corn is the right degree. Nowhere have I found a line saying, "Pull sweet or field corn at thus and such a time." In the seed books, under the most tempting ear you have ever seen, will be these words: "Golden Bantham Corn will be ripe in sixty days from the planting." In our case it would be the second Wednesday after the first Monday in April. Alas, it doesn't work out that way. Frankly, I agree that sixty days from dropped seed to butter-slathering time is plenty where the rightful appointed place for tender ears or creamed corn is—namely on the plates of corn-hungry folk.

Books and old folk plainly tell you hen eggs will hatch in twenty-one days; and you had better have the coop ready for the hen and her brood. If you set a turkey or duck hen, don't bother to build your coop until the eve of the twenty-seventh day. Even our ice cream freezer came with a big tag saying, "Freezing time eight minutes." Every time, its eight minutes, no more, no less.

Along about the time the corn silks look right for making moustaches and goatee-like chin beards (you remember, dear one, how to do these elegant face decorations? Smear top lip and chin with sticky molasses, press dried silks in place and talk with only your lips moving, but gently), I begin to pull open a few ears, here and there. Always I am armed with a spool of silk thread to tie the shucks snug over the not-ready ears, for I have hoped too soon. Dale assures me the silks must be brown and droopy. My eyesight isn't the same as others'; if I wait until the silks look brown and droopy, the corn is so hard it takes a horse with good teeth to eat it boiled.

Picking peas is a snap! Okra is tested with a thumbnail. Squash picked the moment finger length is reached, a cucumber is ready well before it has developed a seed. I can pick butterbeans with my eyes closed, strawberries must be real red, and anybody with hands can feel a cabbage head and tell if it is fit for the salad bowl.

Yellow apples must be yellow before pulling, green apples stay green even when ripe, grapes turn purple when ready for making jelly or wine, elderberry flowers must be golden before picking for wine, and, of course, the elderberries must be purple-black before picking for pies, wine or jelly.

I can tell when a maypop is ready to eat; never do I gather sheep sorrels before just right for snipping into salad bowls. Cotton picking, pshaw! Anybody—even Rose Budd—knows it must be open, white, and dry. Pecans open their hulls and spill out the nuts. Wild plums to be eaten with cow salt hang ready in mid-October. But corn?

Our sons know the very day in the fall when muscadines and possum grapes get ripe. They have a sixth sense for fish grabbing. Even without the law that says dove must be hunted from this day to that day, they can tell when that first day arrives by sniffing the breezes that come from the west.

Dale is a perfectionist at pulling watermelons, with never a green one in a car load. He can judge the weight of a fat steer ready for the freezer; he tells me to call the freezer plant and say, "He will dress out at around 400 pounds." And the steer does, give or take a few pounds.

I can churn and tell the minute the butter comes without lifting the churn lid. However, be warned! If I am around and you need a mess of corn pulled for a meal or to freeze, don't send me: it will be half pops and the rest fit only for the birds.

Asparagus and Macaroni Casserole

1 No. 2 can asparagus, drained (save juice)
2 cups cooked macaroni
2 or 3 hard-boiled eggs
2 cups cheese sauce

Put a layer each of asparagus, macaroni, egg slices and cheese sauce in casserole. Bake for about 15 to 25 minutes at 375 degrees. I like to add pie crust to the top for a pretty surprise dish.

Cheese Sauce

2 cups asparagus juice or milk
5 or 6 T. flour or 2 T. corn starch
½ to ¾ pound grated cheese
½ to 1 stick butter

Melt butter slowly in heavy boiler; stir in flour. Add liquid, a small amount at a time, stirring constantly. When smooth add cheese and cook until thick.

What a lucky farm wife to have the makings of beautiful decorations right on the farm. My newly constructed table decoration is a dream. I took my biggest tray, piled six dark orange squash in a helter-skelter fashion; green and red peppers were placed at vantage points, three purple onions were added along with a white onion for color contrast, and a bunch of wine red grapes was placed right on top. Later on I will make a new centerpiece of ruby red sweet potatoes, green winter squash, white onions, and polished nuts.

Corn and Asparagus is a dish that can be made, frozen, and cooked days later. With this almost a meal-in-one dish, you will like tiny, very hot biscuits made with ham or a bit of bacon. A peach stuffed with pecans, cream cheese, and a bit of mayonnaise to hold it together, with a sharp lemon dressing poured over is just the salad to accompany this dish. Green beans from the freezer go nicely, and for dessert why not try hot gingerbread with applesauce or a slice of old-fashioned chocolate pie.

Corn And Asparagus

3 T. butter
4 T. flour
½ tsp. salt
¼ tsp. paprika
¼ tsp. celery salt
2 cups sweet milk
1½ cups cooked corn
1 cup canned asparagus
½ cup bread crumbs
⅓ cup grated cheese

Melt butter, add flour, and stir until well-mixed. Add seasoning and stir, pouring in the milk. Cook slowly, stirring constantly until a creamy sauce forms. Add corn and asparagus. Pour into a shallow, buttered baking dish, cover with bread crumbs, dot with butter, sprinkle cheese over top and bake 20 minutes in 350-degree oven.

Broccoli Casserole

⅔ stick margarine
½ cup chopped onion
½ cup chopped celery
2 boxes frozen broccoli spears
1 tsp. salt
1 pkg. (roll) garlic cheese
1 can cream of mushroom soup
Bread crumbs (Italian)
White bread crumbs

Saute onions and celery in margarine until soft but not brown. Add cheese and mushroom soup. Mix together until cheese melts. Pour over cooked and drained broccoli. Sprinkle "bought" Italian bread crumbs over this, then spread real bread crumbs on top. Bake in 350-degree oven until brown and bubbly.

Baked Cabbage

Head of cabbage
Cooking fat or oil
Onion, chopped
2 eggs
Cayenne pepper to taste
Salt to taste
2 T. butter
Bread crumbs from 2 slices of bread

Trim down and wash a solid white head of cabbage. With sharp knife, cut off top cross section, and hollow out head, leaving a thick shell. Cut up heart of cabbage that was removed; put in frying pan with a little cooking fat and sliced or chopped onion and bread crumbs that have been soaked in water and squeezed dry. Cook until cabbage is barely tender, then turn into bowl. Add 2 eggs, cayenne and salt to taste. Stuff mixture into cabbage, place top on. Tie whole cabbage up in a clean cloth and boil in broth or salted water to cover. When tender, remove from water and remove cloth; place cabbage in baking dish or pan, put butter on top, and brown in oven.

Ground meat—ham is especially good—may be cooked and added to the cabbage mixture before stuffing cabbage. Serve with a corn casserole, corn bread sticks, hot tea, and for dessert, applesauce with lemon cookies.

What have you cooked differently for your family in the past few days? We are all hankering for new turnip greens, smarty radishes, baby carrots, and green onions. Water corn bread is a must with these spring goodies. For those who enjoy a big dish of smothered green onions coated with eggs, certainly nothing could be more delicious than a pan of fluffy egg bread, cut in large pie-shaped pieces, each piece split and heaped with a generous serving of the onion-egg mixture.

If one listens carefully on a hot still day in July the sound of corn growing can be heard; that is if you happen to be close by a field of lush beautiful corn.

To my way of thinking beauty is rampant in a corn field; I feast my eyes on blue-green curving leaves, drooping so gracefully, fruited with two ears, and once every five or six stalks three ears. A great field of corn rustles and sighs, clapping its hands and tossing tassels in small breezes blowing from over the far away hills. How pretty are the drooping silks, some snow white, others pink, and here and there a few dried brown-black.

I like to walk in a field of laid-by corn—much higher than the tallest man on Shady Rest it towers. How faint the sun filters through the millions of leaves laced this way and that, making golden coins on mellow earth.

I remember the year Dale and I decided to sucker this very field of corn and almost worked ourselves to death keeping the suckers pulled off. We'd carry great

Cabbage And Apple Casserole

1 small head green cabbage
1 small head red cabbage
1 cup green bell pepper, minced
3 cups diced apples
½ cup brown sugar
Juice of 1 lemon
½ cup butter
Salt
Pepper
Nutmeg
Bread crumbs

Grind cabbages separately. Season red cabbage with salt and pepper, place in greased casserole, and dot with half of butter. Add sugar, lemon juice, and nutmeg to apples. Place on top of red cabbage. Mix green cabbage with green pepper; season with salt, pepper, and nutmeg. Place over apples. Dot with rest of butter. Cover with buttered bread crumbs and bake in moderate 375-degree oven for about 25 minutes. Makes 6 or 8 servings. Serve with biscuits, crisp fried bacon, and sliced pineapple.

Boiled Corn

Corn on the cob, fresh from the garden
1 tsp. sugar
½ stick butter

Full well do I know the heady taste of fresh corn just reaching the milk or dough stage, for we have feasted on several varieties: golden bantham, white sweet corn, and yellow sweet corn. Now that the "sweets" are almost gone, we will wait a little while and begin fattening as well as feasting on field corn: a corn so yellow, a dish of fried or baked corn looks as if Mother Nature threw in an extra measure of color—that's a treat!

At our house we are fortunate that we can have freshly churned butter at least three times a week. Nothing goes with tender boiled corn like butter just lifted from the churn, washed well, and salted lightly.

When the corn is boiled, the water becomes faintly yellow. One year, I saved this corn water and used it to water my ferns. While I have no idea if this water had any value other than being wet, the ferns grew fronds longer that any I had grown in other years.

Sweet corn must be taken directly from the stalk to the boiling water for best results. I will allow time to remove the shucks, but if you leave a few of the tender inner shucks, not over three or four on each ear, the taste will be improved (if at all possible).

Have a big pot of water boiling. Add 1 teaspoon sugar. Add corn and let boil approximately 9 minutes. Remove at once. Melt ½ stick of butter in a long deep dish. Turn each ear over in butter. Place on platter and serve. Each person seasons to taste.

armfuls of the lush green suckers to the milk cows and how they enjoyed the crisp green food as a dessert to a day of clovers and grasses of the pasture. Suckering the corn did nothing for it; in fact, the rows we left made just as good, if not better, corn. But we learned a valuable lesson: Never toil to sucker corn; it amounts to nothing. Old heads had tried to tell us, but we had to see for ourselves.

Back in my little girlhood, I faintly remember Bo-Diddle telling of corn he had heard his grandfather talk about. They raised it for cattle feed and there was no outside shuck on the ear. Each grain or kernel was enclosed in a separate husk.

Listen with your ears as well as your heart if you chance to be in a corn field in July.

Corn Fritters

1 cup flour
½ tsp. salt
1 egg
¼ cup milk
½ T. butter
1 tsp. baking powder
1 cup whole-grain drained corn

Corn Fritters are especially good with a plain vegetable dinner, such as green beans, beets, potato salad, and lemon pie for dessert. Children like them served with tartar sauce, and they are delicious if served with tart plum jelly. Back when I was a child coming in from school and very hungry, Mama would often fry corn fritters for use with syrup or jelly.

Corn Pudding goes well with wilted lettuce salad, smothered round steak, hot biscuits, wild plum jelly, iced tea, and spice cookies for dessert.

The person who sent me this recipe for German Style Cucumbers wrote: "I got this recipe from people in a German community in Michigan. They said their ancestors brought this recipe with them from Germany before 1850. They said salting out the liquid from the cucumbers makes them more digestible for those who say they can't eat cucumbers."

I enjoy German Style Cucumbers with thin, hot

Mix dry ingredients. Add milk and well-beaten egg. Add corn and melted butter. Drop by teaspoonfuls into hot fat and fry until brown.

Corn Pudding

1½ cups fresh yellow corn cut from cob
   (make sure to scrape milk from cob)
¼ tsp. salt
⅛ tsp. pepper
1 tsp. sugar
3 eggs
1¼ cups sweet milk
¼ cup melted butter

Combine corn and corn milk, salt, and sugar. Beat eggs and add to corn mixture. Add milk and melted butter. Pour into greased casserole dish. Set in pan of water. Bake at 350 degrees for 60 minutes.

German-Style Cucumbers
(Michigan-1850)

3 large cucumbers
Salt
1 small white onion
Black pepper
½ tsp. sugar
Vinegar
Mayonnaise

Peel and wash cucumbers; slice into paper-thin rounds and put into a large bowl. Lightly salt and let stand at room temperature at least 2 hours. With hands squeeze out all liquid and place squeezed-out cucumbers in another bowl. Thinly slice onion into cucumbers and generously sprinkle with black pepper. In a kitchen teaspoon such as you would eat with, place half a teaspoon of sugar; add just enough vinegar to moisten. Add to cucumbers. Then add as much good quality mayonnaise as you like to moisten the cucumbers well. Chill and serve.

Eggplant Pizza-Style

1 medium eggplant
1 beaten egg
⅓ cup fine, dry bread crumbs
Salad or olive oil
Salt
Pepper
1 8-ounce can seasoned tomato sauce
1 tsp. oregano
2 T. chopped parsley
¼ cup grated Parmesan cheese
4 to 6 slices Mozzarella cheese

Pare eggplant and cut in ½-inch slices. Dip in beaten egg, then coat well with bread crumbs. Let dry a few minutes, then lightly brown on both sides in hot oil. Overlap slices in lightly buttered 10 x 6 x 1½-inch baking dish. Sprinkle with salt, pepper, oregano, parsley, and Parmesan cheese. Top with mozzarella cheese. Pour tomato sauce over all. Bake in 350-degree oven for 20 minutes or until sauce is bubbly and cheese melts. Makes 5 or 6 servings.

Elder Bloom Fritters

Cut whole head of blooms from an elderberry bush, dip up and down in clear water, drain, and

buttered biscuits, a slice of boiled ham, small new Irish potatoes seasoned with butter and chopped parsley, hot tea, and a slice of fresh huckleberry pie with pouring cream for dessert.

I am a firm believer in cooking several vegetables for the noon meal; I certainly don't see anything funny about having beets, green beans, cut corn, squash, cabbage salad, peas. and potatoes fixed two ways for a meal.

Once when we had unexpected company I was a little put out that I had Irish potatoes cooked three ways: boiled to eat with melted butter, cooked in milk gravy, and a big dish of chips. Not every person ate of all three, but most helped themselves to two dishes, even though I had five other vegetables on the table.

Mama often has potato salad and creamed potatoes at a meal; I notice guests helping themselves with a lavish hand when the creamed dish is passed, for nobody can fluff a potato better than Mama. She pounds the daylights out of them with an old fashioned masher. But wait a minute. She shakes the boiler over a hot flame to dry every drop of water out of the boiler. While the mashing is going on Mama has half sweet cream and milk along with

then divide clusters of blooms. Make up a fritter batter using flour, sweet milk, sugar, and salt—about like pancake or batter cake mixture. Dip bloom clusters in fritter batter and drop in hot fat. Let cook until light brown or until you think they are done enough for your family. You can cook squash bloom fritters this way, too.

Hominy Balls

Form cooked and cooled hominy into small balls about the size of a walnut. Roll in fine, soft bread crumbs; dip into mixture of beaten egg and 3 tablespoons milk. Roll again in crumbs and fry in hot deep fat until browned. Serve in place of potatoes. These are especially good with crisp bacon and tart, wild plum jelly.

Lima Bean Casserole

1 small can green lima beans, drained
¾ cup water
2 T. chili sauce
2 T. butter
2 T. chopped green pepper
1 small onion, chopped
Grated cheese

Combine all ingredients except cheese. Bake in covered dish about 1 hour at 350 degrees. Uncover and sprinkle cheese on top the last 10 minutes of baking. Serve with hamburger patties, corn bread muffins, and iced tea. Berry cobbler with pouring cream is perfect for dessert.

Stewed Okra

1 pound okra, sliced
1 No. 2 can tomatoes or pint of home-canned
   tomatoes
4 strips bacon, cut in small pieces
1 medium onion, chopped
Salt and pepper

Fry bacon and remove from fat. Add onion to fat, cook until tender but not brown. Add okra, cook about 10 minutes. Add cooked bacon and tomatoes. Season to taste. Cook over low heat until tender, stirring occasionally.

Fried Okra

Okra is delicious when cut in 45-degree slices and worked gently with your hands to get it slightly slimy. (If you are using frozen okra, slice it frozen, and let it sit a couple of hours before you are ready to cook it.) Next add a bit of self-rising flour and work to coat each piece. Sprinkle meal over okra slices and work very gently. Have a deep iron kettle filled with fresh cooking oil, and drop in okra a few pieces at a time. As they rise to the top, remove to brown paper to drain. Keep hot until served.

Onion-Potato Dish

1 big white onion
3 medium white potatoes
1 quart sweet milk

a piece of butter the size of an egg heating to the just-before-skim-forming-point. The milk is added just a little at a time, and the potatoes are whipped well after each addition.

Daddy has been eating Mama's creamed potatoes at least six times a week for over forty years and not once has Mama ever added cheese, crisp bacon or any of the other nonsense things some cookbooks tell us to add. At our house we do stoop to brown gravy spooned over a helping of potatoes, once in a blue moon.

Store mushrooms in a paper sack in the refrigerator to keep them from turning brown.

You can hasten germination of peas by soaking them overnight in water. Drain water off the next morning and let peas stand on a piece of absorbent toweling for an hour or so before planting. Remember, peas do best in rich soil that has been conditioned with well rotted manure and commercial fertilizer. Bush peas mature in 55 days and tall-growing varieties in 60 to 80 days.

Once we planted a long row of peas called telephone peas, and never have I seen such tall vines. Dale put two three-foot pieces of chicken wire down the double row, making the so-called stakes six feet tall. I am a mere five feet and scant two inches tall so I had to get a stepladder to pick the peas.

1 can cream of mushroom soup
Grated cheese

Boil onion and potatoes until done; mash and cream well. Place over hot water while heating milk. Mix potatoes, onions, and hot milk. Add soup; heat very hot but not boiling. Pour in big bowls and grate a little cheese over on top. Serve with thin corn bread or crackers. All you need with this to make a meal is a custard or Jell-O and your favorite drink.

Peas in a Pot

Bacon
3 T. flour
Peas, washed not drained
    (Crowder, Cream, Silver
    Cream, Purple Hull,
    Whipporwill)

Cut bacon in medium-thick slices and fry a little in the bottom of the pot. Remove the bacon and add the flour (you will have to temper the amount of bacon and flour to the amount of peas you have) and brown slightly. This will make a roux that is the basis of your pea liquor. Add the washed, un-drained peas and stir over and over until they are well-coated with the grease and flour mixture. Of course, the flame will be low under the pot all this time and you will never stop turning the peas. After 5 minutes of this, add 1 cup of water and cover tightly. Cook slowly and add water as need-ed, only a little at a time. The resulting peas are grand, and the liquor will be slightly thick, just fine for eating out of a sauce dish.

Lye Hominy

First you must have a wooden hopper—or a wooden barrel will do—with a wooden spout at the bottom. You must get five or six water buckets full of ashes from the fireplace (hickory and oak are best) and put them in the hopper. Place a wooden or glass container under the spout. Then pour enough hot water over the ashes to cover and then a bucket to spare. The water will slowly drip through the ashes, leaching lye into the container. This is all done outside in the yard, of course. Once you have four cups of lye drippings, you are ready to start on your hominy.

You will need a black iron washpot that holds at least 15 gallons of water, including the lye water. Shell 20 big ears of white corn or lots of small ones. Pick out the bad grains, saving them for the chickens. Put corn in the washpot, add lye water, and fresh well water. Make a nice to middling fire under the pot and let it boil gently for eight or nine hours. (Certainly you would want to start this at good daylight.)

When the grains get big and begin to crack and swell, pull the fire away from the pot. Dip corn into a big tub, take to the creek or branch, and wash, wash, wash, rubbing the grains to remove the husks and black specks at the end of each grain where it grew on the cob. (Some folks never bothered to get these black specks off, saying the black pepper used to season the hominy looked just the same.)

Once the washing is over, the corn should be put back in the iron pot, and cooked in clear water for about four hours, or until done enough to suit your family. At the end of this time you should have a nice big amount of hominy ready to be drained and put in stone crocks and then stored in a pantry or smokehouse. Pieces of clean cloth should be tied over the crocks.

Lye hominy was on many plates back in the Depression. A food easy to digest, it could be prepared in many ways once the hard work was over. If there were corn in the crib and ashes in the fireplace, the family could whomp up a batch of hominy within a day or so. Dale says he remembers going by the lye hominy crock, getting a handful, and eating it as if it was popcorn.

Hominy can be served with melted butter or stirred into the frying pan where a slice of pink home-cured ham has been sizzled. The hominy will take up the bits and pieces left in the skillet. Seasoned with lots of black pepper, this is a nice dish to serve with hot biscuits and quince preserves. I know families who always add a big dish of cabbage cooked with apples to round out the meal.

But may I make a suggestion to all you lovers of lye hominy? Buy a can at the grocery store. You will save yourself much misery, money, and many sore muscles.

For those who want to know what you are missing, the recipe appears on these pages.

For several years we have enjoyed poke sallet plants growing in out of the way places in our yard. One very thrifty plant grew to over ten feet, smack in the middle of the last compost pile. Another pushed its dusky ruby stems from beside a Boston Terrier pen.

Longing for a "poke salad" in an exact spot became a "thing" with me. I saved and planted seed, dug, and planted roots; even small plants were carefully lifted and put out. Nothing happened to boost my faith in my "once green thumb," for the seeds failed to sprout, the roots curled and turned black (How do I know? Well, I dug them up after a month or so), and the transplanted plants grew pale and finally waned away. All the while down in the bare spots in the barn yard many, many poke sallet plants poked tender crisp green leaves to the sun. These I cut before the sun reached them on the fourth day, and cooked them for delicious greens and water corn bread.

Mother's Day, Dale came inside and invited me to come see what he had

Poke Sallet

In early spring when finger-high poke sallet leaves are tender green, gather your apron full to make a batch of these prized greens. Back in my salad days the old folks cooked several batches, or "messes," to clean out a person's system. After a winter of no fresh vegetables, poke sallet was welcome.

Wash poke sallet leaves with gentle hands, then scald through three waters. Melt bacon grease in a black iron skillet. Cook the scalded greens by turning over and over in bacon grease. They will turn dark green with moisture forming. Add salt and pepper and a hard-boiled egg, peeled while hot, and sliced over the greens.

New Irish Potatoes in Cream Gravy

6 medium size Irish potatoes
2 cups cold water or enough to cover (Should be at least 2 cups)
1 tsp. salt
3 T. butter or margarine
2 heaping T. plain flour
¼ tsp. pepper
1 cup sweet milk

Scrape new potatoes leaving bits of pink skin. Cut in 1 to 1½-inch cubes. Put in heavy boiler, add cold water and salt, bring to boiling point, reduce heat and cook until tender, about 15 minutes. Do not drain. Remove from heat. Mix milk, flour, and pepper in cup until smooth—add a bit of potato water, stir again; add more potato water and stir—

then add to potatoes and water. Cover boiler and cook on low heat; stir until sauce thickens. Set aside for at least 10 minutes before serving. The cream sauce is delicious served over hot egg corn bread.

New Irish Potatoes in Brown Gravy

5 medium-sized new Irish potatoes
Cold water to cover
1 tsp. salt

Wash potatoes well—scrub with stiff brush—leaving pieces of the thin pink skin on. Cut in large pieces, each potato in about eight pieces. Cover with cold water; bring to boil, reduce heat, and cook until done (test with fork). Drain, saving water for gravy.

For brown gravy: Fry two slices of bacon for each person; remove bacon to platter to keep warm. Pour off most of grease, reserving about 4 tablespoons to make gravy. Put grease in heavy skillet, add about 3 level tablespoons plain flour and cook till dark brown, taking care not to let it burn. Remove from heat; slowly add potato water, stirring all the time. Place over low flame and cook gravy until flour and water is thickened. Pepper well. Pour gravy over potatoes, let come to a boil, remove from heat, and let ripen for at least 10 to 15 minutes.

Serve with bacon, corn meal muffins, wilted lettuce salad, and for dessert, canned pears and spice cookies. A good meal for an early spring supper.

discovered for my extra special Mother's Day present. Imagine my delight to find not one but three of these lovely plants growing where I had planted seeds several years ago. Perhaps I was too anxious, eager and not willing to wait until Mother Nature gave the nudge to the wee seeds, to get growing.

Already I am enjoying round clusters of knobby buds, ready to bloom. The pleasing shade of pinky-red stems, against the spring green leaves is a cooling, refreshing sight any time of day.

Most times Mother Nature provides for sallet plants in likely places: fence corners, in zigzags of rail fences, beside old barns, sheep sheds, even in lower gardens and back yards.

Know how she does this? In late fall when the poke berries are ripe, birds feast on these reddish purple berries. When they sit on fences or barn eaves, they pass these seeds through the process of elimination. How clever of Mother Nature! Seeds are deposited along with a dap of fertilizer in apt and likely places. Along about early March, the second season after the planting by birds, you will be able to gather finger-high tender green leaves.

Once a patch of poke sallet is established, there will be potato-like roots. Not too long ago we were cleaning a place below our playhouse where a thriving patch had provided us with messes of nature's broom for at least thirty-five years. Thinking we were dealing with a tree root, we dug and dug. Imagine our pleasure when we turned out a great root which weighed eleven pounds. (Sure, I brought the kitchen scales to weigh this surprise.) At once we made plans to chop the root and boil it for making a 'tea-wash' for poison oak or ivy, or any summer rash that vinegar water will not cure. Anyone for a pint of Rose Budd's poke tea? Bring your own bottle! Or you can dig a small root and plant it in your own nook or corner, assured it will grow and soon you will have a poke sallet patch of your very own.

Potato Pancakes

If any mashed Irish potatoes are left over, be happy. At the next meal form small cakes from them, dip in flour, and brown in a bit of bacon fat. These potato pancakes can be served with jelly, meat, cheese, sauce, or vegetables.

Scalloped Potatoes

4 cups thinly sliced potatoes
2 T. butter
2 cups sweet milk
2 T. flour
½ tsp. salt
⅛ tsp. pepper
¼ cup chopped onion
Green pepper rings (optional)
Parsley (optional)

Melt butter; blend in flour. Gradually add milk. Cook over low heat until thick, stirring constantly. Add salt, pepper, and onion. Place half of potatoes in buttered casserole and cover with half of sauce. Top with remaining potatoes and rest of sauce. Cover with lid or foil and bake in 350-degree oven for 30 minutes. Garnish with pepper rings or perky parsley for a bright trim.

French Fries

To my way of thinking, a big platter of French fries, crisp on the outside and tender on the inside, can't be beat. Before I go to the field, I peel a pot of potatoes, cover with ice water, and leave in the refrigerator. When I come to the house to milk, I slice them in finger-sized slices, add salt, and pepper well. Then I heat a heavy skillet and add fat that had either bacon or ham fried in it, until smoking. Next I add drained potatoes and turn the flame down low. Then I cover with a heavy lid, and go milk. As soon as I wash my hands, I take the batter cake turner and turn the potatoes over in one cake. I brown them for a few minutes, for they have cooked through. Break potatoes apart before serving.

They are delicious with cold corn, butterbeans, green peppers, salad, chicken stew, and corn bread. Plenty of cookies and cold milk will fill everyone to bursting.

Cut off the flat bottom of an onion and let it drain on a paper towel a few minutes before eating or cooking. The milky liquid absorbed in the towel is responsible for tears and adds to indigestion when eating onions.

Squash Drumsticks

Small, tender yellow squash
   (about 2 per person)
1 beaten egg
1 T. water or milk
Cracker crumbs
Salt
Pepper
Paprika

Leave squash whole and cook until tender in strong onion water. When tender, but not too much so, drain and cool. Dip in beaten egg that has been diluted with 1 tablespoon water or milk and again slightly beaten. Dip in cracker crumbs, seasoned with salt, pepper, and paprika. Fry in deep fat until golden brown.

Are you tired of yellow squash cooked in casseroles, stewed down low with onion, baked in the oven, or stuffed with any kind of meat or other vegetable? Then have a platter of Squash Drumsticks for supper tonight. They're truly delicious when served with a side dish of chili sauce.

Hurry, hurry to the seed store and get some English pea seed. Many smart gardeners have peas up, and I hear tales of Irish potatoes already snug in the ground. The woods rabbits and the semi-tame ones that live in the edges of your garden during the winter months must be shut out of the garden; now is a fine time to go around the garden and weave a piece of wire in every hole large enough for a skinny rabbit to slip through. Takes a little time, but it surely will save a lot of woe and wails some near-spring morning when you visit your garden only to discover a rabbit and his family have feasted off your peas during the night.

Paper tied on sticks stuck here and there over the garden doesn't work on these modern-day rabbits. I well remember putting sheets of crumpled newspaper tied on sticks in my garden years ago; however, I believe the rabbits had found better feeding grounds and if they had come to my garden, the paper wouldn't have bothered them one whit.

Squash a la Originale

3 tsp. ketchup
Salt
Pepper
Buttered bread crumbs
1½ pounds yellow squash
1 small can tomatoes
2 large onions, sliced

Scrub squash and slice. Place squash and onions alternately in buttered casserole. Pour remaining ingredients over top. Bake 35 minutes in 350-degree oven. Add crumbs and bake 15 minutes longer.

Sweet Potato Balls

Roll mashed sweet potato around a marshamallow to form a small ball. Dip balls in 1 egg diluted with 2 tablespoons water, then in seasoned bread crumbs. Fry balls in deep fat or bake in moderate oven. Serve with any meat.

Sweet Potato Casserole

3 medium sweet potatoes, baked and mashed
2 to 4 T. honey or sugar
½ cup milk
¼ stick butter
½ to ¾ cup coconut
Marshmallows

Mix first 4 ingredients. Put in baking dish, sprinkle coconut on top, then press marshmallows down into mixture. Bake 25 minutes at 350 degrees. I find today's marshmallows don't stand up as well as they did when this recipe was first used back in 1940. I suggest adding marshmallows the last 10 minutes of baking.

Spiced Sweet Potato Casserole

3 pounds sweet potatoes
¾ cup light brown sugar
3 T. butter
Pinch salt
½ tsp. cinnamon
½ tsp. nutmeg
½ tsp. ginger (optional)
¾ cup whole milk
½ cup raisins, plumped in warm water
½ cup toasted pecans, broken in pieces
2 well-beaten eggs
1 cup sweet milk

Pare and boil potatoes. When tender, mash well, and add rest of ingredients. Put in greased casserole and bake in 350-degree oven for 20 minutes. Top with whole marshmallows and brown. If any is left over, serve cold with whipped cream for dessert the next day. This freezes nicely and can be made weeks ahead of time.

Cinnamon Sweet Potatoes

2 large sweet potatoes
½ cup fresh butter

This is the time of year when no farm woman can call her time her own. The second patch of corn in the lower garden is at its peak, and one must work like mad to get it from the garden to the freezer or jars. It can and does get too hard in a matter of several hours. What is perfect at five in the morning will be tough by five in the afternoon.

If you pull an ear open and it isn't ready, have a spool of thread in your apron pocket, smooth the shucks and tie several wraps of thread around the ear. The birds are not so apt to peck and insects won't enter in and sour it. If you pull ears that are too hard, let the children cut grains off close to the cob for the laying hens.

When the last ear is pulled off a stalk, break the top over so the boys will be sure to cut that stalk for the milk cows. Milk cows love the fresh green stalks of corn, and the pail will be filled to overflowing.

Juice of 2 oranges
1 cup white sugar
1 cup brown sugar
Cinnamon to taste

Peel potatoes and slice into thick chunks; place in deep pan or skillet. Add butter, orange juice, sugars, cinnamon to taste, and water to cover. Place in stove and bake until juice is thick. This can be used as a dessert or with cold meat.

Rice Croquettes

1 cup raw rice
4 T. butter
4 T. sugar
2 egg yolks, well beaten
Milk
Salt to taste
Bread crumbs or cracker meal

Add raw rice to 8 cups boiling water. Cook rapidly for about 25 minutes. Drain in colander, rinse under hot running water. Whip the butter and sugar into hot rice and season with salt. When partly cooled, add 2 well-beaten egg yolks; moisten with enough milk to hold form when molded with hands. Mold into balls or cakes, dip in beaten egg, roll in fine bread crumbs or cracker meal, and fry in either deep or shallow fat. Serve hot. Makes 8 nice-size croquettes. These are a nice addition to scrambled eggs and currant jelly.

Garden Odds and Ends

2 quarts of sliced okra
2 large sweet onions, chopped
4 peppers—2 red, 2 green—chopped

6 large ripe tomatoes, peeled and chopped
Salt and pepper as needed
4 T. chicken fat

Put 4 tablespoons of chicken fat in heavy iron pot. Put chopped vegetables on top of fat. Put heavy lid on; cook over low fire for about 45 minutes. Add a little hot water if needed. Season to taste. Serve with lettuce salad, corn bread muffins, and the last of the smoked ham which has been put down in lard. Iced tea for grown ups and children. Lemon cookies and apple sauce for dessert.

Stuffed Cabbage

(from Mrs. J.K. Sanders)

1 medium-size head cabbage
1 egg
½ cup milk
1 T. grated onion
1 envelope (1½ ounces) cheese sauce mix
1 cup soft bread crumbs
1 pound lean ground beef
1 1-pound can tomatoes
salt to taste

Remove core from cabbage; then hollow out center of cabbage, leaving a 1-inch shell. Beat together egg and milk. Stir in bread crumbs, ground beef, and onion; mix lightly. Spoon mixture into the center of cabbage. Place hollow side down in deep casserole. Stir together contents of sauce mix envelope and tomatoes, and pour over cabbage in casserole. Cover tightly and bake at 375 degrees for about 1 hour or until tender. Cut in wedges and serve with tomato and cheese sauce.

Right now is the time to make hot pepper sauce for winter eating. Pick and wash enough green, red, and yellow pods to fill a pretty shaped bottle. Heat vinegar to boiling and fill bottle. After a few hours the peppers will have absorbed a little vinegar; fill to the top again. Let set a few days. Always put the bottle on the table when you serve collards, turnip greens, mustard, pig feet, and blackeyed peas.

New English peas cooked with marble-size new Irish potatoes, slices of soda corn bread, buttermilk, ginger bread, and ginger sauce make a mighty fine spring meal.

Preserves, Pickles, & Relishes

Here on Shady Rest I am elbow-deep in jam, jelly, and marmalade making. The first two crates of strawberries were made into luscious jam. I simply cannot bring myself to make strawberry jelly and throw away the pulp—entirely too much good eating, to my way of thinking.

The old fields are yielding a heavy harvest of plums, both red and yellow. Along the ditch banks and in clumps the plum trees seem to huddle together, forming a canopy of deep green, spiked with ornaments beautiful and flavorful—namely, the plum.

My children, thank goodness, see beauty in most things, like the heavily-fruited plum trees, for all the world like a Christmas tree in June. We go in the late afternoon and gather the sun-warm, ripe plums. A foot tub holds the small deeply yellow ditch fruits, a big bucket filled and heaped with bright red field plums. Once Rose Jr. and I "toted" the buckets to the house. Now that we are the proud owners of a wheelbarrow with a tire filled with air, we ride the plums in style.

Carefully the plums are sorted, the specked ones in one pile for our newest Shady Rest member—a fat, already spoiled guinea pig, sure to grow into a hog one of these days. The clear-of-specks plums go into a deep dishpan for washing and cooking. The biggest and fattest of the red plums go into a special bowl for chilling icy cold, to be eaten after supper while we sit outside on the patio, enjoying the stars, scent of rose, the flash of lightning bugs, shadows cast by a full moon, the night breezes, and the plaintive call of the whippoorwill.

Tomorrow is to be a big day, for I plan to make thirty pints of jelly, marmalade, and a few jars of plum preserves. Some tell me that jam, jelly, and the like can be bought cheaper than it can be made at home. Maybe so, but I get pleasure and joy out of canning and having extra to share with friends. I love to open a cupboard and see the fruits of my labor there in colorful array.

We have a daughter who must be taught these arts and skills, and who can do it better than I? I want my daughter to learn to work with her hands, take pride in winning a prize at the fair for her efforts, or if no prize, see where she can better her product. Our sons tell me they had rather have a jar of my yellow plum marmalade for eating with roast pork, beef, or chicken than any bought sweet. So you see how easy it is for such talk to lure me into a whole day of sweet making?

Apricot Jam Deluxe

1 pound dry apricots
1 No. 2 can crushed pineapple

Cover apricots with water and cook gently until done. Put through food mill or mash with potato masher; add pineapple and sweeten to taste. Cook until thick, stirring often. This filling or jam is simply wonderful if spread between hot ginger-bread squares and topped with whipped cream. If your family leans toward fried pies or tarts, use a tablespoon of jam on a square of dough. Fry in deep fat, or for less work, place dough on well greased baking sheet, dot butter and bake in 350 degree oven until done; top with jam.

It's August and elderberry time is just over a month away. Berries hang in lush clusters everywhere you look in old fields, fence rows, barnyards, wildflower fields, and along roadsides. I'm sure these lovely bushes and berries were put here as special treats for our bird friends; however, many of my readers enjoy a few jars of elderberry jelly.

Old Time Elderberry Jelly

1 pint elderberry juice
1 pint apple pectin mixture
1 pint granulated sugar

Cover 2 pints berries with water; bring to boil and boil for 2 minutes. Remove from heat and turn into jelly bag. Bring juice and pectin to boil, add sugar; stir and boil rapidly until it will "sheet" from spoon. Skim, pour into hot jars and seal.

Ripe Elderberry Jelly

3 cups of prepared berry juice
2 pounds white sugar
¼ cup lemon juice
1 box Sure-Jel fruit pectin

Take 3 pounds of ripe elderberries (remove stems before weighing). Crush fruit one layer at a time until all are crushed. Heat gently until juice starts to flow. Cover and simmer 15 minutes, stirring occasionally, strain. Measure sugar and set aside. Stir Sure-Jel and lemon juice into berry juice, place over heat and let come to full boil. Stir in measured sugar and bring to a full rolling boil that cannot be stirred down and boil hard for one minute. YOU MUST STIR CONSTANTLY. Remove from heat, skim off foam, and pour into clean jars. Wipe tops with clean hot damp cloth and seal

Homemade Pectin

When you peel tart apples, save the peels and cores (leave seed in). Wash and cover with water, then boil for 10 minutes. Strain, can in jars, and use for delicate jellies.

Orange and Quince Marmalade

7 pounds quinces
3 quart water
8 oranges
9 pounds sugar

Pare and core quinces; boil parings and cores in water to cover until tender, then strain through jelly bag. To this juice add the quince, chopped fine, and the rind of two of the oranges, chopped fine. Simmer until quinces are tender, then add sugar, slightly heated in the oven, and juice of all the oranges. Simmer together for 2 hours, stirring occasionally to prevent scorching, or until mixture gels. Seal in sterilized jars.

When my grandmother made this jelly, she used homemade pectin made from the peelings and cores of apples she had canned in late August and September before elderberries got ripe.

Do you know how to tell when and if your fruit juice has enough pectin? Mother always used one teaspoon of cooked juice and stirred in one teaspoon of grain alcohol. DO NOT TASTE. If the juice was rich in pectin, it formed a large amount of gelatinous material; if poor in pectin, only a small flaky sediment was formed. Apples, grapes, plums, and cranberries have generous amounts of pectin, and they combine well with raspberries, pineapple, cherries, and strawberries, all of which are notoriously short on pectin.

Once, when the apple man was part of the scene or farm folk had apple trees in the back yard, orchard, or even down in the old stump field, women canned for winter pies and other

goodies. Sometimes they dried a supply for making tarts, a spread for hot cinnamon, a spread for hot biscuits, or just for eating out of hand. Housewives then had a great store of peels and cores to make all the pectin they could use.

Don't put preserves in quart jars. When a jar is opened so long, the family will get tired of the same flavor and the preserves seem to lose some of their fragrance and to darken. Pints are fine and for small families, half-pints are better.

With a bowl of peach preserves and a pan of hot buttered biscuits, there is no need for a dessert at the end of a meal. Mammy's Peach Preserves are made by a real old-fashioned recipe and will please many tastes. Pear preserves can be made using the same recipe.

Muscadine Preserves

Wash muscadines (can use scuppernongs), remove stems and drain. Separate pulp from hulls by pressing between fingers. Cook pulp in its own juice until soft and press through sieve to remove seeds. Add just enough cold water to cover hulls, then boil slowly over low heat about 20 minutes or until tender. Add pulp to hulls, measure, and add 1 cup white sugar to each cup of fruit mixture. Cook until thick, stirring to keep from sticking. Put in hot sterilized jars and seal. Store in dark place.

Mammy's Peach Preserves

Select firm peaches of a variety that will not cook to pieces (cling stones are best), peel, and cut in halves as much as possible. Using a large enamel or stone vessel, put a layer of peaches and a layer of sugar; alternate until you have covered all peaches with sugar. Let stand overnight. Dip out peaches and place in another vessel while you strain juice (syrup) that has come from the peaches while they sat overnight. Use that juice and as many pounds of sugar as you have peaches in making a syrup that you bring to a boil before dropping in the pared soaked peaches. Be sure to have enough syrup to keep peaches from sticking. Cook at high heat until bubbly; then turn as low as possible to keep preserves simmering. Cook until peaches take on a transparent look and the syrup is good and thick. Let stand in syrup overnight. Next morning heat and seal. Cook a few seeds in the syrup for an extra delicious flavor.

Country Brandy Peaches

1 bushel ripe freestone peaches
6 pounds sugar
1 yeast cake or 1 pkg. active dry yeast

Scald and skin peaches and place them in a 5-gallon earthenware crock. Add sugar. Cover crock with a plate or lid and tie a cloth over the top. Set aside in a cool, dark place. On second day, stir mixture gently to help dissolve sugar. On third day, stir again. Remove a little of the peach juice and dissolve yeast in the liquid. Add dissolved yeast to peaches in crock. Place a clean, weighted plate inside the crock on top of the peaches to keep them submerged while juices ferment. Cover crock with clean cloth tied down and store in cool dark place. Every second day, open crock and stir peaches, with gentle hand. When peaches sink to bottom and remain submerged on their own, they may be used or removed to jars, sealed, and processed in a hot-water bath for long-term storage.

Mother-in-Law Pear Relish

2 quarts pears, after grinding
1 quart small onions, before grinding
4 hot peppers, ground
4 green bell peppers, ground
2 red bell peppers, ground
6 medium dill pickles, chopped very fine
2 cups sugar
3 tsp. dry mustard
2 T. white mustard seed
2 T. salt
1 tsp. turmeric powder

Grandmother Budd did not waste a thing when working with peaches. I never remember grandmother dipping peaches in hot water to scald them for easier peeling. Indeed not! She wanted those peelings for canning so she could make fried peach pies in the cold winter months.

Once the peelings were off the peaches, it was Aunt Phleta who washed them well, put peelings in a heavy boiler, covered them with boiling water, and cooked them until they were tender. The cover was removed and the peelings boiled hard to evaporate the water. The peelings were mashed and packed in hot pint jars, popped into a hot water bath, and boiled for twenty minutes.

As a rule there would be five pints of peels waiting for adding sugar (to taste) when the family had a taste for fried peeling peach pies. Now the peelings can be cooled, packaged in pint size freezer containers, and frozen.

One sure sign of fall to me is the falling of the pears. In the night a little wind will come stealing across the west forty and gently shake the tall pear tree just outside my window. I hear a thud as a great juicy pear hits the ground. I make a mental note to get up before the chickens do in the morning, for they love to take deep pecks from the fallen pears. Always I fill my apron with at least a dozen green and russet beauties, just enough to make a few jars of pear mince meat, or perhaps pear relish.

And speaking of pear relish, I know every cook reading this will want to make at least eight pints of this delicious, yellow-flecked-with-green-and-red relish. It has no peer for use with cold meats and winter vegetables.

Different pear trees bear different fruit, of course. I take my time about picking up preserving pears and often let them stay on the ground overnight. Not so with the delicious eating pears. The crop is small and

1 quart vinegar
4 T. flour

Mix dry ingredients, then mix with ground vegetables. Cook for 15 minutes, stirring often. Seal in clean hot jars.

Pear Relish

2 quarts pears, after grinding (use coarse blade for all vegetables)
1 pint white onions, after grinding
1 hot pepper, ground
4 large green bell peppers, ground
2 red bell peppers, ground
6 medium dill pickles, ground
3 tsp. dry mustard
2 T. mustard seeds
2 T. salt
1 tsp. turmeric powder
1 quart vinegar
4 T. flour
2 cups sugar

Mix dry ingredients, then mix with ground vegetables and pears. Cook for 15 minutes after it comes to a good boil. Stir often. Seal in clean, hot jars. Makes 8 pints, with a little left over for supper.

Pear Honey

11 pounds ground pears
6 pounds sugar
1 pound coconut
1 large can crushed pineapple
2 large oranges, seeded

Grind pears, oranges and coconut; add pineapple and juice, mix with sugar; cook slowly until thick and clear. Seal in hot jars.

Pear Mincemeat

7 pounds peeled and cored pears
3 pounds sugar
1 pound seedless raisins
2 large apples
2 oranges, unpeeled
1 lemon, unpeeled
1 cup vinegar
1 cup grapejuice
1 T. cloves
1 T. allspice
1 T. cinnamon
1 tsp. nutmeg

Grind fruits and sugar together; add remaining ingredients. Boil 2 hours and seal in hot clean jars.

Plum Jelly and Butter

Clean and wash plums, cover with water. Let come to almost a boil and sit for 10 minutes. Drain the juice off. This is for jelly. Follow directions on box of bought fruit pectin. When the plums are cool, force all the pulp off the seeds, using a colander. Use the pulp and hulls for making plum butter, using 1 cup of sugar to 1 cup of pulp. If the hulls won't go through the colander, pick them out with your hands, for the hulls are delicious in the butter, and it makes an interesting texture. This mixture has to be watched with an eagle eye because it burns easily, but the results are worth every minute of your time.

the eating so satisfying. For the smooth, soft feathery thump that says, "Here is something really tasty for canning or eating out of hand," I drop whatever I am doing and rush outside and bring in this lovely bit of goodness.

They are wrapped in newspaper and put in a pasteboard box with holes cut in it. This, in turn, is pushed under my bed where the pears lie in secret darkness and develop their natural sugar, until they are so juicy you have to hold them over a saucer or go outside to eat them.

The plums are beautiful. Under the trees a carpet of fallen ones give dinner to ants, bees, and other forms of insect life. Each day I make several jars of plum butter, jelly, or marmalade to add to my store of delicious winter eating. I lean toward the old fashioned plum, the red ones make such sparkling jelly. In our yards we have apricots that reach small peach size; they are delicious eating, grand for cooking, and for canning whole there is nothing better; still I think the wild plum superior for jelly and butter making.

Homegrown or bought berries make delicious preserves, and believe me, if you want ten recipes, ask as many cooks! From whole berries dipped in thick sugar syrup, then dried on panes of glass in the hot sun, to a cold preserve using pectin for thickening, you get a wide range of strawberry preserves. This Strawberry Preserves recipe is very tasty and bright red if the berries are of the deep red variety.

The recipe says: Cover with medium syrup and freeze. There are your beautiful berries ready for the freezing cups. You rack your brain: just how do you make medium syrup? Given below is some very helpful information, and the wonderful thing about this syrup is that you can keep it in the refrigerator in a gallon jug, ready for freezing a small or large amount of fruit.

Strawberry Preserves

1 quart perfect berries
2 quarts boiling water
3 cups sugar

Wash berries in cold water. Cap, using teaspoon so as not to ruin thumbnail. Pour 2 quarts of boiling water over berries; drain at once. Discard water. Add 1 cup sugar and boil 5 minutes. Add 2 cups sugar and boil 15 minutes. Pour in a large dish. Let stand at room temperature overnight to plump up the berries. Pour or dip into glasses; seal with wax. Do not try to make a double measure: the berrries will get mashed and the results simply will not be up to perfection.

Mock Strawberry Jam

2 cups ripe figs, peeled and mashed
  (measure after mashing)
2 cups white sugar
1 large or 2 small pkgs. strawberry gelatin

Combine ingredients in heavy sauce pan. Bring to a boil and cook for 5 minutes. Pour into hot, sterilized jars and seal. Store in cool dark place. This jam is delicious with hot buttered biscuits.

Canning Syrup

Thin Syrup: 1 cup sugar to 3 cups water. Stir well before heating and bring slowly to a boil. For use with naturally sweet fruits or to give the effect of fresh fruits.

Medium Syrup: 1 cup sugar to 2 cups water. Prepare as for thin syrup. Good for general canning of fruits not highly acid.

Heavy Syrup: 1 cup sugar to 1 cup water. Stir and boil very carefully to prevent crystallization and scorching. For very sour fruits like rhubarb; suitable for dessert use.

Most freezing recipes for fruits call for a medium syrup. It is wise to make up a gallon at a time and keep handy.

Tomato Preserves

4 cups red-ripe tomatoes, peeled and
　　finely cut
1½ tsp. pickling spices
¼ tsp. powdered ginger
2 cups sugar
1 lemon, thinly sliced with seeds removed

Put tomatoes in steel or enamel-ware boiler. Heat slightly; pour off a generous amount of the juice that forms. (Save the juice to drink or add a little cream to make a cream soup.) Tie pickling spices in a muslin bag; add with remaining ingredients to tomatoes. Simmer slowly, stirring often, until tomatoes become transparent, about 20 minutes. Remove boiler from heat. Cover and let stand. Eighteen hours later, reheat and simmer slowly for 30 minutes. Stir frequently, as it scorches easily. After removing the sack of pickling spices, pour mixture into small jars, sealing each with paraffin. Store in a cool dark place and serve with whole wheat rolls and butter.

My mother always made a list of things to be canned or dried when spring came. One of the foods she made sure to can was plenty of fresh tomatoes. Of course she put up soup mix using tomatoes, tomato paste, tomato chili, tomato sauce, even tomato conserve, which is a sort of relish with brown sugar, spices, broken pecan meats, and slivers of lemon peel.

Here in 1988 I remember her fresh tomatoes, beautiful in blue-green glass canning jars. They were whole tomatoes about hen egg size canned in extra thick, fresh-made tomato juice. In winter when fresh vegetables and fruit weren't to be had, how we enjoyed Mama's fresh tomatoes (canned without salt).

Vine-ripe tomatoes were gathered in early morning, hand-peeled, then heated in tomato juice until just simmering. Next the tomatoes were put in quart jars, covered with the hot tomato juice, then the jars were well-sealed with red rubber rings and Mason jar tops. When eight jars were ready, a water bath for 20 minutes finished the canning process. When cool, storage in the deep recesses of the dark pantry kept the bright red of the fresh tomatoes from fading.

Cauliflower Pickles

Wash and clean cauliflower. Place in salty water (salty enough to float an egg). Leave cauliflower in salty water for 7 days. Remove on eighth day. Rinse well and place in alum water strong enough to pucker your tongue. Leave in alum water 1 day. Next day rinse well and place in jars. Mix 1 quart vinegar and 2 quarts sugar; bring to boil. Pour over cauliflower in jars; do not seal. Drain jars and reheat juice for 3 days. On fourth day drain and heat juice; seal jars. (Do not remove cauliflower from jars. Just drain off and heat; be sure it boils.) Wipe jar tops well, boil jar flats according to directions on box, place on jars, use sealing rings, and tighten. I never process these pickles. I also put loose spices in a few jars.

Every year I make about 20 quarts of pickles using this recipe for Four Day Pickles. It is foolproof and the results—well, try them and see for yourself.

Four Day Pickles

1 gallon cucumbers, after slicing
2 heaping T. lime
½ gallon white vinegar
8 cups sugar
1 box pickling spices

Add lime to cucumbers; cover with cold water. Let stand 24 hours and wash through 4 waters. Mix remaining ingredients and pour over cucumbers; let set for 24 hours. Simmer in mixture for 20 minutes; let set for 24 hours and seal cold in pint or quart jars. If you start on Monday at nine o'clock, by Thursday the same hour you should be packing the pickles into the jars.

Garden Dill Pickles

Gather as many big cucumbers (about the length of a quart jar) as you have, wash and pack into clean quart jars. Add 1 tablespoon of salt and a big bunch of dill. Fill jars with cold vinegar and seal. Let set at least 30 days before opening. Sometimes I hollow out the cucumbers and fill with shredded cabbage; can in the same way. A clove of garlic may be added to the dill pickles.

Ice Box Pickles

3½ pounds thinly sliced cucumber
2 large onions, chopped fine
7 bell peppers, chopped fine
3½ cups sugar
2 cups vinegar
¼ cup salt

Mix vinegar, sugar, and salt until sugar dissolves. Pour over the cucumbers, peppers, and onions and mix together well. Stir every 10 or 15 minutes for 2 hours. Put into jars and keep in refrigerator.

Mustard Pickles

1 gallon vinegar
1 cup salt
1 cup sugar
1 cup ground mustard
1 cup ground horseradish
A little piece of alum
Cucumbers

Some folks have it and others don't. Grandpa Causey had that sense of knowing when to cover up his beans and watermelons and any other garden sass that might get nipped by Jack Frost coming in late March or early April. He listened to the thunder in February, marked it accordingly on the March and April calendar, and, on the right dates, he and the hired men brought down from the loft over the small corn crib, newspapers, pieces of cardboard, and brown paper bags—all saved with such days in mind.

Days when the temperature dropped degrees in a few hours and the air was sharp and frost was sure to cover the farm with a mantle of white, Grandpa could fashion cunning little paper caps for a hill of beans with a few twists of his work-gnarled hands. A slender stick was used to fasten the cap together; this in turn was gently placed over a tender light green bean, and the whole thing was anchored with a heavy clod of dirt. Always the Causey farm had beans, melons, and truck to sell long before other would-be-gardeners knew what was happening—all because Grandpa was a weather watcher and did something about it.

Of course, he couldn't make paper caps big enough to cover his fruit trees, but he did something to save his baby apples, peaches, and grafted plums. He and Grandmother stayed up all night when a frost was coming, keeping several fires going in the orchard—fires that were smothered down and allowed to smoke and keep the air stirred. All during the winter when a slack period came, a few loads of fat lidered, along with some big logs, were carried to the orchard against such days.

Once I spent the night with my Causey grandparents and had the wonderful experience of staying up all night, snuggled close by a smoky fire, watching and hoping the trees would be saved.

Only once do I remember an apple crop failure. People came from far and wide to buy green apples, and Grandpa had no apples to sell. In fact, that year there were no apples for

Mix the vinegar with the dry ingredients. Wash and wipe the cucumbers and put them into a crock containing the mixture. Put a plate and a stone over the top. Add a few cucumbers every day until the crock is filled. Let set 3 weeks, then pack in jars, pour liquid over and seal.

Mustard Bread and Butter Pickles

1 quart tiny green tomatoes
1 quart large green tomatoes
2 or 3 heads of cauliflower
1 pint large cucumbers
1 pint midget cucumbers
½ pound ground mustard
3 cups sugar
½ cup salt
6 green peppers, diced
1 pint to 1 quart tiny onions, or 1 pint large onions, quartered and sliced
1 gallon vinegar
2 cups flour
2 T. powdered turmeric
Vinegar to make paste

Quarter and slice the large tomatoes, making one quart. Break the cauliflower into flowerets. Dice the peppers; quarter and slice the large onions; slice the cucumbers. Add all the vegetables except the cucumbers to the gallon of vinegar; let come to a good scald and remove the vegetables. To this vinegar add the mustard, flour, sugar, powdered turmeric, and salt, which have been mixed together with enough vinegar gradually added to make a smooth paste. Let boil, stirring; add the vegetables including cucumbers, bring again to boil, and seal in jars.

Pickled Peppers

(from Lora Hughes McAlpin)

1 gallon green bell peppers,
    cored, sliced and washed

Blanch peppers for 10 minutes in boiling water. Drain this water and pour fresh boiling water over peppers to cover; bring to another boil. Drain and pack in jars and cover with liquid.

Liquid: Combine 1 quart vinegar, 2 cups sugar, 1 cup water, and 1½ tsp. salt. Bring to boil and pour over peppers in jars. Seal and process. Makes 4 quarts or 8 pints.

Sliced Sweet Pickles

2 gallons cucumbers, 3 to 5 inches in length
¾ cup salt
14 small white onions
4 large green peppers
10 cups sugar
1 T. turmeric
¼ cup mustard seed
1 tsp. celery seed
1 tsp. ground cloves
2½ quarts vinegar

Slice the cucumbers into ⅛-inch slices without paring. Slice the onions likewise and cut the peppers into fine bits. Mix the salt through the combined cucumbers, onions, and peppers. Place a weighted lid on them and let stand 3 hours. Drain and add sugar, turmeric, mustard seed, celery seed, cloves, and vinegar. Place over low heat, heat thoroughly, but do not boil, stirring often. Pack into jars and seal. This makes a very crisp sliced pickle.

Grandmother to core, then cut in rings, these in turn to be strung on heavy strips of cloth or on cane poles, then taken to the garden and dried in the sun and later piled loosely in cheese cloth bags and hung in the attic to mellow until winter.

I didn't get much from Grandpa Causey—some cut glass salt dishes, a mirror in a walnut frame—but I did get the love of work and the courage not to be afraid of what life might hand me from him.

A *farm woman has a time when so many things are ready to can at one time. For instance, right now on my back porch, waiting to be canned: one bushel of purple hull peas, a wash tub of tomatoes, two zinc buckets of butter beans, a foot tub of shelly beans. The children are sick of the sight of things to be shelled and peeled for canning, and I don't blame them. Today, instead of making them help me, they are going to play and have fun. Little feet and fingers can't be expected to stay still and work for something that to them is as nothing.*

I think the tomatoes can be washed, the bad spots cut out, and cooked whole. Tomato juice will be fine on cold mornings this winter. The peas can wait until afternoon, and the butter beans and shelly beans will make a cooker to be gotten out of the way before dinner. That gives the long afternoon to shell and pick over the peas, and tonight they will be canned— fourteen quarts of them. Time must be taken out for a quick swim this

Pickle Relish

7 medium cucumbers, grated (you can use a few more)
3 medium-sized onions, ground
3 large green bell peppers, chopped fine
3 large red peppers (you can use 6 green if you don't have red), chopped fine
1 pod hot pepper (leave whole; discard before canning)
5 T. salt
3 cups sugar
3½ cups water
1 cup white vinegar
1 T. turmeric
¼ tsp. ground cinnamon
¼ tsp. allspice
¼ tsp. ground cloves
½ tsp. celery seed

Mix vegetables together; add salt and let set overnight in refrigerator. Drain and rinse. Make syrup of remaining ingredients and bring to a boil. Add vegetables. Simmer for a few minutes; pack in sterile jars and seal.

Beet Relish

1 quart cooked beets
1 small head cabbage
1 cupful grated horseradish (prepared horseradish may be used)
2 cups sugar
3 T. salt
2 T. mustard seed
2 tsp. celery seed
1 pint vinegar

Put the beets and cabbage through the food chopper and add the other ingredients in the order given. Let stand at least 24 hours. This relish will keep well in a covered crock with a little salad oil poured over it.

Green Tomato Mincemeat

1 peck green tomatoes
2 lemons
4 pounds brown sugar
2 pound seedless raisins
1 T. salt
1 tsp. cloves (ground)
1 tsp. allspice
1 tsp. cinnamon
½ tsp. mace
1 cup vinegar

Scald and peel tomatoes. Put through food chopper using coarse blade. Add sugar, raisins, vinegar, and spices. Bring to a boil and cool slowly for an hour. Pour into sterilized jars and seal. Of course, you remove the seeds from the lemons. Grind the whole lemon, peel and all. If your tomatoes are very small and tender there is no need to peel them. When you are ready to make your pie, use two crusts. One pint of mincemeat will make a nice pie for slicing for company. It keeps if well-covered.

Mrs. Thomas's Relish

1 quart chopped celery
1 quart chopped ripe tomatoes
1 quart chopped bell pepper, green
½ cup chopped bell pepper, red

afternoon, and I think cookies and lemonade will be fine for a little picnic by the spring branch.

July days are little gems—each one a day to be welcomed with open arms. Sure, it is hot, and if we are to believe the weather man, it is going to be hotter.

Years ago I was of the school "I am going to be hot, so why not do my work while I am hot as can be, then enjoy the cool hours of the morning and late afternoon pleasuring myself and being lazy as a cat in the sun." This I did until I reached forty, and only then did I realize that even though I was still young, I felt better and not so many little snags popped up in my days if I got up bright and early, even before the first bird opened a beady eye to view the coming dawn.

Now, if I have jelly or jam to make, I try to get to

bed by nine and I am up at three, measuring sugar, and cooking juice. What a wonderful time to make a batch of biscuits, put them on top of the water heater so they will be faintly sour by breakfast time. Get out one of your pretty relish or jam dishes and dish up for breakfast some of the fresh goodness you are cooking.

Helpful hint to keep relishes from sticking in middle of pot while cooking: put five silver dimes in the bottom of the pot. When you stir, the dimes will go back and forth. Be sure to use real silver dimes. The ones I use are so old and worn there are no markings on them.

½ cup chopped hot pepper
1 cup carrots, diced
1 cup small snap beans
1 pint small whole onions
5 T. mustard seed
1 tsp. celery seed
1 tsp. turmeric
4 cups vinegar
2 cups sugar

Soak tomatoes, peppers, and onions overnight in salt water to taste. Drain off brine, mix with mustard seed, celery seed, turmeric, vinegar, and sugar. Add other vegetables. Let stand 2 hours. Cook until mixture is clear. Seal in clean hot jars. Grand when served with cold pork roast and wonderful with dried lima beans.

Chow Chow

1 quart chopped cucumbers
1 quart chopped green tomatoes
1 quart chopped cabbage
2 large chopped onions
½ gallon vinegar
2 T. mixed spices
4 cups sugar

Soak vegetables overnight in salt water (not too salty). Drain and then squeeze out all the water you can, without bruising the vegetables. Mix vinegar with sugar and spices, bring to boil. Add vegetables, bring to boil again and boil for 10 minutes. Put in clean hot pint jars, seal, and store in cool dark place. Be sure to save a small dish of chow chow to serve with spring vegetables.

Rose Budd's Chili Sauce

1 peck tomatoes
6 large white onions
¼ cup salt
2 cups vinegar
6 large green bell peppers
¾ cup sugar
1 tsp. ground cloves
1 tsp. allspice
1 tsp. black pepper

Scald, peel, and slice tomatoes. Bring to boiling point. Add peppers and onions that have been chopped fine. Add sugar, salt, vinegar, and spices. Boil slowly until thick, about 3 hours. Seal in sterilized jars (pint) or wide-mouth bottles.

Chili Sauce

12 ripe tomatoes
4 white onions
2 green bell peppers
2 T. salt
1 T. celery seed
½ cup brown sugar
2 cups white vinegar

Peel tomatoes and cut in ¼-inch slices (crosswise). Put in heavy boiler and add onions, chopped peppers, and remaining ingredients. Bring to boiling point, then reduce heat and let simmer 3 hours, stirring once or twice, to keep from sticking right in the center. When done, put in clean jars, seal, and store in a cool, dark place. If you have no dark storage place, wrap in newspaper or place in paper bag.

August is a hot month—hot, so hot you can wave your bare arm and feel the delicious goodness that is warm air. I like the deep red-leafed canna bushes that are blooming and—strange as it may seem—their orange blooms are beautiful in the heat of August. The four o'clocks hang heavy with yellow, pink, white, and red flowers, and the ripe black seeds of falling flowers keep the hens jumping high for these tasty tidbits.

Mid-afternoon is my favorite time of day in August. The dinner dishes are out of the way, the morning work is behind me, the children are swimming, and Rose Jr. has been coaxed into taking a nap. I take my patching to the shade of the chinaberry tree to enjoy the many and varied scents of a hot August afternoon. The tomato vines are wilted limp, and they add their heady smell to the drifting aroma of cut hay over beyond Wagoner Creek. I breathe deeply of the spicy odor coming out the kitchen window, as my chili sauce bubbles very slow and gentle for at least three hours. Perhaps you would like my recipe for this delightful sauce, so easy to make and so tasty with winter meats and dried vegetables.

Homemade Ketchup

2 gallons tomato juice
6 T. salt
1 heaping tsp. paprika
2 tsp. black pepper
4 tsp. cinnamon
12 small hot peppers
½ cup mixed spices (tied up)
2 quarts red vinegar
3 cups sugar
3 tsp. red pepper
1 T. dry mustard
3 large onions
1 large bell pepper
2 tsp. whole cloves

Put in a large container and let cook to desired thickness. Before putting in bottles or jars, remove cloves, onions, peppers, and tied up spices. Important: Toward the last of the cooking, stir ketchup with a wooden spoon.

Homemade Tomato Juice

Wash ripe tomatoes; add just enough water to keep them from sticking. Let come to a boil and stir several times. When tender run through a Foley's food mill or a sieve. Heat juice, pour in jars, add ½ tablespoon salt to a quart (1 teaspoon to a pint). Follow directions on jar lids for sealing and processing.

Walnut Ketchup

Young tender walnuts
Vinegar
2 ounces black pepper
2 ounces ginger
1 ounce cloves
1 ounce nutmeg
Large pinch cayenne pepper
Shallot, minced fine
Thimbleful celery seed
Salt

Bruise walnuts with a wooden billet and place in a large jar with sufficient water to cover them, adding a handful of salt for every 25 walnuts. Stir them twice a day for 14 days; then drain off the liquor into a sauce pan (save liquor). Cover the walnuts with boiling vinegar, crush to a pulp; strain through a colander into the liquor in the sauce pan. For every 2 quarts, add above measures of spices, all tied up in a muslin bag. Boil all together for an hour, remove muslin bag and bottle. It is suggested you dribble melted bees wax around top of sealed bottle. Serve with cold meats and vegetables.

Canned String Beans

(from Lora Hughes McAlpin)

1 gallon string beans, snapped and washed
½ cup white vinegar
¾ cup sugar
4 tsp. salt
Enough water to cover beans

Place all in large canner or dutch oven and boil for 30 minutes. Place in jars and fill with liquid. Seal and process. Makes 4 quarts or 8 pints.

This recipe was handed down from a great-great-grandmother. When I tried it, this recipe turned out fair. My family wondered why I would bother when I knew only tomato ketchup suited them.

ON THE SIDE

S. BEIBERS

Beverages

Leaf tea came in beautiful tin boxes. In each box there was a pasteboard dipper. A scoop or dip would be enough for a glass of tea. My grandmother never bothered with the dipper: she had a square of white muslin used to hold the tea. She would reach in the tall gold colored tin and gather what could be held in a clenched hand. After the tea was placed in the muslin square, the corners were brought together and tied closely with a selvage torn from the same material.

The homemade tea bag would be placed in the tall blue granite tea pitcher. Boiling water (from a granite kettle) would be poured over the tea. Allowed to steep until the sides of the pitcher were lukewarm, the bag would then be lifted out and squeezed against the side—every drop was precious.

Our Aunt Phleta knew how much more water to add to weaken the tea. This water had been sweetened and heated to dissolve the sugar. Poured into the tea pitcher, stirred, and covered with a clean cloth, it was put on the back porch "water shelf" to rest until the time when the beautiful amber liquid would be poured into tall glasses filled with crushed ice .

After the tea was made, the tea leaves were boiled in lots of water for about five minutes and set aside to cool. This water was used to water Grandmother's prized box ferns and angel wing begonias. The tea leaves were scattered up and down the sides of the front walk where cinnamon pinks and thrift grew in rank profusion—all due to tea leaves, so said our Aunt Phleta.

The tea square was rinsed and hung to dry until company came and tea was a treat.

Elderberry Cordial

Berries
Water
Sugar
Cloves
Ginger
1 yeast cake

Strip the berries from the stems and to every 3 gallons of berries add 2 gallons of boiling water. Press them down under the water and cover close-ly. Let them remain in this condition 24 hours. Press the juice from the fruit by thoroughly squeezing though a bag. To every gallon of juice add 3 pounds of sugar, 1 ounce of cloves and 1 ounce of ginger. Boil all for 20 minutes, thoroughly

skimming off any scum that rises. While still warm put in a stone jar or large glass demijohn. Fill full and add a yeast cake on top to make it work. In about 8 or 10 days it is ready to cork up. Let stand some weeks to clarify, then drain off carefully and bottle.

Elderberry Wine

3 pints berries
3 gallons water
9 pounds sugar
Juice of 2 lemons
1 yeast cake
2 pounds seedless raisins

Mix all ingredients in enamel pan; let come to a slow boil and boil gently for 3 minutes. Cool to lukewarm (be sure it isn't too hot) and add yeast cake. Stir well. Cover and let stand 9 days. Strain and add seedless raisins. Let stand 5 days. Strain and bottle. Seal with cap and sealing wax. Store in cool, dark place. In case of sickness, old folks especially relish this. Fill glass with finely crushed ice. Pour 2 tablespoons wine over the ice; sip and enjoy.

Elder Blossom Wine

1 quart elder blossoms
   (bloom in May and June)
9 pounds white sugar
1 yeast cake or 1 pkg. dry yeast
3 gallons water
3 pounds seeded raisins (seeded, not seedless)
½ cup lemon juice

Now that elder blooms are hanging heavy in every nook and cranny, families enjoy "putting up a few bottles" of elderbloom wine. There is one thing to remember: the blooms used for making this delicious, clear, golden wine are the ones that grow in large, round heads, which look when fully open like a creamy cauliflower head.

The elder blossoms should be carefully picked from the stems and the quart measure packed full. Put the sugar and water together over the fire and stir well until sugar dissolves. Then let boil without stirring for 5 minutes. Add the elder blossoms, then stir well; remove from fire at once and cool to lukewarm. Add the dissolved yeast and lemon juice. Put in an earthen jar (a churn will do) and let stand 6 days, stirring 3 times daily. The blossoms must be stirred from the bottom of the jar or churn each time.

On the seventh day, strain through a cheese cloth. This will fill 6 half-gallon fruit jars as full as the jars should be—not quite full, as you should leave 2 inches from the top of the jars for fermenting. Divide the 3 pounds of seeded raisins into 6 equal parts and put the same amount of raisins into each jar. Cover tightly and put up; do not bother until just before Christmas when you open up the jars and strain out the raisins. Then put the wine in bottles. You can use the raisins for mince pies or puddings. Some dry the raisins and serve with cracked peppermint candy and little crackers or pecans. This recipe is very old and comes from way before the time of bottled lemon juice. Don't risk making it with bought, bottled lemon juice. Use real lemons that you squeeze. Beware of using plastic containers that have been used to store anything greasy. You know you cannot remove grease from most plastic wares.

Fruit Punch

For a refreshing punch, mix one quart apricot and blackberry syrup with one quart cold water. Pour over glasses filled with crushed ice and serve with sugar cookies to hot, tired children.

May is a month when the world is always fresh and clean. Mornings are pearl smooth and the early rising sun is a special treat—that is, if you have already had a cup of fresh made coffee.

Now, I am as saving as the next farm wife, but deliver me from having warmed-over coffee that has been left over from supper. Coffee, to be at the peak of its perfection, should have a good chance to present itself in the best light, and in these days of high prices, who would dare make coffee that isn't delicious to the last drop.

First of all, this means a clean pot, one that has been scrubbed with plenty of suds and elbow grease. I find that an occasional sunning makes the pot fresh and sweet. Next, after the coffee is made, I believe pretty cups and saucers should be a must, even for "at home" folks.

If you have time for a walk in the woods, pay close attention to arching blackberry briars, loaded with green, red, and ripe blackberries, made more attractive with pleasingly shaped and textured leaves. Do watch out for the thorns so cleverly hidden. And be reminded that wasp nests are loaded this time of year, and the wasps seem dearly to love protecting their nests from reaching hands—no matter if only for berries!

Blackberry Acid

12 pounds of berries
2 quarts water
5 ounces tartaric acid
1½ pounds white sugar

Place berries in a stone, enamel or glass container. Bring to a boil 2 quarts water in which tartaric acid has been dissolved. Pour over berries and cover; let stand 48 hours. Turn into cheese cloth or flour sack to drip. Do NOT squeeze the bag. Measure juice, and to each pint of juice add 3½ cups white sugar. Stir and stir until the last crystal of sugar has been dissolved. Do not reheat. Bottle and seal. Store in a dark place, and when ready to serve pour over finely crushed ice. A small amount will be plenty as it is quite strong. Refreshing and tasty and fine for a sick stomach.

Many years ago, a recipe for Cranberry Punch came my way. It was contributed to a cookbook by Mrs. Elden Wells of Jackson and became a great favorite with my family. It's pretty to the eye, delicious to taste, and goes well with little party sandwiches and cookies.

Cranberry Punch

½ cup sugar
1 cup water
2 16-ounce bottles cranberry juice
½ cup lemon juice
¾ cup orange juice
1 12-ounce bottle ginger ale

Combine sugar and water. Cook over moderate heat for 3 minutes. Cool. Add cranberry juice, lemon juice, and orange juice. Chill. Just before serving, add ginger ale and fruit cubes (optional).

Fruit Cubes: Place strawberries and thin wedges of lemon in the sections of an ice cube tray. Fill with water, freeze. Place 2 in glass and add cranberry punch.

Chocolate Sauce for Cocoa

3 squares unsweetened chocolate
¼ cup butter or margarine
1½ cups confectioner's sugar
1 small can evaporated milk
Bit of salt
½ tsp. vanilla extract

Combine all ingredients except vanilla in the top of a double boiler. Cover and heat over boiling water. Stir together when chocolate is melted. Cook 30 minutes, stirring now and then. Add vanilla. Makes about 1 pint and will keep for weeks if covered air-tight in the refrigerator. For a cup of quick cocoa, heat milk and add enough of this sauce to suit your taste.

Egg Nog

½ cup sugar
3 egg yolks
¼ tsp. salt
4 cups scalded milk
⅛ tsp. salt
3 egg whites
¼ cup sugar
½ tsp. vanilla extract

Pay careful attention to your cooking as you make this dainty, tasty, refreshing drink. Beat ½ cup sugar into egg yolks, add ¼ tsp. salt, stir in scalded milk. Cook in double boiler until it coats spoon; stir constantly. Cool. Add ⅛ tsp. salt to egg whites and beat until stiff. Add ¼ cup sugar; continue beating until stiff again. Add vanilla to cooled custard and fold in egg whites with an over and

This recipe for Chocolate Sauce is foolproof, yummy, and as easy as falling off the proverbial log.

How long has it been since you have given a Christmas party? Not a dinner or family get-together, but a real stomp down Christmas party with goodies beautiful to the eye, delicious to taste, and fattening to the figure?

This year we plan a Christmas party about a week before real Christmas week, making the decorations we hope to gather from our woods do double duty for the party as well as Christmas Day and until the New Year. Holly, green vines, mistletoe, pine cones, cedar, and other delightful smelling winter

hardy branches will be placed at vantage points. Tinsel, glitter, and home-whipped snow also will be used to add cheer as well as beauty.

To my way of thinking, nothing can add more to a Christmas party than a lovely decorated table, where Egg Nog is served along with thin slices of fruit cake and an assortment of wee cakes and cookies.

over movement. Mix until all egg white is coated with custard. Chill at least 4 hours. Serve in punch cups; sprinkle with nutmeg just before serving. For those who like the flavor of sherry, substitute for vanilla extract. Make sure the vanilla is real and have the nutmeg fresh from a grated nutmeg nut, or open a new box. Be sure to use whole milk.

Ginger Beer

4 oz. dried ginger root
1 gal. water
Juice of one lemon
1 package dry active yeast
½ pound sugar

Pound ginger root to bruise, then boil in ½ gallon water for 20 min. Remove from stove and set aside. Mix lemon juice with dry yeast in cup of warm water in which ginger root was boiled. Pour in remaining ½ gallon of water, let mixture set for 24 hours. Strain out the root and stir in sugar. Bottle and place in refrigerator. DO NOT store at room temperature; bottles may explode. Makes ten 12-ounce bottles.

Note: Root beer, ginger beer, lemon beer, and a host of similar drinks had little or no alcholic content. Such beverages were fermented briefly with the same kind of yeast used for making bread, then bottled and stored; the fermentation served only to make them fizzy. Old fashioned root beer is difficult to make because of the rarity of its ingredients: spice wood, prickly ash, and guaiacum, to name a few.

Lemonade

Wash a lemon for each person. Slice in thin slices. Put into a a deep dish and cover with sugar. After a few minutes, take a wooden spoon and start pounding on the sliced lemons. Continue to do this until the sugar is syrupy. Add crushed ice and one 8-ounce cup of water for each lemon. Taste, and if not sweet enough, add more sugar. Serve in large glasses, with a bit of the lemon hull and lots of ice in each glass. (This method came to me from *McCall's* magazine and is the best I have ever used.)

Muscadine Juice

It's muscadine-picking season again, and this brings many calls about harvesting and processing the juice of this superb native grape. Whole muscadines run about six pounds to the gallon, which in turn produces about a quart of juice. Crush the berries, add a little water, and simmer for a few minutes to get the most juice for your efforts, then freeze until ready to use.

Peppermint Flip

   1 cup crushed peppermint stick candy
   6 cups milk
   ¼ tsp. salt
   1 tsp. vanilla extract
   1 pint vanilla ice cream

Mix crushed candy with milk. Add salt and heat slowly in double boiler until candy has melted. Cool; add vanilla. Chill until needed. Beat ice cream into mixture; serve in tall glasses. This is nutritious as well as delicious.

Pore Folk's Tea

1 T. sugar
1 T. sweet cream
Touch of cinnamon, if desired

Stir cream and sugar well. Drop in a small rock filled with pores; stir again, fill cup with boiling water, sip and enjoy.

Mrs. Dell Hunter's Party Punch

4 dozen lemons
5 pounds sugar
100 cups water
3 large cans pineapple juice
5 No. 2 cans crushed pineapple
3 large cans orange juice
100 cherries and juice

Squeeze lemons, combining with water and sugar, adding the rinds. Cook for 20 minutes; remove from heat. When cool, place in refrigerator to chill thoroughly. Add remaining ingredients and serve over ice in punch bowl. This recipe serves more than 150 portions in punch glasses. The syrup may be made several days ahead of time. Always remember to remove lemon rinds before chilling.

It has been told in our family for many years, going back to the late 1700s, that Pore Folk's Tea was a standard drink when there was no coffee or tea. Those early morning wake-up brews were to be had only when someone ventured over Natchez way to tote home necessary things for keeping body and soul going.

The secret to this tea is a small rock filled with pores that you drop into a sugar and sweet cream mixture.

At one time I had two of these rocks, but one morning after sipping my tea on the patio I removed the rock from my cup and placed it on the low wall beside me. I forgot all about the little rock that came with our foreparents across the waters. Then our youngest son spied a nice rock that he put in his pocket and went hunting with his sling shot. He spent a fine time shooting rocks high in a tree, and kerplunking a rock or two at wee minnows in the wet weather branch, even

Homemade Soda Pop

1 quart water
4 cups sugar
4 tsp. cream of tartar
1 T. vanilla extract
3 egg whites, beaten stiff
Tartaric acid powder
Bicarbonate of soda

Heat water to near boiling; dissolve sugar and cream of tartar in it, add dash of vanilla. Cool, add beaten egg whites, stir thoroughly. Bottle and store in refrigerator. To make the actual soda pop, dissolve 2 tablespoons of the syrup, plus ⅛ teaspoon tartaric powder per 8-ounce glass of very cold water. Add ½ tsp. bicarbonate of soda and stir. Half a teaspoon of fresh lemon juice can be added for the tartaric acid per glass. Or, you can eliminate the soda and tartaric acid and use carbonated water instead of the very cold water.

Summer Drink

2 cups strong tea (5 T. tea to 2 cups water)
5 whole cloves
4 cups sugar
1½ cups lemon juice
4 cups grape juice
1 quart ginger ale
2 quarts ice water

Put cloves in tea, pour hot water over, and let stand. Drain while hot and pour over sugar. Let cool. Add lemon juice, orange juice, and grape juice. Chill. When ready to serve, add ice water and ginger ale that has been well chilled.

bringing home a brown thrasher to be cooked for his tomcat.

Alas, my Pore Folk's Tea rock was gone, and 35 years later I still look for the little rock that came from the country where shamrocks grow and the wearing of the green is celebrated on March 17.

This is the day of instant drink powders, canned and bottled drinks. Is it any wonder there are some people who yearn for the old days of having homemade Summer Drink, delicious and very refreshing?

Sassafras Tea was a standby for a tasty drink when winter winds caused chickens to huddle in sheltered places and people to long for something hot to drink. Mama would send Brother and me to the sassafras patch in the corner of an old field where we dug up roots of the small trees. We chopped the dug roots into pieces once we reached the house, washing them first. There was an old milk safe on the back porch where the roots were dried for winter use.

Sassafras Tea

10 or 12 pieces of sassafras root
1 gallon boiling water
Milk
Sugar

Boil root in water for about 20 minutes. Set aside to steep until the water cools. Add heated milk and sugar to each cup. Remove root and discard.

Shrub

1 quart cider vinegar
3 quarts ripe strawberries
1 pound mild flavored honey

Add berries to cider vinegar; let stand for a day. Strain and add honey. Simmer for 30 minutes over low heat, and store in refrigerator when cool. Make shrub by adding 2 tablespoons of the concentrate to a glass of water.

On hay-making day Brother and the other farm children would trot to the fields with jugs of Switchel. It was a chore they loved. I, too, was allowed to tag along and feel important carrying a quart of Switchel in a striped hunting sack hung across my neck, one arm through the strap.

Switchel

2 cups sugar
1 cup molasses
¼ cup cider vinegar
1 tsp. ground ginger
1 gallon water

Heat ingredients in 1 quart of water until dissolved, then add the remaining water. Pour into a gallon stone jug, wrapped in a dampened crocker sack, and hang from tree limb so that breeze can cool it.

Syrup Drink For The Children

Have sweet milk nearly frozen in the bottle; add grated nutmeg and a tablespoon of molasses to a tall glass of cold sweet milk. Have a straw to sip the drink through, and if the children are hungry, a cookie or two goes well with this.

Tomato Juice Cocktail

3½ cups tomato juice
1½ T. lemon juice
1¼ tsp. sugar
½ tsp. salt
1 tsp. onion juice
3 or 4 drops Tabasco sauce
1 dash each black pepper, cayenne pepper, and paprika

Mix all ingredients together; chill. Serve ice cold as a drink. To serve in sherbet cups at table, double recipe, pour into uncovered molds, and freeze. Unmold into chilled sherbet cups and top with stuffed olive. This is refreshing on a hot day.

Breads

Right about now—September—is the time of year country folks start living off the fat of the land: sweet potatoes in half a dozen recipes, pecans beginning to fall, peanuts for boiling and drying for winter parching. Best of all is the joy of having new cornmeal for cooking. I forget from one year to the other how wonderful it is to have new meal for corn bread dressing and thickhoe cake baked on top of the stove.

What a contrast getting our first batch of new meal this year against the days when the boys were small. This year I shelled a peck of corn, put it in the car, drove to the grist mill, waited about fifteen minutes, and brought the warm sack home, where I made a small pone of water bread for Dale and myself.

When the boys were home, they would go into the patch below the barn to pull enough corn to shell the big sack full. This was tossed on top of the crib to take the sun for about a week. Come Saturday, Joe and Tim would saddle their horses, tie the corn behind Joe's saddle, and off they would go for a full morning of fun and frolic. At the community blacksmith shop and grist mill many folks would gather, and talk would flow. The boys picked up some news and some new cuss words, played mumble peg and hopscotch, and pitched washers and horseshoes.

Angel Biscuits

1 pkg. dry yeast
¼ cup warm water
2½ cups plain flour
½ tsp. soda
1 tsp. baking powder
1 tsp. salt
⅓ cup shortening
1 cup buttermilk

Add warm water to yeast; set aside. Mix dry ingredients; cut in shortening. Add buttermilk and yeast mixture; blend thoroughly with spoon. Refrigerate or make into rolls. (It's better if made today and used tomorrow.) When needed, shape into rolls and let rise 1 hour at room temperature. Bake in 375-degree oven for about 15 minutes or until brown. Makes about 3 dozen.

Such excitement here at the Stevens family—getting ready, talking, planning what to wear. One would have thought Papa and the boys were getting ready for a trek into darkest Africa. Joe took my year-before-last hat with the veil that came down over his face. (Never mind that the back of his head was exposed.) Tim borrowed a veil from his grandmother.

Why all this excitement? Dale, on one of his fishing jaunts, had discovered a wild honey tree right next to a muscadine vine, so he knew the honey was of the very best kind. They got fixed up and went down to rob the tree. They carried old rags to burn a smudge and make the bees drunk, water to throw on them if the smoke treatment didn't work, and a bottle of stuff bought at the drug store said to repel insects.

Dale had me get nine syrup cans. He said the honey was running out a knothole four feet from the ground and the tree was three feet in diameter, so there must be at least ten gallons, if his figuring was right. He thought the bees would eat at least a gallon when they started to cut on the tree.

Anyway, they came back three hours later with three gallons of honey—very top grade honey, at that—along with red eyes, singed brows, lashes smoked black, and forty-one stings among them. (Some were so close together we had to average them on the low side, at that.)

Hot biscuit, butter, honey, and ice cold milk was a steady diet here for several meals running, until I could feel the extra pounds weighing heavy on me. Then I put a stop to this honey business. I do want to have enough for frosting my jam cakes this summer.

Cheese Biscuits

2 cups sifted flour
Dash cayenne pepper
¾ cup butter
2 T. ground pecans
1 tsp. salt
½ pound Old English cheese
1 egg, slightly beaten

Mix and sift dry ingredients. Put cheese through food chopper and mix thoroughly with butter and flour to form a firm paste. Roll out on board, cut and brush with egg, and sprinkle with pecans. Cook at 300 degrees for 15 to 20 minutes.

Foolproof Biscuits

4 cups self rising flour
2 tsp. baking powder
½ cup shortening
1½ cups milk

Combine flour and baking powder; stir well. Cut in shortening until mixture resembles coarse meal. Sprinkle milk evenly over flour mixture, stirring just until dry ingredients are moistened. Turn dough onto a lightly floured surface; knead lightly 10 to 12 times. Roll dough to ½-inch thick, with a 2½-inch cutter. Place on greased tin; bake at 425 degrees for 12 minutes or until lightly browned.

Sour Dough Starter

1 medium-sized Irish potato, cut and peeled
1 cup sugar (white)
3 cups cold water
3 cups plain flour

Peel potato and cut into small cubes, make flour paste using water, and stir until all lumps are gone. Mix with sugar and potato. Let stand in stone, glass, or enamel container (a gallon size at least) for three days. When a cup of starter is taken out for biscuits, add one cup of cold water, one-half cup flour, and one tablespoon sugar to the remaining starter, so there will be a supply for the next batch of biscuits.

Sour Dough Biscuits

1 cup starter
¼ cup soft shortening
½ tsp. salt
1 cup flour (approximately)

Mix all ingredients, adding enough flour to make dough easy to handle. Roll to about ½-inch thickness on floured board. Cut out and place on greased baking sheet. Bake at 425 degrees for 20 minutes. Serve hot.

Harvey Patton's Sourdough Biscuits

First get a crock. Avoid use of metal as it will rust in time. The amount of baking governs amount

These are the days we begin to call for Sourdough Biscuits and thick slices of bacon fried in the black iron skillet. A breakfast served at six o'clock must last until twelve and then it has to be more than juice, toast and cereal. My family is fond of steak, brown gravy, and hot biscuits for their early morning meal. Cold milk and tomato juice satisfies them, and keeps them from getting too hungry. They certainly don't turn up their noses at thin slices of roast beef, hot gravy poured over slices of crisp toast, and hot cocoa, either.

Harvey Patton is well-known in cooking circles for his sourdough biscuits.

Rose Budd's Recipes for Country Living

*S*omeone once asked me what soot was used for, other than messing up the house. I can tell you any number of things soot was used for back in my salad days and on into my first married years. In fact, only last week Dale and I were hard-pressed to find enough soot to "mark a setting of eggs" to satisfy one fussy hen that longed to be a mother.

Our fireplace is closed for the summer, so I finally lit a candle, let it smoke against the bottom of an old piece of broken plate, added a dab of grease to the soot and made nice marks around a dozen eggs. The hen settled down nicely, will share the nest with some stragglers that refuse to lay in other nests nearby, and the marked eggs will be left for 21 days, when I hope to "take off" future flyers.

to be mixed. Start small by mixing one cup of flour and one cup of water mixed into a smooth paste. Set mixture in a warm place for about a week and allow to sour. This process may be speeded by adding a package of dry yeast, making mixture ready in about 3 days. Each time sourdough is removed some must be left for a starter. Add additional flour and water to the starter for your next baking.

2 cups flour
1 tsp. salt
2 tsp. baking powder
¼ tsp. soda
½ cup shortening, butter or lard
⅔ cup sourdough
½ cup cold water

Never mix the wet dough with hands. Use a knife to stir in liquids. Sift flour, salt, baking powder, and soda together. Blend shortening with them and hollow out the center of the mixture. Pour in sourdough and cold water. Mix well with knife until moisture is taken up, then turn on well floured surface and cut. Place on greased pan; brush with melted butter and bake in 450-degree oven.

Superior Biscuits

2 cups flour
4 tsp. baking powder
½ tsp. salt
½ tsp. cream of tartar
2 tsp. sugar
½ cup shortening
⅔ cup milk (less 1 tablespoon)
Melted butter

Sift dry ingredients; cut in shortening until finely blended. Add milk all at once. Stir gently with fork. Then stir vigorously until dough follows the fork around the bowl. Turn out on lightly floured waxed paper or rolling board; pat or roll out ⅓- to ½-inch thick. Cut with round cutter cutting down (do not twist cutter). Place on heavy, lightly greased baking sheet. Brush tops with melted butter. Bake 12 to 15 minutes in 450-degree oven.

Pumpkin Bread

3 cups sugar
3½ cups sifted plain flour
1½ tsp. plain cinnamon
1 tsp. nutmeg
1½ tsp. salt
2 tsp. soda
⅔ cup water
½ tsp. baking powder
¾ cup raisins
¾ cup chopped nuts
2 cups cooked pumpkin
1 cup cooking oil
4 eggs

Mix all dry ingredients. Add liquids and beat well. Grease and flour 4 1-pound coffee cans or 2 loaf pans. Pour coffee cans half full of batter and bake at 350 degrees for about 50 minutes. Let cool and remove from cans. This bread freezes very well.

Soot was used by Mama to make marks around our legs when we were taken wading by a non-swimming person. We were allowed no deeper than the band of soot around mid-calf. Soot mixed with lard made an excellent blacking for work shoes that were worn for Sunday, since one pair of shoes served two purposes. Soot mixed with spider webs made an excellent packing to stop bleeding from cuts, gashes or any wounds. And soot mixed with red clay helped chink many a chimney crack.

*I*s there any chore more of a pleasure than making Salt Rising Bread? Last night I "set" my yeast to making and at nine this morning it was just right with that flat sour smell that goes with making your own yeast. I do so enjoy working the dough, kneading it until it springs back at the merest touch. When the loaves are cooled, they are wrapped in a clean cloth and stored in an air-tight box.

Salt Rising Bread

1 cup fresh milk
¾ cup home-ground meal
1 tsp. sugar
¼ tsp. salt
¼ tsp. soda
1 cup scalded milk
1 cup water
¼ tsp. soda
3½ to 4 cups sifted flour
4 cups flour
3 T. shortening
2 tsp. salt
3 T. sugar

The Yeast: About 5 p.m., scald one cup of fresh milk, sift together ¾ cup meal, 1 teaspoon sugar, ¼ teaspoon salt, and ¼ teaspoon soda. Add these dry ingredients to scalded milk and pour into a pint jar. Close lid tightly; wrap in a cloth and place on top of gas water heater until 9 a.m. Then it should be puffy and filled with bubbles. You will notice an odd odor. If it doesn't have this odor, don't use it, because the success of salt-rising bread depends on the yeast.

The Batter: To the yeast add 1 cup scalded milk cooled with 1 cup water, ¼ teaspoon soda, and 3½ to 4 cups of sifted flour to make a stiff batter. (Rinse your yeast jar with a little warm water.) Beat well; cover and place back on gas hot water heater until it doubles its size and is quite puffy, about 1½ hours.

The Dough: Sift 4 cups flour; put 3 cups into a bowl. Make a hole in the center; put into that 3 tablespoons shortening, 3 tablespoons sugar, 2 teaspoons salt and the batter. Knead well, using hand to work in fat and to mix. Add flour as needed to make a soft dough (use flour that is already in bowl). The fourth cup of flour will be used to sprinkle on rolling cloth and to knead the dough. Divide the dough and place it in well-greased pans; brush tops with melted butter. Keep in a warm place, covered, until it rises twice its bulk. Bake at 325 degrees until done. Remove from oven, turn out onto rack and cover with cloth until cool.

Strawberry Bread

½ cup margarine, softened
½ cup sugar
1 tsp. vanilla extract
2 eggs
2 cups sifted all purpose flour
½ tsp. salt
¼ tsp. baking soda (omit salt and baking soda if you use self rising flour)
1 cup strawberry preserves
½ cup buttermilk
½ cup chopped pecans, walnuts or almonds

Preheat oven to 325 degrees. In large bowl, cream margarine or butter, sugar, and vanilla; beat until fluffy. Add eggs, one at a time, beating well after each addition. Sift together flour, salt, and baking soda. In a small bowl, combine preserves and buttermilk; stir to mix. Alternate dry ingredients with preserve mixture and add to egg mixture. Beat only until well blended.

Spoon into greased 8½ x 4½ loaf pan. Bake for 1½ hours (bread will be moist). Cool in pan for 15 minutes. Turn out of pan, cool completely, and wrap loaf in plastic wrap or aluminum foil. Store overnight in a cool place for easy slicing. This bread is good with a meat dinner.

*S*alt Rising Bread is a favorite to serve with vegetable dinners or with salads made with fresh vegetables.

I for one know a family cannot live off corn bread, fat meat, and syrup or molasses. However, I do know corn bread can be eaten in so many ways one should not tire of it in a whole month of eating.

Do you make corn bread often? In many homes, especially in the country, a small skillet of bread is *made each noon meal to go with vegetables. As a rule, these same bread eaters will enjoy a glass of milk with corn bread crumbled in, allowed to soak for a few minutes, then eaten with a spoon at the night meal.*

When we were small, Mama relied on several forms of bread and milk to keep our hunger within bounds, such as slices of hot bread buttered and served with a small glass of milk. Often when we walked in the kitchen from school on cold winter days, Mama would already have a good fire going in the stove. A good fire was one hot enough to bake something in the oven.

As we shed jackets and overshoes, Mama would be busy buttering slices of store bread, thick with butter, two each, and these would be put in the oven to get crusty and slightly brown. Whole milk would be heating very hot, but not boiling. Bread slices would be put in soup bowls, sprinkled with sugar, and lightly dusted with cinnamon. The hot milk was poured over the bread and we would be given spoons to eat this custardy goodness.

Easy Corn Bread

¾ cup yellow cornmeal (self-rising)
¼ cup self-rising flour
½ T. sugar
½ cup plus 1 T. milk
1 egg

Preheat oven to 425 degrees. Place one tablespoon bacon grease or shortening in small iron skillet. Have skillet hot when you pour batter in. Sift together meal, flour, and sugar; stir in milk and egg. Beat well. Pour into heated skillet. Bake 20 minutes or until done. Turn out and cut in pie-shaped wedges.

I like to sprinkle meal in skillet before pouring batter in. Serve with green beans, smothered yellow squash, and spiced pear pickles. Dessert: hot gingerbread with vanilla sauce.

Egg Corn Bread

1 cup white or yellow cornmeal
¼ cup flour
½ tsp. baking powder
1 large egg
1 cup buttermilk
¼ tsp. salt
¼ tsp. soda
2 T. bacon grease or melted shortening

Sift together cornmeal, soda, flour, baking powder, and salt. Add egg, buttermilk, and shortening or bacon grease. Mix and stir beat well. Pour into greased, hot iron skillet. Have oven at 450 degrees and bake until brown, about 20 minutes.

Corn Muffins

2 cups sifted all-purpose flour
4 tsp. baking powder
1½ tsp. salt
6 T. sugar
1½ cups yellow cornmeal
2 eggs, well-beaten
1⅔ cups sweet milk
⅓ cup melted shortening

Sift flour once, measure; add baking powder, salt, and sugar and sift together in a bowl. Add cornmeal and mix well. Combine eggs and milk. Add to flour mixture, add shortening, then mix. Mix only enough to dampen flour. Bake in greased muffin pans in 425-degree oven for 25 minutes or until done.

Cornmeal Dumplings

5 or 6 cups beef stock, consomme, clear
  soup, or vegetable stock
1 cup cornmeal
¼ cup all-purpose flour
1 tsp. baking powder
½ tsp. salt
2 eggs
½ cup milk
1 T. melted butter

Simmer stock. Sift together dry ingredients. Beat eggs and milk together. Combine dry ingredients with egg mixture. Stir in melted butter. Drop batter from a spoon into the hot stock. Cover pan

Bantie eggs are just right for making corn bread, and if you are lucky enough to have guineas on the farm never use the eggs for anything but making bread. They are so rich for their size and make the bread so very yellow, one almost thinks cake is the offing. I love to hunt the little nests of the wandering guinea hens, for it is truly a battle of wits when one finds a nest.

*T*om Rusty was often served
hot with a fresh vegetable
dinner—turnip greens, new
Irish potatoes in milk,
garden lettuce salad,
buttermilk—a real farm
dinner.

*M*ama always made
crackling bread when hogs
were killed and lard
rendered. She canned quart
jars of cracklings to have
for summer corn bread—so
good with vegetable dinners.
Here in 1988 cracklings
can be bought in the meat
department at the
supermarket—or you can
make your own: Take one
pound of salt pork, cut in
cubes and rendered out
until light brown. Save fat
for greasing sweet potatoes
before baking, for greasing

tightly and simmer dumplings for about 15
minutes. Remove at once from the liquor.

Tom Rusty

1½ cups cornmeal (home ground)
½ tsp. soda
Pinch of salt
1 cup molasses
1 egg—2, if small

Sift meal, soda, and salt; add molasses and egg,
mix thoroughly. Pour into a size 7 iron skillet that
has been greased and floured. Bake at 350 degrees
for 15 minutes; lower heat to 250 degrees and bake
until done.

Crackling Bread

1 cup pork cracklings (not the ones bought in
    plastic bags and eaten like potato chips)
2 cups cornmeal
2 eggs beaten
1 cup buttermilk
1½ tsp. baking powder
½ tsp. soda
2 T. bacon grease
1 tsp. salt

Sift cornmeal, soda, salt, and baking powder in
mixing bowl. Combine beaten eggs, buttermilk,
and fat. Stir liquid mixture into cornmeal mixture; mix well. Add cracklings and stir until well
mixed. Spread mixture in hot greased iron skillet.

Bake in 425-degree oven for 20 to 25 minutes. Top should be raised in center. This bread is good sliced and toasted for breakfast.

skillets and bakers for breads and cookies, or for frying cottage type Irish potatoes.

Basic Dough For Rolls

1 cup milk
¼ cup sugar
⅓ cup shortening or salad oil
5 cups sifted all purpose flour
1 tsp. salt
2 pkgs. quick acting yeast
¼ cup lukewarm water
2 eggs

Scald milk. Add sugar, shortening, and salt; stir until dissolved. Dissolve yeast in water; add to milk mixture. Beat eggs and add to milk mixture. Gradually add flour, mixing to form smooth, soft dough. Knead on lightly floured board until smooth and satiny. Place in greased bowl, cover, let rise in warm place until double in bulk. Pinch off pieces, shape in rolls, place in greased baking pan and allow to rise until double in size. Bake in 400-degree oven until brown, about 10 to 15 minutes.

Buttermilk Rolls

1 pkg. dry yeast
1 cup lukewarm buttermilk or beaten clabber
¼ tsp. soda
1 tsp. sugar
3 T. melted shortening (not hot, lukewarm)
2½ cups flour
1 tsp. baking powder
1 tsp. salt

Crumble yeast into mixing bowl. Add buttermilk, soda, sugar, and melted shortening; stir to dissolve completely. Sift together flour, baking powder and salt. Mix well, turn out on board, and knead smooth. Roll out and form into any shape rolls you like. Set in a warm place to rise, usually about an hour. Bake. If you make these very small, they are nice to serve with salad to your bridge club.

Cheese Beer Rolls

3 cups biscuit mix
¾ cup sharp cheddar cheese, grated
1 cup beer

Mix all ingredients, shape into rolls. Bake at 450 degrees until golden brown.

Never Fail Rolls

1 cup lukewarm water
1 pkg. dry yeast
2 T. sugar
¼ tsp. salt
⅔ cup shortening

Soften yeast in warm water; add sugar and salt. Add shortening which is at room temperature. Mix enough all purpose flour to make a dough just right to roll out. Cut with biscuit cutter, crease a little over halfway with a knife, and fold over on this line. Gently does it; do not press down at all. Place in a greased pan and let rise 2 hours in a warm place; bake at once. They simply do not take to refrigerator keeping or waiting longer than 2 hours. If you like rolls crisp on all sides, place far apart on cookie sheet. Snuggle them close together if you like soft crumb on the sides.

Never Fail Rolls are a surefire hit with young and old. The rolls are tasty, easy to make, and if any are left over, excellent when buttered and toasted for a snack, spread with jam or jelly.

Quick Rolls

1 pkg. yeast
⅓ cup lukewarm water
⅞ cup buttermilk
1 tsp. sugar
1 tsp. salt
¼ tsp. soda
1 T. shortening
2 cups flour

Dissolve yeast in water (about 5 minutes). Heat buttermilk, stirring in sugar, salt, soda, and shortening. Mix with yeast. Positively do not let the milk or yeast be above lukewarm temperature or the yeast germ will be killed. Add flour to make a stiff dough; mix well and let set 10 minutes. Knead slightly, roll out, and cut or shape as you wish. Let set until double in bulk. Bake at 425 degrees for 10 to 20 minutes.

Refrigerator Rolls

2 pkgs. active dry yeast (not cakes)
2 cups warm water
½ cup sugar
2 tsp. salt
1 egg
6½ to 7 cups sifted flour
¼ cup soft shortening

Dissolve yeast in water; add sugar, salt, and half the flour. Beat thoroughly 2 minutes; add beaten egg and shortening. Mix well. Gradually beat in remaining flour. Do not use a mixer, mix by hand until smooth. Place in large bowl or crock and grease top of dough. Cover with foil or damp cloth

No matter how fluffy the whipped potatoes, golden brown the fried chicken, pink or red the sliced tomatoes, buttery the boiled corn, crisp and crunchy the carrots and radishes, something in the hot bread line is almost necessary to please the men folks. Pass a plate of hot rolls (homemade, of course), already buttered and covered with a snowy white napkin, and watch to see the looks of pleased happiness.

and place in refrigerator. Punch down every once in a while. Two hours before baking, cut off amount needed and shape in three small balls; put in muffin tin. Make as many cloverleaf rolls as needed. Bake at 400 degrees for 12 to 15 minutes.

Sixty-Minute Rolls

5 cups flour
1 cup warm milk
2 yeast cakes or two envelopes dry yeast
½ cup warm water
1 tsp. salt
1 tsp. sugar
3 T. shortening

Dissolve yeast in warm water; add to milk in which shortening has been melted. Sift flour, salt, and sugar together. Add liquid mixture to this. Mix well and knead until smooth using only enough flour to keep from sticking to hands. Make into rolls, place in buttered tins. Allow to rise 60 minutes. Bake in 400-degree oven until brown.

Note: Dough can be kept in refrigerator several days. If so, more time should be allowed for rising. Dough should double in size before baking.

Rolls

5 cups self rising flour
1 scant cup shortening
½ cup lukewarm water
1 pkg. yeast
2 tsp. sugar
2 cups buttermilk with 1 tsp. soda
   dissolved in it

Cut shortening into flour. Mix yeast, water, and sugar well. Add buttermilk with soda to yeast mixture. Add to flour mixture, mixing well. Knead on a floured board. Roll dough to ½-inch thickness. Cut and place rolls close together on a lightly greased sheet. Do not let dough rise. Bake at 450 degrees until golden brown. Leftover rolls can be split, buttered and toasted to serve with other meals.

Potato Rolls

1 cup mashed potatoes
2 eggs, beaten
5½ cups sifted all purpose flour
2 cakes compressed yeast
1 cup scalded milk
⅔ cup butter
½ cup sugar
1½ tsp. salt

Soften yeast in ½ cup lukewarm water. Combine milk, butter, sugar, salt, and mashed potatoes. Cool to lukewarm. Add softened yeast and half the flour mixture. Beat well. Blend in eggs. Add remaining flour, mixing thoroughly. Knead dough on floured board 5 to 10 minutes until smooth. Place in greased bowl. Grease top of dough lightly. Cover. Let rise in warm place for 1 hour or until dough is doubled in bulk. Punch down dough. With buttered hands form dough into any shape rolls desired. Place in greased muffin pans and let rise in warm place for 30 minutes. Brush tops of rolls with melted butter. Bake in 375-degree oven for 15 to 20 minutes.

Homemade Yeast

For homemade yeast, boil 6 large Irish potatoes in 3 pints of water. Tie a handful of hops in a small muslin bag and boil with the potatoes. When thoroughly cooked, drain the water in enough flour to make a thin batter. Set this on the stove or range and scald it enough to cook the flour (this makes the yeast keep longer). Remove it from the fire, and when cool enough, add potatoes (mashed), plus ½ cup sugar, ½ tablespoon ginger, 2 tablespoons salt, and a teacupful of yeast from a former batch. Let it stand in a warm place until it has thoroughly risen, then put in a large-mouthed jar and cork tightly. The jar should be scalded first. Two-thirds of a coffee cupful of this yeast will make 4 loaves of bread.

This recipe for Liquid Yeast was sent to me by a reader. Here's what she wrote: "My mother didn't have the hop vine. I don't know how she got the start, but she saved a bit of the yeast each time. I was about six or seven. Oh, what bread she could make. There was never any doubt that the bread would be good. Sometimes she cooked the loaves in a Dutch oven in the yard. Everyone loved Mrs. Alice Ashley Thornton's bread."

Liquid Yeast
(from a 100-year-old recipe)

Early in the day, boil 1 ounce of of best hops in 2 quarts water for 30 minutes; strain, and let liquid cool to warmth of new milk. Put in an earthen crock or bowl and add 4 tablespoons each of salt and brown sugar. Now, heat 2 cups of flour with part of the mixture and add remainder, mixing well together. Set aside in warm place for 3 days, then add 1 cup smooth, mashed, boiled Irish potatoes. Keep near range in a warm place and stir frequently until well-fermented. Place in a sterilized wide-mouth jug or glass fruit jar. Seal tightly and keep in a cool place for use. It should keep well for 2 months and improve with age. Use same quantity as other yeast, but always shake jar well before pouring out. For dry yeast, add flour to make a thick batter; stir in 1 tea-spoon salt and set to rise. When risen, add dry corn meal to form a mush; let rise again, knead and roll out. Cut in cakes. Dry slowly and thoroughly. Keep in cool, dry place. It keeps for 6 months.

Buttermilk Yeast Cakes

To make buttermilk yeast cakes, put 1 yeast cake or package of dry yeast in 1 pint of lukewarm water. Add one tablespoon each of salt, sugar, and meal. Mix and let stand overnight. Boil 1 pint of buttermilk. Mix 1 cup of water with flour, as for starch (use raw flour for this, about 3 tablespoons). Stir into the boiling buttermilk and boil until thoroughly cooked. When cooled take the yeast cake mixture and stir all together. If the weather is cool, let stand until the next day as it must sour. After it sours put into tray and work meal into it until it becomes stiff. Use flour to keep it from sticking. Roll out about ½-inch thick, cut in squares and dry in shade—not in the stove oven. The squares should be about ½-inch square. One of these yeast cakes will be enough for 1 batch of rolls.

Plain Muffins

2 cups sifted flour
3 tsp. baking powder
½ tsp. salt
2 T. melted shortening
2 T. sugar
1 egg
1 cup milk

Sift together flour, baking powder, salt, and sugar. Beat egg and add milk and melted shortening. Add egg mixture to flour mixture, stirring only until

Years ago farm women had to depend on yeast cakes which must be kept on ice. There were no such things as packages of dry yeast. When yeast cakes were obtained, my grandmother made her own yeast cakes that required no ice to keep them.

flour is moistened. Fill greased muffin pans ½ to ⅔ full and bake at 425 degrees for 20 minutes. Nut muffins are delightful with a meat salad, when served at the noon meal. Simply add ½ cup of chopped nuts to flour mixture and put a nutmeat on top of each muffin.

Sour Cream Muffins

1¾ cups flour
2 tsp. baking powder
2 T. sugar
½ tsp. salt
1 large egg
1 cup sour cream
1 T. water
½ tsp. soda

Sift dry ingredients into mixing bowl; beat eggs well, add sour cream, then soda mixed with water. Mix with sifted dry ingredients. Beat vigorously until dry ingredients are moistened. Fill muffin tins ⅔ full and bake about 20 minutes at 425 degrees.

Hot Flour Muffins

2 cups flours
¾ tsp. salt
1 tsp. soda
1 T. cornmeal
1 egg
1½ cups buttermilk
3 T. butter

Sift dry ingredients together. Add milk, butter, and well-beaten egg. Beat thoroughly. Bake in hot

On real cold days Mama would make a batch of Hot Flour Muffins ready to be eaten when we put our books and lunch boxes away. Mama often said, "You take the muffin! A little bit of heaven, cold or hot, sweet or not, it can fill the bill in many ways." Mama felt it a pity more cooks didn't cozy up to the muffin pans and treat their families.

greased muffin pans. Have oven at 450 degrees when you put the batter in.

Hominy Drop Cakes

1 T. butter
2 cups boiled, drained hominy
2 beaten eggs
1 tsp. salt

Stir butter into hot hominy. Add eggs and salt. Mix well and have a greased biscuit pan (cookie sheet with raised edges will do) ready; drop batter on it by spoonful. Bake at 450 degrees until brown. Makes 1 dozen.

Mr. Black's Special Hush Puppies

Grind fine:
  2 medium onions
  1 toe of garlic
  1 pint dill pickles
  2 large sticks of celery
  ¾ pound of boneless fish

Mix:
  6 cups corn meal
  3 cups flour
  8 heaping tsp. baking powder
  4 tsp. salt
  4 tsp. pepper

Method: Mix thoroughly ground ingredients with the dry. Add tap water until the dough is thick enough to drop ½ teaspoon into hot fat and fry. This amount makes enough for twenty.

The men are off to put out set hooks on the creek banks. I dream of crisp brown catfish, green salad, hush puppies, and lemon pie for dessert. There will be coffee for everybody, even the children. It's such an easy meal—no fuss, no bother, no planning, no nothing. Just open a bottle of homemade ketchup and feast. We have a deep black iron pot to fry the cut up fish and we use homeground meal to roll the fish in. Dale is our fish fryer. I make half a measure of special hush puppies from this recipe sent me from over in Louisiana.

Red belly perch, hush puppies, green onions, thin crisp biscuits to eat with muscadine jelly, and lots of tea and coffee makes a good Saturday supper, so the whole family can get in the house early to listen to the radio, study Sunday school lessons, and have good baths, for tomorrow is church and we must be up and at the work early so as to be in town at 10 sharp.

Hush Puppies

2 cups flour
2 cups sifted meal
4 level tsp. baking powder
4 eggs
4 T. sugar
Grated onion or garlic
Enough hot water to make stiff dough

Mix and drop by teaspoonful into hot fat. This will form into a lopsided ball when it hits the fat. Chopped (fine) green onions add extra zip to these delicious bits of goodness.

Pineapple Dressing

1 stick butter or margarine
1 scant cup sugar
4 eggs
6 slices sandwich bread
1 cup crushed pineapple (unsweetened)

Cream butter and sugar; add eggs one at a time and mix well. Cube bread, add with pineapple, and bake for 1 hour at 350 degrees.

Mrs. Herrington's Tomato Dressing

Make up a skillet of corn bread. Bake, then let rest a few hours to dry out a bit.

1½ cups sifted cornmeal
½ cup plain flour

4 tsp. baking powder

1 tsp. salt

1 heaping T. good grade mayonnaise

Enough sweet milk to moisten, making a nice pouring batter

Grease black iron skillet (medium size); heat in 400-degree oven until hot; sprinkle with sifted meal (just a bit). Pour in batter, bake until done. The top should be nicely rounded and golden brown. When bread is rested and cold, crumble in large bowl and moisten with fresh chicken broth. Add 1 cup of chopped onions with green tops. Add 1 teaspoon black pepper, 1 teaspoon sugar, and 3 tablespoons melted butter or margarine. Add 2½ to 3 cups of real ripe red tomatoes, peeled and chopped, but not too fine. Mix together with light hand; pour in greased baking dish. Bake at 350 degrees until light brown on top. Serve with chicken fried steak, baked rabbit or pork roast.

Turkey (Or Chicken) Dressing

3 cups biscuit crumbs

2 cups egg bread crumbs

2 eggs, slightly beaten

2¼ cups broth

2 T. melted butter

1 T. minced parsley

2 tsp. minced green pepper

¼ cup minced celery

¼ cup minced onion

½ tsp. black pepper

½ tsp. salt

¼ tsp. sweet marjoram

½ tsp. baking powder

Turkey, goose or baked ham for Thanskgiving can be extra special if you make a batch of delicious stuffing or dressing, or "cush," as it is called in some places. Many cooks wait until they are ready to make their stuffing to whip up a batch of corn bread and pull out a loaf of fresh bread. To be at their best, both should be at least a day old. If you must add rice, steam it until it is as dry as dry. The secret of good dressing is to handle it lightly, stuff the fowl lightly or pile it with a light hand into a baking dish.

Our Aunt Mae, wife of Daddy's brother Will, could not eat onions. When she and Uncle Will came for Christmas dinner Mama always made a small dish of cush special for Aunt Mae.

This is a moist dressing used in the South. Omit part of the liquid if a dry dressing is desired. Toast bread, break in small pieces or grind with coarse blade, then measure. The corn bread may be plain egg bread, muffins or corn sticks freshly made. Add seasonings. Add broth. Let stand 1 hour for moisture to penetrate. Add slightly beaten eggs and blend with a fork. Blend in baking powder; turn dressing into a greased baking dish. Bake covered 20 minutes, then uncovered 20 minutes at 350 degrees. Triple recipe to stuff a turkey. You can add ½ cup cooked rice if desired; just add ¼ cup more broth.

Note: The dressing used to stuff the bird should not be as moist as that cooked in baking dish because it absorbs moisture from the fowl.

Cinnamon Buns

½ cup butter
½ recipe basic roll dough
½ cup broken pecans
¾ cup brown sugar
3 tsp. cinnamon
½ cup raisins
6 T. butter

Cream butter and spread on bottom and sides of a 9-inch skillet. Roll dough in ⅛-inch thick oblong. Spread with remaining butter; sprinkle with remaining sugar, nuts, raisins, and cinnamon. Roll up like a jelly roll; cut dough in 1½-inch pieces; place cut side down in skillet. Cover, let rise until double in bulk. Bake in 350-degree oven for 30 minutes.

Mrs. Newell's Lost Bread

Soak 4 slices of day-old white bought bread in 1½ cups sweet milk with 1 level tablespoon of regular white sugar added. Set aside while you beat 2 egg yolks well. Beat whites until medium stiff. Add yolks to whites gently. If desired, add a few grates of nutmeg. Spread in flat dish. Using a wide spatula, dip each slice of soaked bread in the egg mixture and fry in mixture of 6 tablespoons pure lard and 1 tablespoon real butter. Fry until lightly browned, turn and fry the other side. Remove from skillet, sprinkle with powdered sugar if desired, keep warm until all slices are ready. It's best to serve Lost Bread piping hot. Be sure to have the syrup pitcher ready, or tart preserves to spread on this special bread.

Polske Paczki

(Polish Doughnuts)

    1 cake yeast
    4 egg yolks
    ½ cup sugar
    ½ tsp. vanilla
    About 7 cups flour
    1 pint milk, scalded and cooled
    1 whole egg
    ½ cup shortening or butter
    Grated rind of ½ orange or lemon
    1 tsp. salt

Dissolve yeast in lukewarm milk, add 2 cups flour. Let stand in warm place about ½ hour. Then beat eggs, sugar, vanilla, grated rind, and salt and add to dissolved yeast. Add melted butter, then 5 cups of flour. Cover and let rise until double in bulk.

Turn on floured board and pat to ½-inch thickness. Cut with doughnut cutter; cover, let rise until light, and fry in deep fat.

You can't go wrong with a good Waffle recipe, as any meat can be served with a waffle and there are all manner of extras that can be added to a standard recipe. Creamed chicken or ham hash go well with waffles. Regular pouring syrup or molasses along with fried eggs and bacon make a great light supper on cold winter nights.

Waffles

⅛ cup sweet milk
2 cups flour
½ cup melted butter
3 tsp. baking powder
½ tsp. salt
2 eggs, separated

Beat egg yolks and add milk. Add flour to make a stiff batter. Add melted butter and salt. Add baking powder. Fold in stiffly beaten egg whites. Bake batter on hot waffle iron.

SWEETLY BE

Cakes

When we were small, Mama and our grandmother often used a colored streak through a cake, making the cake something special. A pink streak that curled through and about in a white cake would call for delicate pink boiled icing. If Mama mixed cocoa with a bit of batter and used this for a streak, then the icing would be cocoa or chocolate.

The best thing I remember about Mama's baking was the delicious little "try" Mama would cook for each child, whenever a batch of batter was mixed. Lives there a soul over 35 who doesn't remember the dab of cake batter baked in a small tin plate or the lid of a baking powder tin "to see" if enough baking powder had been added, or too much sugar, flour or milk. All of these questions were answered by the simple method of baking a "try."

We were allowed to grease and flour our own "try" tins into which Mama would dip a level full tablespoon of batter.

When I make a cake I always leave several spoons of batter in the bowl. I do the same for the filling and icing. Then one of the boys "socks the bowl," as they call licking the bowl. I hate for the boys to grow up, but one thing I will like about it—I'll get to lick the bowl myself!

Dried Apple Cake

2 cups dried apple
1 cup sugar
2 eggs
1 cup butter
1 cup sour milk
2 tsp. soda
1 cup raisins
1 cup nuts (chopped)
1 tsp. cloves
1 tsp. cocoa
4 cups flour (plain)
1 tsp. cinnamon
Other fruits if desired
1 cup molasses

Chop and soak apples overnight. Cook in molasses until thick. Cream butter and sugar; add eggs, beat well. Sift flour with cocoa and spices. Mix soda with 1 tablespoon of warm water and add to sour milk. Fold apple-molasses mixture into sugar-egg

Thanksgiving is about three gobbles away. In some homes the national bird is a must on the table for the big family dinner. Others make do with baked hens, ducks or perhaps a goose, and others bake a ham all slathered with brown sugar and pineapple. Whatever the main course, mold a festive salad, pinch off pieces of yeast dough and come up with nose-tingling hot rolls, candy some sweet potatoes, cook a pot of green beans, and slice enough Dried Apple Cake for seconds.

Rose Budd's Recipes for Country Living

Nothing is nicer than having a water house: A water house is a long shelf (boxed in with lattice or not, suit your taste) on the back porch where the water bucket, the white stone wash bowl, the terripan shell for a soap dish, the nail brush, the little bottle of coal oil (for sweet potato gum, pine resin, paint tar and pitch) and my prize pot of sweet gum ivy is kept. In the long plank Dale shaped a round hole for the stone bowl to sit in. The shelf is too low for grown folks, but just right for little fellows. There are more little fellows here than grown folks. To the side is the roller towel, two mirrors, one for Dale and one for the boys (Dale refuses to stoop to shave and comb his hair) and a shelf for my powder and paint. Of course a nice bathroom would be nicer but not having a bathroom we make the best of what we have.

mixture, then add flour and soda-milk mixture alternately, beginning and ending with flour. Fold in nuts and raisins, turn into a greased, and then floured tube pan. Bake at 350 degrees about an hour or until a straw stuck in the middle comes out clean. I like to pour warm water over my raisins about an hour before making the cake so they will plump up, and I also dust the nuts with a bit of flour before sifting with the spices. If you bake in layers, 30 minutes or less is about the right time.

Applesauce Cake

2 cups sugar
1 cup butter
4 cups cake flour (save 1 cup to flour nuts and raisins)
2 cups unsweetened applesauce (canned or fresh from 6 fresh apples will make about 2 cups)
1 tsp. soda, dissolved in applesauce
4 cups nut meats
1 box puffed seeded raisins
1 T. allspice
1 T. cloves
1 tsp. nutmeg

Cream butter and sugar. If sweetened applesauce is used omit 1¼ cup of the sugar. Sift flour 3 times, after adding spices. Mix flour mixture with applesauce, a small amount at a time, beating after each addition. Add floured raisins and nuts. Candied cherries and pineapple may be added if desired. Bake in large tube pan, which has been greased and lined with brown paper, at about 300 degrees for about 3½ hours.

Rose Jr.'s Birthday Cake

8 egg whites
1 cup butter
2¼ cups sugar
1 tsp. flavoring
4 level tsp. baking powder
Pinch salt
1½ cups sweet milk
4 cups cake flour plus
1 T. corn starch

Remove 1 tablespoon flour from sifted flour, add corn starch, and resift with salt and baking powder. Cream butter until creamy and add sifted sugar a little at a time until light and fluffy. Add flour and milk alternately, beginning and ending with flour. Beat egg whites until stiff (I use a wire whisk for this, as the volume is greater than if an electric mixer is used), fold into the cake batter until well mixed. Add flavoring toward the last foldings over. Pour into heavy tube pan—about a 10-inch one—that has been greased and floured. Bake in 350-degree oven for about an hour.

Mrs. Carey Young of Liberty gave me this Birthday Cake recipe years ago. Only one time have I made a failure. I added baking powder twice and it came up, up, and up over the top, making a real mess. This cake is grand if baked in two layers, or two loaf pans, or in one large sheet. It cuts in party squares without crumbling and can be decorated with flowers, candies or flavors. Use your favorite icing to decorate.

Banana Cake

¼ pound butter
½ cup Wesson oil
2 cups sugar
4 eggs
½ cup raisins (cut up)
2 cups chopped pecans
3 cups plain flour
2 tsp. soda
1½ tsp. cloves
½ tsp. salt

If you are looking for a delicious cake that keeps well for several days, this one will suit your taste as well as those coming home for the holidays. Some of the cake if left need not be thrown away; freeze this Banana Cake for another day.

2½ tsp. cinnamon
6 ripe bananas
½ pound candied cherries (optional)

Cream butter, oil, and sugar. Add whole well-beaten eggs. Add nuts, cherries, and raisins that have been rolled in a little flour. Mix and sift flour, spices, salt, and soda; add alternately with bananas that have been mashed to a pulp. Bake in large tube pan (loaf pans can be used) in very slow oven for about an hour (350 degrees).

Mary's Apple Cake

4 medium apples
3 cups plain flour
1 tsp. cinnamon
1 cup chopped nuts
1¼ cup cooking oil
2 cups white sugar
2 eggs
2 tsp. vanilla
2 tsp. soda

Mix as for any other cake, grating or chopping the peeled apples fine. Fold the apples and chopped nuts in last. This is excellent if baked in a sheet cake, 3 layers or in a tube pan. Bake at 350 degrees until done—50 or 60 minutes for the tube pan, 40 minutes for the sheet cake. You will want to glaze the cake or use the glaze for filling. A few pecan halves will pretty the cake when placed around the top layer.

Glaze For Apple Cake

½ cup sugar
¼ cup warm water
3 T. butter
2 tsp. rum extract

Mix sugar, water, and butter in sauce pan; cook until it is a syrup. Add rum extract and pour glaze over still warm cake.

Bishop's Cake

1 cup butter
2 cups sugar
2 cups plain flour
3 eggs
¼ tsp. salt
1 tsp. vanilla
½ tsp. lemon extract

Cream butter well, adding sugar gradually, creaming all the time. Sift salt with flour and add alternately with the eggs. Beat well after each addition of flour and eggs. Add flour last, then flavorings. Place cake in cold oven; turn to 325 degrees and bake 1 hour and 15 minutes. Remove from oven and cool before storing in an air-tight stone or pottery container; no tin, please.

Bishop's Cake is delicious, heavenly to smell, and freezes well. People ask for seconds, and if you bake it, notice how pretty the top cracks and then sugars.

Banana Nut Cake

2 cups flour
1 tsp. baking powder
1 tsp. soda

¾ tsp. salt
1⅓ cup sugar
½ cup butter
½ cup buttermilk
1 tsp. vanilla
1 cup mashed bananas
½ cup chopped nuts
2 unbeaten eggs

Stir butter until soft, sift in dry ingredients; add ¼ cup milk and mashed bananas. Beat 300 strokes. Add eggs, nuts, and rest of milk and beat 150 strokes. This recipe makes 3 medium or 2 large layers. Bake 25 minutes at 375 degrees.

Buttermilk Cake

3 cups flour
2½ cups sugar
1 cup buttermilk
2 tsp. lemon flavoring
Pinch salt
2 sticks butter or margarine
5 eggs
½ tsp. soda
Rind of 1 lemon, grated

Cream butter and sugar, add yolks all at once, mix well. Add half of the buttermilk with the soda dissolved in 1 tablespoon of warm water. Add flour and balance of buttermilk and flavoring. Fold in egg whites after they have been beaten stiff. Set oven at 350 degrees. When cake begins to brown, cut oven to 200 degrees and bake until done.

Talking about the advantages of living in the country: When I make a cake and the recipe says butter or butter substitute, what is that substitute they are talking about? I use butter and nothing else. Have you ever tasted hot butter cake with fresh churned butter spread on instead of icing? Try it sometime. With a glass of buttermilk, nothing could be better. If you want cold butter cake, double the recipe, for if the family gets into the hot cake, it's gone. Cottage cheese—in town a little package is 22 cents. Here I use a whole crock of clabber, cream and all, dripped out in the yard overnight and served with fresh sweet cream, cinnamon rolls, and stewed fruit. Who wants to live in town?

Chocolate Eclair Cake

1 box graham crackers (whole)
1 large carton Cool Whip
2 pkgs. French Vanilla instant pudding mix
3 cups cold milk

Mix pudding mix with milk; fold in Cool Whip. Line pan with graham crackers. Put half of pudding mixture over crackers, then another layer of crackers, then the remainder of pudding mixture, ending with crackers over pudding. Top with topping made of 1 cup sugar, ⅓ cup cocoa, and ½ cup canned Pet milk. Boil 1 minute and add 1 teaspoon vanilla and 1 stick margarine. Freezes well.

Rich Cupcakes

½ cup butter
1½ cups sugar
3 eggs, unbeaten
1½ tsp. vanilla
⅔ cup sweet milk
2⅓ cups cake flour
3 tsp. baking powder
1 tsp. salt

Cream butter and sugar until soft and fluffy. Add eggs, one at at time, beating well after each addition. Sift flour, baking powder, and salt together 3 times and add alternately with milk and vanilla. Bake at 375 degrees until lightly browned. This recipe makes 50 small cupcakes. Or, you may bake this cake in a large square pan and cut in diamonds or squares as suits your fancy.

When you are feeling in a very gay mood, frost a batch of these Rich Cupcakes and decorate with bright candies or make your own decorations from the many interesting things to be bought in the stores. These cupcakes are so rich and delicious they will melt in your mouth. When served with a cold fruit bowl or a frosty drink, you will have to fill the plate a second time.

Dark Velvet Cake

4 squares unsweetened chocolate
1 cup sugar
½ cup butter
1 tsp. vanilla
3 eggs
1 tsp. soda
½ tsp. salt
⅔ cup milk
2 cups sifted cake flour

Melt chocolate in ½ cup hot water in top part of double boiler over boiling water. Cook, stirring constantly, until thickened. Add ½ cup sugar and cook for 2 or 3 minutes, stirring constantly. Cool to lukewarm. Cream butter well; add remaining sugar gradually, beating until light and fluffy. Add vanilla. Add eggs, one at a time, beating well after each addition. Add sifted dry ingredients alternately with milk, beating until smooth. Add chocolate mixture and blend. Pour into 2 9-inch layer pans, 1½ inches deep, lined on the bottom with paper and then greased. Bake in 350-degree oven for 50 minutes or until done. Let stand 5 minutes; cool on wire racks.

Remember a long time ago I promised you a chocolate cake recipe that would make a mare kick her colt? Here it is, and I promise you it will be delicious and the very best you ever made if you follow directions and use real clabber or sour buttermilk.

Red Devil's Food Cake

2½ cups plain flour
1 tsp. soda
1 tsp. baking powder
½ tsp. salt
½ cup fresh butter
¼ tsp. cinnamon
1½ cups sugar
1 tsp. vanilla

2 eggs
1 cup sour milk
⅓ cup hot water
½ cup cocoa
Few drops red food coloring

Sift flour once, measure and mix with soda, baking powder, cinnamon, and salt; sift three times more. Cream shortening and add sugar gradually, beating well after each addition. Add vanilla, then well-beaten eggs and beat until fluffy. Add food coloring at this time. Beat in flour mixture alternately with sour milk. Mix cocoa and water to form a paste; beat into batter. Pour into 2 9-inch pans and bake in moderate oven (350 degrees) for 30 to 40 minutes. Cool, spread fudge icing between layers and top with 7-Minute Frosting.

One-Egg Cake

2 cups flour
½ tsp. salt
2½ tsp. double-acting baking powder
⅓ cup soft shortening
⅓ cup granulated sugar
1 egg
2 tsp. brown sugar
¾ cup skim milk
1 tsp. vanilla extract

Grease bottom of 2 8-inch cake pans and lightly dust with flour. Preheat oven to 350 degrees. Sift the flour, salt, and baking powder together. Cream shortening until light and fluffy; beat in sugar and cream well. Add egg and beat until very light and fluffy. Add one at a time: flour mixture, brown sugar, milk, and vanilla, beating only until

One-Egg Cake will serve twelve and each serving will boast only 120 calories, including the Eggo Filling. This is fare for a dieter who likes to end a meal with a little something sweet.

smooth. Turn mixture into prepared pans and bake 30 minutes or until a cake tester comes out clean. Cool on cake rack.

Eggo Filling can be used as a low calorie dessert. Serve cold in pretty dessert dishes.

Eggo Filling

1⅓ cups no-cal cream soda
2 envelopes low-calorie chocolate pudding
1 tsp. unflavored gelatin
4 tsp. cocoa
1 T. cornstarch
1 T. brown sugar

Mix all ingredients in a blender. Then place in a pot and bring to a boil, stirring constantly. Chill until set, then fill cake and sprinkle powdered sugar on top and serve.

Eggless, Butterless, Milkless Cake was used during the Depression. Since we lived in the country and had milk and butter to spare, I often wondered why Mama would make this cake. She finally told me: "I sold the butter to buy things to run my household.

Eggless, Butterless, Milkless Cake

2 cups water
2 cups sugar (1 cup brown and 1 cup white, if you prefer)
1 cup shortening
1 cup raisins
2 cups flour
½ tsp. cloves
1 tsp. cinnamon
1 tsp. nutmeg
1 tsp. soda
1 tsp. salt
2 tsp. baking powder

Put water, sugar, shortening, and raisins in boiler and let boil about 1½ minutes; cool. Sift dry ingredients together 3 times, add to cooled mixture. Mix well. Add 1 teaspoon vanilla and ½ cup chopped nuts (peanuts will do, pecans are better). Bake in a greased and floured loaf pan at 350 degrees until broom straw inserted in center comes out clean.

Grandmother Budd's Fantastic Fruit Cake

4 large fresh eggs
1½ cups butter or shortening (do not use oil)
1½ cups sugar
1 cup molasses
4 heaping cups plain flour
1 tsp. soda
½ cup flour to dredge nuts in
½ tsp. salt
2 tsp. cloves
2 tsp. cinnamon
2 tsp. allspice
1 pound raisins (dark)
½ pound each: candied lemon peel and candied orange peel
½ pound green and red candied cherries (mixed)
½ pound each candied yellow pineapple and candied green pineapple
¼ pound currants
½ pound citron
1½ pints fig preserves (well-drained)
2 quarts nuts, measure after chopping

Sift spices with 4 cups flour, salt, and soda. Cream sugar and butter well; add eggs one at a time, stirring well to mix. Chop candied fruit (not too small) and dredge fruit and chopped nuts in

My 96-year-old mother made this cake all her cooking life. Now she lets her three daughters have the pleasure.

My grandmother, my mother and I used a citron melon that grew wild on our fields to pare, slice and "sugar down" this cake recipe. In the last few years I bought citron for my cake. The melons no longer grow here.

Once again it is time to enjoy the pear blossoms, so I mosey down to the spreading tree in the hog pasture and break off generous limbs, loaded with beautiful five-petaled blooms. The many stamens in the center of each bloom are tipped with dark brown, and truly there's nothing quite so breathtaking in the spring as the pear blossom centerpiece I have on my polished pine table.

My grandmother Budd gave each of her grandchildren a stone crock when she grew too old to handle the heavy things. The one that came my way is bronze-red with faint streaks of yellow here and there under the heavy glaze. The leaves on the pear limbs are green in the center and edged with bronze-red. I use plenty of blooms and tuck in a few daffodils for color appeal.

A ray of sunshine adds a sheen over the arrangement, and the two pottery ducks sitting close by seem to cock an eye toward the sunshine.

Springs smells are everywhere, and I like to do my bit to add something to the already heavy laden air. The quickest way is to bake

the ½ cup of flour. Add to the above mixture, folding to mix well. Add molasses and cut up drained figs. Stir to mix or fold in. Set oven at 350 degrees. Grease large tube pan with generous amount of unsalted lard. Line pan with brown wrapping paper and grease well. (This recipe is so old foil paper had not been invented. Be sure to use a brown paper bag or brown wrapping paper.)

Add batter and bake for about 2½ hours, depending on your stove. Insert a broom straw or a toothpick at end of 2 hours to test for doneness. Be sure to have a pan of water in the oven at all times to create steam. Have water in shallow pan beneath the cake pan so the steam will rise. Keep pan half-filled with water at all times. When done, let cake cool about 30 minutes in the pan. Remove and let cool completely.

Spread large white cloth on table; slice tart apples over top of cake. Wrap cloth around apples and cake. Store in stone churn or crock, or a very clean tin box. (Peel paper off carefully so cake won't tear.) Your taste or way of life will guide you as to pouring spirits over the cake.

Don't make the mistake of planning to whip this cake up in a few minutes before leaving for work in the morning. Everything should be at room temperature before beginning. This was in the days before the mixer; grandmother used her hands to mix and stir. Store at least 10 days before slicing. Hold a slice up to the light; it should look like a piece of stained glass. Do not ice this cake.

Gold Cake

⅛ cup sugar
¾ cup butter
8 egg yolks

2½ cups cake flour
3 tsp. baking powder
¼ tsp. almond extract
½ tsp. vanilla
6 cups milk

Combine flour and baking powder and sift 3 times. Sift sugar once. Cream butter and sugar well. Beat yolks until light; add to mixture. Add flavoring to milk. Add flour alternately with milk in about 3 parts. Beat batter after each addition until blended. Bake in greased 9-inch tube pan in 350-degree oven for about 45 minutes. Ice if desired.

Dale's Family Jam Cake Recipe

1 cup butter
2 cups sugar (white)
6 egg yolks
4 cups sifted flour (plain)
1 tsp. cinnamon
1 tsp. nutmeg
2 tsp. soda
½ cup sour cream
6 egg whites
2 cups blackberry jam

Cream butter and sugar until light and fluffy. Beat in egg yolks, one at a time. Mix well. Stir in jam. Add flour and spices—that have been sifted together three times—alternately with sour cream, ending with flour. Fold in egg whites that have been beaten to stage where peaks stand firm. Bake in 4 9-inch layers in moderate (350-degree) oven until center springs back when pressed with forefinger. Cool on clean cloth on wire rack. Ice

a spicy jam cake, and indeed the children come wandering kitchenward with questioning eyes asking to lick the mixing bowls. My daughter dips a pink finger tip into the rich purple batter. She gets out the baking tins and cuts waxed paper to fit. Soon the delicious fragrance of baking spice cake fills the whole house. The kettle sings and Mama Cat rumbles deep in her breast.

as desired, and may I beg of you to make boiled frosting—the kind where sugar and water are boiled to thread stage and then drizzled over beaten egg whites.

How often our hearts remember delicious food cooked by mothers and grandmothers. A letter from a gentleman from north Mississippi remembered a Jelly Coconut Cake his mother made each year at Valentine's. It was his pleasure to grate the coconut and his sister would choose the jelly to be used. She always chose wild plum jelly. How pretty and tasty the cake was, high on the beautiful cake stand, his mother's only possession saved from a family fire.

I like to cook on dark, dreary days. Cookbooks tell of icings not doing their best when the air is damp. I

Jelly-Coconut Cake

1 cup butter or margarine
2 cups sugar
4 eggs, separated
3 cups plain flour
¼ tsp. salt
3 tsp. baking powder
1 cup milk
1 tsp. vanilla extract
1 pint jelly (your favorite)
1 can coconut (moist type)

Grease and flour 4 layer cake pans before beginning cake. Cream butter or margarine until fluffy. Add egg yolks one at a time, beating well after each addition. Sift dry ingredients together 3 times; add alternately with milk and vanilla to creamed mixture. Beat after each addition until smooth. Fold in stiffly beaten egg whites. Pour in cake pans and bake in a 350-degree oven for 35 to 40 minutes. Test to see when done using toothpick or listen to see if cake is crying. While layers are warm, spread with jelly and top with coconut. Stack the layers, but do not frost or put jelly or coconut on top and sides of cake.

Layer Cake and Icing

1 cup butter or shortening
4 eggs
2 tsp. baking powder

1 T. pure vanilla
2 cups sugar
3½ cups flour
1¼ cups water
½ tsp. salt

Cream butter and sugar until light and fluffy. Add eggs one at a time, beating well. Add flour sifted with baking powder and salt about half of the mixture, then one cup of water, more flour, the rest of the water, ending up with flour. Mix batter each time water or flour is added. Add vanilla and mix. Grease three layer cake tins—square or round. I use square ones, and this recipe fills the pans to the brim when baked. Bake at 350 degrees until top springs back with touch of finger tip.

The icing is simple: in a large boiler put 2 cups of white sugar, ½ cup butter, 1 cup cream, and a few grains of salt. Cook over low heat until a few drops form a soft ball in cold water. Add 1 teaspoon vanilla, cook a few seconds longer, let cool, then beat until creamy. Spread between layers and on top of cake. Chopped nuts may be added if you desire.

Seven Layer Lemon Cake

(from Ella Lucas)

3 cups plain flour
2 tsp. cream of tartar
1 tsp. baking soda
2 cups sugar
1 cup butter or margarine, softened
¾ cup milk
4 eggs, room temperature
¼ cup milk
1 tsp. vanilla

pay no attention to such advice and usually come up with a fair example of cooking art. Take last week, for instance. I wanted a cake that didn't smack of cocoa, lemon, or of any of the other fillings or icings used by modern day cooks. I began thinking of the cakes my grandmother made and suddenly there came to my mind an icing so simple and requiring few ingredients. As I remembered it, the layers were thick and yellow, the icing silvery, soft, creamy, and delicious! Here is the recipe I used for the cake, a modern verison of the one my grandmother Budd used, but the results are beautiful. The icing is one I put together the best I remembered from twelve years of age. Dale and the children loved it.

Sift together first four ingredients into large mixer bowl. Add butter and ¾ cup milk to flour mixture and beat 2 minutes at medium speed. Add eggs and vanilla, the remaining ¼ cup milk and beat 2 more minutes. Prepare 7 9-inch round layer cake pans. (If you don't have 7, you can divide dough into 7 small bowls. Dip batter with a ½-cup measuring cup to divide evenly.) Cut 7 rounds of wax paper to fit bottom of pans. Grease and flour only the bottoms. Smooth batter into pans. Bake at 375 about 12 minutes. They should be done but not very brown. Turn out onto towel or brown paper bags to cool. Peel off waxed paper while warm.

Filling:
> 3 eggs, well beaten
> 1½ cups sugar
> 3 T. butter

Mix above ingredients well in top of double boiler. Add to egg mixture the grated rind and juice of 3 lemons and cook over boiling water until thick, about 20 minutes. Stir very frequently. Spread between layers while warm. There should be about ¼ cup for each layer. This recipe serves 12 to 15 persons.

In a hurry on Saturday morning? make up one recipe of my Lightning Cake. While it is baking, peel enough Irish potatoes to have plenty creamed for your family; put on to boil. Cut lettuce into a deep bowl, add two hard-boiled eggs, dash of dry mustard, tablespoon ketchup, one

Lightning Cake

1 egg
½ cup sugar
1 tsp. baking powder
¼ tsp. lemon extract
¼ tsp. salt
¼ cup milk
3 T. melted butter
½ tsp. vanilla

Beat egg and add sugar while beating; add flour that has been sifted with baking powder and salt. Then add milk, melted butter, and flavoring. Turn into skillet or 2 oiled layer pans. Bake in moderate oven (350 degrees) for 25 minutes. When partly cool, split layer if baked in skillet; butter bottom side. Pile sliced peaches that have been lightly sprinkled with sugar and nutmeg on top slice and cover with whipped cream. Slice into 6 pieces and serve. Sometimes I make this cake and mix up a package of Jell-O pudding and use for filling. It must all be eaten at one meal as it isn't the kind of cake that takes to waiting.

'Malgamation Cake

8 egg whites, stiffly beaten
2 cups sugar
1 tsp. soda
1 tsp. baking powder
1 cup butter
1 cup milk
3 cups flour

Cream butter and sugar. Add milk, baking powder, and soda, then add flour, followed by the stiffly beaten egg whites. Pour into 3 9-inch layer cake pans and bake at 350 degrees for about 25 minutes. For the filling, cream 1 cup butter and 2 cups sugar. Add 8 beaten egg yolks to mixture and cook until a drop hardens in cold water. Remove from heat and add 1 cup raisins, 2 cups pecans and 1 cup grated coconut. Spread between cooked cake layers and on top.

green pepper, and season with salt and pepper; then add two tablespoons of sweet cream, add a little lemon juice, mix well, and sit in a cool place. Fry slices of slab bacon, serve with salad, creamed potatoes, bread, tea, and cake, and there's your Saturday dinner.

Amalgamation: a coming together, drawing near—hence a recipe bringing good things together.

There is compensation in the cold days we are having: great big, wonderful wood fires to toast one's shins by; to roast foil-wrapped potatoes in the ashes; to tuck three foil-wrapped, buttered cold biscuits with smoked ham under a layer of coals until sizzling hot. The coffee pot keeps merry company right by the hearth. This dinner is a filling one, one that completely satisfies the mind as well as the stomach— how good a book reads when you can nibble and read.

The cold days have

Molasses Cake

1 cup homemade syrup
⅔ tsp. soda
½ cup shortening (bacon fat is best)
½ cup buttermilk
2 cups sifted self-rising flour
Vanilla or spices to flavor
2 eggs

Heat molasses. Beat soda into heated molasses; then add shortening or melted bacon fat, sifted flour and buttermilk, beginning and ending with flour. Add spices or vanilla. Add the eggs, one at a time, and beat well. Bake in 3 layers in 8-inch cake tins. Bake at 350 degrees until done. See frosting recipe page 186.

Molasses Cake

½ cup butter
½ cup brown sugar
½ cup molasses
1 egg
½ cup milk
3 tsp. baking powder
½ tsp. salt
¼ tsp. soda
2 cups sifted plain flour
1 tsp. mixed spiced (optional)

Cream butter with sugar, stir in molasses, add beaten egg. Resift flour with other dry ingredients. Add sifted ingredients alternately with milk. Beat batter after each addition until blended. Bake cake in greased 1-inch tube pan in moderate 350-degree oven for about 45 minutes—or 30 minutes if baked in party square pan.

Frosting:
   1½ cups sugar
   ¾ cups sweet cream
   Pinch of salt

Cook sugar, cream, and salt to a soft ball stage and allow to cool slightly. Beat until creamy and spread between layers and on top. Do not ice the sides of this cake.

No-Milk Cake

   1 cup vegetable shortening
   4 whole eggs
   2 tsp. baking powder
   1¼ cup cold water
   1 tsp. rum flavoring
   2 cups sugar
   3½ cups flour
   ½ tsp. salt
   1 tsp. vanilla

Cream shortening and sugar, add eggs one at a time, beating well after each addition. Blend in rum and vanilla flavoring. Sift flour, salt, and baking powder together and add alternately with the cold water (not ice water). Grease a tube or 2 deep layer cake pans well, pour in batter, and bake at 350 degrees until cake springs back when touched with fingertip.

brought a flock of redbirds to my yard. How I enjoy watching them as they vie for a favorite limb in the quince tree where I have tied pieces of beef fat studded with sunflower seeds, cracked corn, and a cob well daubed with peanut butter. If you haven't tried peanut butter for the birds, do so; they seem to relish it. The timid wrens fill themselves in the hen yard from the laying mash trough, and Rose Jr. wants to know if they will begin laying before the proper season, now that they are fed on laying mash.

These cold days call for a big molasses cake, and this recipe makes one that is fat and moist. If you want a huge cake, double the recipe and bake in sheet or party square pans.

This recipe is ages old. It came handwritten inside my cake pan and I've used it over and over, in many guises and variations. It has been baked in layers, sheets, loaves, cupcakes, muffins, and drop cookies if the milk is omitted from the recipe.

One-Two-Three-Four Cake

1 cup butter
1 cup sweet milk
2 cups sugar
2 tsp. baking powder
3 cups plain flour
4 large fresh eggs
Pinch salt
Vanilla flavoring to taste
   (be sure it is pure)

Cream butter until it is light, add sugar a little at a time, creaming after each addition. Sift flour with salt and baking powder three times. Add egg yellows one at a time, beating with firm beats. Add flour alternately with milk, adding a bit of flour last. Add beaten egg whites, using a folding over and over method; add flavoring. Turn into a well-greased tube pan and bake in 350-degree oven until top springs back when pressed with forefinger. This takes about 45 minutes.

Some guests or callers in our home like a choice of cake, and I try to always have something on hand to share the jam cake plate. I have found that an Orange Loaf Cake keeps well, tastes grand, and freezes beautifully.

Orange Loaf Cake

2 cups sifted flour
1¼ cups sugar
1½ tsp. baking powder
1 tsp. salt
½ cup soft shortening or butter
½ cup orange juice
1 tsp. orange or almond extract
2 eggs
1½ T. grated orange or lemon rind

Sift together flour, sugar, baking powder, and salt. Add remaining ingredients. Beat 2 minutes. Bake at 350 degrees for 60 minutes for loaf cake, 30 to 35 minutes for two layers. Frost with boiled frosting flavored with grated lemon or orange rind.

Orange Filled Coconut Cake

1 cup shortening
2 cups sugar
½ tsp. almond extract
4 eggs
3 cups sifted cake flour
2¼ tsp. baking powder
¾ tsp. salt
1 cup milk

Cream shortening well; add sugar gradually, beating until light and fluffy. Add flavoring, then eggs one at a time, beating well after each addition. Add sifted dry ingredients alternately with milk, beating until smooth. Pour batter in 3 round 9-inch layer pans. Bake 25 minutes at 375 degrees. Let stand 5 minutes, then cool on racks.

Orange Filling

½ cup sifted cake flour
1 cup sugar
¼ tsp. salt
¼ cup water
1¼ cups orange juice
¼ cup lemon juice
2 T. grated orange rind
Grated rind of 1 lemon
4 egg yolks

What happens to your cooking failures? Do you leave them around as living proof that you slipped up? Of course, we can't be perfect at all times, but I can see no point in waving your failures in the family face. If there are chickens and hogs on the place, they will relish a fallen cake; too much soda in the biscuit will never be known if eaten by the dog. A pie that failed to stand firm will serve fine for a pudding if dipped into little custard cups.
Remember, no husband can brag with a clear conscience: "My wife is the best cook in the county," if he can see in his mind that lopsided cake you left on the sink last week. So be safe instead of sorry: get those flops out of sight.

December is the tissue paper month, a month wrapped in silver morning frosts, tied with sparkling rays of sun as it peeps over the little pine forest. December is a month of hidden presents, hushed voices, much anticipation and joyous expectations. December is a red bow on the package of your life, the month when we count anew our blessings and see where we failed in the months now gone forever; taking mental tucks in the remiss places. December is the month when we take new life and hope for the coming year.

Mix flour, sugar, and salt in heavy sauce pan. Add water and mix until there are no lumps. Add orange juice, lemon juice and grated rinds. Cook over low heat until mixture thickens and becomes almost transparent. Beat egg yolks slightly; add hot mixture slowly, stirring constantly. Return to sauce pan. Stirring constantly, cook about 5 minutes or until it thickens again. Cool.

Coconut Frosting

1½ cups sugar
⅛ tsp. salt
½ cup egg whites
½ tsp. cream of tartar
¼ tsp. almond extract
2 cups shredded coconut

Combine sugar, cream of tartar, salt, and ½ cup hot water in sauce pan. Cook without stirring until it forms soft ball. Beat egg whites, not dry but stiff. Add syrup slowly to egg whites, beating at high speed. Add flavoring; spread on cake and sprinkle with coconut.

Party Cake

1 large orange chiffon cake (store-bought)
1 pkg. instant vanilla pudding
1 large can crushed pineapple
2 cartons whipping cream

Slice cake cross-ways into three parts. Drain pineapple; use juice to mix with instant pudding. Whip cream. Fold in pudding mixture and pineapple (a gentle hand is necessary). Spread between layers and frost entire cake. Refrigerate for several hours before serving.

...e Cake

- ᵥ. cup butter
- 1½ cups sugar
- 2½ cups flour
- 2 eggs beaten separately
- 1 cup cooked unsweetened prunes (chopped coarsely)
- ½ cup sour buttermilk
- Pinch salt
- 1 level tsp. soda
- 1 cup chopped walnuts

Cream butter, sugar, and egg yolks together (be sure to add yolks after mixing sugar and butter). Add prunes that have been cooked tender in a small amount of water and drained; next add buttermilk, cream well. Sift flour, soda, and salt together; add separately with chopped nuts. Last, fold in stiffly beaten egg whites. Bake in 350-degree oven using 2 9-inch layers—square pans make such an imposing looking cake. Ice with your favorite frosting.

Emma Tallison's Black Walnut Pound Cake

- 1 cup shortening
- 2 cups sugar
- 4 eggs, separated
- 3 cups all purpose flour
- ½ tsp. soda
- ½ tsp. baking powder
- ¾ tsp. salt (I leave this out)
- 1 cup black walnuts
- 1 tsp. vanilla
- 1 cup sour milk

The ducks are going at this setting business with an earnestness that amazes me. I take away the eggs as fast as they lay and still they lay and continue to set on an old door knob, a white bone, a smooth rock, and any other thing they can find and roll into their nest. Down on the branch we hunt and find a nest here and there—behind a fallen log, under a great clump of water grass, in a hollow log, and one nest is right out in the open in an old thrown away dishpan. The duck eggs make fine angel food cakes and we keep one cooking or in the process of being eaten all the time the ducks are giving us plenty of eggs.

Cream shortening and sugar; add egg yolks and 2 tablespoons milk. Mix well. Sift dry ingredients; add alternately with rest of milk. Add nuts and flavorings and stiffly beaten egg whites. Bake in greased and floured tube pan at 350 degrees until done. Make glaze of powdered sugar and enough milk to trickle over top and sides. Yum, yum.

Of all cakes Grandma made I think I lean toward the pound cake—a pound of flour, sugar, butter and eggs. And it took a pound of beating to get it ready for the oven. When baked it was a smooth tempting yellow cake, with a thick brown crust.

Coconut Pound Cake

1½ cups shortening
2½ cups sugar
5 whole eggs
1 cup sweet milk
¼ tsp. salt
½ T. coconut flavoring
3 cups cake flour
1 tsp. baking powder
1 cup coconut

Cream shortening (1 cup Crisco and 1 stick margarine) well; add sugar, a little at a time, and continue creaming. Add eggs one at a time, beating well after each. Add milk and flavoring; add dry ingredients, beat well. Fold in coconut. Bake 1½ hours at 300 degrees, using a large tube pan. Let cool in pan for at least 20 minutes. This cake needs no icing.

Grandma's Pound Cake

1 cup fresh churned butter
2½ cups white sugar
3 cups cake flour
½ tsp. salt
6 new laid eggs

1½ tsp. baking powder
1 cup sweet milk
1 tsp. pure vanilla
½ tsp. lemon extract

Sift flour once, measure, and sift three times with baking powder and salt. Add flavoring and extract to milk. Cream butter and sugar until light and fluffy. Add eggs one at a time, beating well after each addition. Add milk and flour alternately. Beat well and pour into a tube cake pan. Bake in a moderate oven for 1 hour or until done. I like to grease my pan and then dust with flour; this makes the crust of the cake browner. Mixing time with an electric mixer is about 6 minutes.

Mammy's Pound Cake

3 cups plain flour
2½ cups sugar
9 eggs (whole)
1 pound country butter or 3 sticks
    creamery butter
1 tsp. vanilla

Cream butter and sugar, adding one tablespoon sugar at a time (2 tablespoons if you use an electric mixer). Drop in 1 egg at a time and cream well after each addition. Grease large round tube cake pan very lightly and line bottom with greased brown paper. Put batter in pan and start baking in oven pre-heated to 250 degrees for 10 minutes. Change temperature to 275 for 15 minutes, to 300 for another 15 minutes, and then to 350 for the remainder of the baking time, which should be 40 minutes. Total baking time is 80 minutes. Turn out on rack to cool. (Don't be tempted to look at cake while baking.) This recipe may be baked as cupcakes. Makes about 40 cupcakes when baked in the fluted paper cups.

This recipe makes a heavy cake and one that can be depended on not to stay around until it gets stale. If such a thing should happen, mix up a rich chocolate sauce and serve over slices of the cake. There is no way you can go wrong on this cake, but two words of caution: don't open the oven door and walk easy while it is baking as this is a delicate cake and might fall. A fallen cake has no place in the kitchen of good cooks.

Mrs. Wm. H. Hight of Louisville gave me the recipe for Mammy's Pound Cake many years ago. I wish I had kept count of how many I have made by this recipe.

Have you noticed how good things smell in July? Mid-afternoon sees heat waves simmering over the fields and pastures, but there is a sweet for every sour in this world. Never can a quick dip in the blue hole feel so good as it does on a July afternoon. The very thought of a freezer of ice cream, lush with peaches or strawberries will give you goose bumps, and now that eggs are in every nest and under every bush and lumber pile, do plan to keep big pound cakes on hand.

Prize Pound Cake

1½ cups butter
3 cups sugar (sifted twice)
3 cups all purpose flour (sifted 4 times)
9 eggs
1 T. vanilla
1 tsp. rum extract (or other flavoring of your choice)

Cream butter well, add sugar gradually, and cream mixture each time. Add flour and eggs alternately, beginning and ending with flour. Be sure to add only 1 egg at a time. Pour batter into a greased, lined, and then greased and floured, 10-inch round tube pan. Bake 1¼ hours at 325 degrees in a pre-heated oven. Let cool in pan for 10 minutes, then turn on a clean cloth over a wire rack. When cool, fold cloth over cake and store in an air-tight box. Will keep for at least a week in cool weather and much longer in the freezer.

Thrifty No-Butter Pound Cake

3 cups all purpose plain flour
2 cups sugar
½ tsp. soda
½ tsp. baking powder
¾ tsp. salt
1 cup shortening
4 eggs, unbeaten
1 cup buttermilk
1 tsp. vanilla flavoring
1 tsp. lemon flavoring
3 or 4 drops of butter flavoring, if desired

Sift flour before measuring; sift sugar. Combine shortening and sugar, beating until light and fluffy. Add eggs one at a time, beating 30 seconds after each addition. Stir one-third of flour into creamed mixture and heat well. Combine buttermilk, soda, salt, baking powder, vanilla and lemon flavorings. Stir one-half of mixture into creamed mixture until well blended. Repeat procedure, ending with dry ingredients; scrape bowl frequently. Pour batter into a 10-inch tube pan, which has been greased with shortening and dusted with flour. Bake at 325 degrees for one hour and 25 minutes. Let set in pan for a few minutes; turn out on cooling rack.

Quick Cake

¾ cup sugar
2 heaping T. soft butter
1 egg
1½ cups sifted flour
2 tsp. baking powder
1 tsp. flavoring
Pinch of salt
Milk

Mix sugar, butter, and egg. Then add remaining ingredients, using enough milk to make batter of cake texture. Turn into a black skillet and bake right along with the corn bread. This cake isn't too sweet and takes to berries or fresh fruit like the proverbial duck to water.

If you are missing one egg to complete a cake batter, use a spoon of mayonnaise the same size as an egg.

This is a most delicious, moist, pretty cake that keeps well. It freezes beautifully and is grand for gift giving to a neighbor.

A Real Good Tasting Cake

1 box yellow cake mix
4 whole eggs
⅔ cup cooking oil
1 cup apricot nectar

Glaze:
½ cup apricot nectar
1 cup powdered sugar

Mix cake mix, oil, and nectar; add eggs one at a time, beating well. Pour into well greased and floured pan; bake in moderate oven for about an hour. Turn out on rack to cool, and while still very warm, but not hot, glaze with a mixture the apricot nectar and sugar. Dribble over cake until surface is covered. Some will run off the cake: scoop it up with spoon and dribble it again over the top.

Sheet Cake

8 egg whites
2¼ cups sugar
4 level tsp. baking powder
1½ cups sweet milk
1 cup butter
1 tsp. flavoring
Pinch salt
4 cups cake flour

Cream butter and sugar until light and fluffy. Add a little flour that has been sifted with salt and baking powder. Add milk and flour alternately to keep from curdling. Beat egg whites stiff and fold in cake batter. Add flavoring of your choice. Bake in big sheet pan at 375 degrees for 1 hour; test with finger after 45 minutes. Ice as desired. If you freeze this cake, freeze without icing. The day you plan to use it, let thaw 2 hours before icing.

Short Cake

1 quart flour (heaped)
2 tsp. baking powder
¼ pound butter
2 eggs beaten with 1 small cup of sugar
1 cup milk

Make into dough; roll out and divide in 2 pieces; put 1 layer of dough on top of the other and bake in a large dish. When baked, separate the layers by running a knife between. Butter well, put sweetened strawberries between the layers and on top. Serve with fresh skimmed sweet cream.

Coffee Spice Cake

2 eggs beaten together
¾ cup white sugar
⅓ cup brown sugar
½ cup strong coffee (cold)
2 cups flour
½ cup butter
2 tsp. baking powder
¼ tsp. mace
¼ tsp. cinnamon
¼ tsp. ginger

Cream sugar and butter, add eggs, and beat well. Sift dry ingredients together and add alternately

This weather calls for something a little more fallish than a chiffon pie or cake, and what could be nicer than a big Coffee Spice Cake? This is a pretty cake, and if you put it on your prettiest cake plate, and serve to callers with steaming cups of perfectly brewed coffee, they will remember coming to visit you with pleasure.

with the coffee a little at a time. Bake in 2 large or 3 small layers in moderate oven until done.

Sour Cream Spice Cake

2 cups cake flour
¼ tsp. soda
2 tsp. baking powder
¼ tsp. salt
¼ tsp. cloves
2 tsp. cinnamon
¼ cup shortening
1 cup brown sugar, firmly packed
¾ cup thick sour cream

Sift flour with soda, baking powder, salt, cloves, and cinnamon. Place shortening and sugar in large bowl and cream until light and fluffy (I recommend your hand for this.) Add whole egg and continue beating for about 2 minutes. Combine sour cream and flour alternately and beat well. Pour into 2 8-inch pans that have been well-greased and dusted with flour. Bake in a preheated (350 degrees) oven for 25 to 30 minutes. When baked, cool on rack and ice. Good is the word for this cake.

Strawberry Cake

1 box white cake mix
½ cup water
¾ cup cooking oil
4 eggs
½ cup frozen strawberries and juice
1 pkg. strawberry flavored gelatin

Mix cake mix and gelatin. Add thawed strawberries, oil, water, and eggs. Beat well. Bake in 3 layers at 350 degrees for about 18 to 20 minutes. Cool layers and fill and ice with icing made of 1 box confectioner's sugar, 1 stick oleo, ½ cup strawberries, and juice. Mix well and spread between layers and on top. If it isn't pink enough, add a few drops of red food coloring.

Sweet Potato Cake

2 cups cake flour
1½ tsp. baking powder
Pinch salt
1 tsp. cloves
1 tsp. allspice
1 tsp. cinnamon
2 T. cocoa
1 cup shortening
2 cups sugar
1 cup mashed sweet potatoes
2 T. hot sweet milk
5 egg yolks
1 cup pecans (measure before breaking)

Mix all dry ingredients and set aside while you cream shortening and sugar, adding egg yolks then potatoes. Mix in dry ingredients and then add chopped pecans and milk. Bake in layers in moderate oven. When cool, ice with 7-Minute Frosting. If you must, lavish freshly grated coconut on the still-soft icing.

I think a Sweet Potato Cake is a delightful ''something'' to have on hand during the holiday season. Try it once and I firmly believe you and yours will say it is ''about the best way we know to eat sweet potatoes.''

Speaking of getting out of the well-worn and known rut, once when I had made about one million egg custards and twelve egg pound cakes I grew faint at the thought of serving another such dessert. Through my cookbook I chanced upon a recipe for Tomato Soup Cake. Ah! Here was something more than once removed from the steady diet of the usual fare fit for the gods. All the while I was mixing up batter, which turned out to be a pale pink, I could hear the remarks my family would make. However, nothing had prepared me for eating Tomato Soup Cake twice a day for five days. I grew so tired of the stuff I gave it to the man who helped me, and he in turn must have given it to Mr. Bones (our dog), for I saw Bones trotting toward the barn with it in his mouth. I always wondered what he did with it.

You can make your own white cake mix and keep it handy when you are ready for a white layer or loaf cake.

Tomato Soup Cake

1 cup sugar
1 can condensed tomato soup
1 tsp. nutmeg
2 cups flour
2 tsp. baking powder
1 cup nut meats
½ cup shortening
1 tsp. cinnamon
1 tsp. cloves
1 tsp. soda
1 cup raisins
1 cup dates (optional)

Cream sugar and shortening; add dry ingredients sifted together. Add soup, fold in nut meats and raisins. Bake in moderate oven for about 40 minutes. Ice with 1 package of cream cheese and 1½ cups powdered sugar, mixed well.

White Cake Mix

1 pkg. cake flour
⅓ cup double-acting baking powder
5 cups sugar
1 T. salt
3 cups shortening

Sift first four above ingredients together 3 times. Cut in shortening and store in covered container.

White Cake:
4½ cups of above white cake mix
1 cup milk
1¼ tsp. vanilla

6 egg whites
¾ cup sugar

Add vanilla to milk. Add ¾ cup milk to mix and stir until mix is thoroughly wet. Add remaining milk and beat until batter is smooth. Beat egg whites (add a pinch of salt) until stiff peaks form. Add sugar and beat until stiff. Fold egg whites into batter and beat until all lumps are out. Pour into loaf or layer pans. Bake at 375 degrees for 25 to 30 minutes.

Yellow Cake

1 cup butter
1 cup sweet milk
3 cups cake flour
1 tsp. vanilla
½ tsp. lemon or almond flavoring
2½ cups sugar
8 eggs (well-beaten yellows)
1½ tsp. baking powder

(If you take the butter direct from the churn to the mixing bowl you will need to add ¼ teaspoon salt.) All measurements are level and are measured in a standard 8-ounce measuring cup.

Cream butter and sugar until light and fluffy; add well-beaten egg yellows. The flour that has been sifted with the baking powder is added alternately with the milk, to which your choice of flavoring has been added. Beat the whites and mix lightly. Bake in a slow oven for about 1 hour and 15 minutes or until the top springs back when pressed with fingertip. I test mine with a clean broom straw right in the middle of one side. A clean straw, the cake is done; particles clinging, bake longer. My sister uses a gas stove and she sets her

If you want to get part of your Sunday dinner out of the way on Saturday, make up a Yellow Cake and rest assured that it will be even better than the day it was baked. It's just plain yellow cake, heavy and close-textured with a delicious brown crust. A thin chilled egg custard poured over slices makes grand eating. We call it ice cream cake, for I always make one to eat with Sunday ice cream.

oven at 350 degrees. I just stick my hand in and can tell if it is too hot or not hot enough. One stick added to the fire keeps the cake baking fine.

Everybody has a favorite pie and cake recipe. While I lean toward a White Layer Cake, filled with lemon jelly filling and iced with boiled frosting for summer, the first cool days of fall find me bringing out the blackberry jam and baking a stack of jam layers. These are put together with a boiled icing of sweet cream, sugar, and finely chopped pecans. The sides of the jam cake are never iced, but I use a heavy hand when spreading the filling between the layers.

Yellow Plain Cake

1 cup fresh country butter
2½ cups sifted sugar
1 cup sweet milk
8 egg yellows, well-beaten
8 egg whites
About 3 cups cake flour
1½ tsp. baking powder
Pinch salt
Extract to taste

Cream sugar and butter until light and fluffy. Stir in egg yellows; sift flour, salt, and baking powder three times and add alternately with milk, beginning and ending with flour. Add extract, fold in beaten egg whites. Bake in stem pan for 1 hour and 15 minutes at 300 degrees until done. Layers and cupcakes take less time, of course.

Yum-Yum Cake

1 pound raisins
2 cups sugar
2 T. butter or margarine
2 tsp. cinnamon
2 tsp. cloves
2 cups water
1 cup preserves, mashed (fig, pear or peach)
1 tsp. soda
¼ tsp. salt
4 cups flour

Combine raisins, sugar, butter, cinnamon, cloves, and water; boil 10 minutes. When cool add the preserves, soda, salt and flour. Mix well and bake in tube pan in moderate oven about 1 hour. This cake can be baked in layers and put together with boiled icing.

Ambrosia Cake Filling

3 ½ T. cornstarch
1 cup sugar
1 egg, beaten slightly
3 T. lemon juice
Grated rind of 1 orange
2 T. butter
½ cup orange juice
2 T. water
¾ cup grated coconut

Combine all ingredients except coconut; cook on low heat until clear and thick—about 10 minutes. Cool and add coconut.

Spread this filling between two or three layers of One-Two-Three-Four Cake and ice with your very best white icing. This makes a real party cake!

Boiled Frosting

2 cups sugar
¾ cup hot water
¼ tsp. flavoring, same as used in cake
Few grains salt
3 egg whites

Boil sugar and water until it spins a thread, pour over stiffly beaten egg whites. Stir over hot water and continue to beat until thick, adding salt and flavoring when it is put over the hot water. Ice cake, making pretty swirls with tablespoon around the sides.

One thing we enjoy around Christmastime is a gooseberry cake. I make a big cake in the tube cake pan, ice it with white icing, and decorate the top and sides with the vine and berries of the gooseberry vine.

Of course, you know what I am talking about. When you walk in the woods, you look down and discover at your feet shiny

little green leaves growing
on a creeping, clinging vine.
Usually there is a lot of
creepy moss nearby and the
pine needles are piled all
around. Push the pine
needles and fallen leaves
away, and there nestled
under the leaves are the red
berries of the gooseberry
vine, plump and firm and
tasteless.

The berries serve no
purpose on the cake except
to decorate it. The
gooseberry cake got started
in this way: Many years ago
when my grandmother on
daddy's side of the family
baked her big white icing
cake for Christmas, she
wanted it to look
"Christmasy." Having no
store-bought ornaments, she
sent the children to the
woods to get the vine and
berries of the gooseberry.
These were washed, drained
dry, then pressed into the
still soft icing. Pretty? Yes,
indeed! The cake stood high
on the cut glass cake stand,
the icing was white as the
snow, and the green of the
vine and the red berries
made a sight never to be
forgotten. We always have a
gooseberry cake on
Christmas. I am counting
the years until I can teach

Cake Filling

1½ cups white sugar
1 cup brown sugar
Pinch salt
Lump of butter size of a large egg
1 cup sweet cream
1 cup cherries or nut meats

Mix and boil until it forms soft ball in cold water. Beat until creamy and spread quickly on warm cake layers.

Chocolate Fudge Icing

1 cup sugar
½ cup sweet milk
2 T. butter
Few grains salt
1 square baking chocolate
½ tsp. vanilla
2 or 3 tsp. cream

Boil first 5 ingredients gently with occasional stirring to the soft ball stage. Remove from heat and set pan in cold water. When bottom of pan feels lukewarm, add vanilla and heat to fudge consistency. Add enough cream to fudge so as to be able to spread on cake. If frosting becomes too thick, thin with a little more cream. This makes enough frosting for a large loaf cake.

Coffee Icing

1 cup white sugar
½ cup brown sugar
½ cup coffee
2 stiffly beaten egg whites

Boil sugar and coffee until it spins a thread; add to egg whites, beating all the while. Continue beating until smooth and cool; spread between layers and on top of cake.

Creamy Nut Frosting

1 stick margarine
2½ T. flour
½ cup sweet milk
1 box confectioner's sugar
½ cup chopped nuts
1 tsp. vanilla

Melt margarine. Remove from heat and add flour, blending well. Add milk, boil 1 minute or until mixture is thick. Stir in sugar, nuts and vanilla. Spread between cooled cake layers and on top of cake.

Devil's Food Icing

2 cups brown sugar
¾ cup water
2 egg whites
1 tsp. salt
2 tsp. vanilla
1 cup chopped nuts

Rose Jr. to make such a cake. And when I am gone, she will teach her grandchildren to make it and say to them, "Your great-great-great Grandmother Budd always made this cake on Christmas."

Cook sugar in water until it spins a thread. Add in thin stream to stiffly beaten egg whites and beat mixture until creamy. Add salt, vanilla and nuts. Delicious on chocolate cake layers.

Fruit Sauce

½ stick butter
¾ cup sugar
1 can concentrated orange juice
1 can apricot and applesauce baby food
Pinch salt
1 T. rum flavoring

Melt sugar with orange juice; do not boil. Add other ingredients and serve over warm cake.

Jelly Icing 1

1 cup sweet cream, whipped
3 T. sugar
½ cup tart red plum jelly

Whip jelly with fork to break into small pieces; stir in sugar. Whip cream and fold into jelly and sugar mixture. Spread on top of cooled cake. All must be eaten at one meal as icing does not keep overnight or even to another meal.

Jelly Icing 2

2 egg whites
¼ tsp. salt
1 cup jelly

Grandma always said, "Wait until you can see the whites of eyes before icing the cake." She made her layers on Saturday and kept them wrapped in several layers of clean cloths. Then after church on Sunday she hurried home before the company came, put the chicken to frying, and iced her cake. Using Jelly Icing was sure to get lots of compliments and never a crumb of the cake was left. I like to make yellow layers for this Jelly Icing and pile the icing high. A cup of wild plum jelly makes a lovely pink icing and one that will tingle your tongue and make you ask for more.

Beat egg whites and salt until stiff. Add the jelly gradually, beating constantly until of a good consistency to spread. Enough for the tops of two 9-inch layers. If your taste runs to cupcakes, bake your batter in muffin pans, and ice top of each muffin.

Pineapple Frosting

1 cup evaporated milk
1 cup sugar
3 egg yolks
½ cup margarine
1 tsp. vanilla extract
1 20-ounce can crushed pineapple, drained

In a sauce pan combine milk, sugar, egg yolks, margarine, and vanilla extract. Cook over medium heat stirring constantly until mixture thickens— about 12 minutes. Add drained pineapple.

Raisin Frosting

1½ cups sugar
½ cup water
½ cup seedless raisins
Pinch salt
2 egg whites
1 T. grated orange rind
¾ tsp. baking powder

Chop raisins fine. Boil sugar and water without stirring until it spins a thread. Add the chopped raisins and boil for a few seconds; then pour over the stiffly beaten egg whites and beat until smooth. Add the orange rind and baking powder and whip thoroughly. Spread between the layers and over the top and sides of cake.

Tutti-Frutti Icing

2 egg whites
1½ cups sugar
¼ tsp. Maraschino cherry juice
1 T. lemon juice
¾ cup chopped, toasted almonds
¼ cup macaroon crumbs
⅛ tsp. grated orange peel
20 Maraschino cherries, cut up

Combine egg whites, sugar, and fruit juice. Cook over boiling water, beating constantly until icing stands in peaks. Fold in remaining ingredients before spreading on cake.

Please, I beg of you, don't flavor this with bottled lemon juice, frozen juice, or lemon flavoring. To be at its best, it should be squeezed right from a fresh lemon. Grate your rind before cutting the lemon. It's also best to ice with Boiled Icing or 7-Minute Icing, not one of those powdered sugar icings that many of us use in a pinch.

Lemon Filling

¾ cup sugar
Dash salt
1 egg, well-beaten
½ cup water
½ tsp. grated lemon rind
4 T. flour
2 T. butter
¼ cup lemon juice

Mix sugar, flour, and salt in top of double boiler. Add water and egg and mix well. Place over boiling water and cook, stirring constantly, about 10 minutes or until thickened. Remove from heat, add butter, lemon juice and rind. Cool. Spread between thoroughly cool layers of cake.

Mocha Frosting

2 cups powdered sugar
6 level T. soft butter
2 tsp. strong coffee
2 tsp. milk
½ tsp. vanilla
Dash cinnamon

Put all ingredients in a bowl and mix with a fork or mixer until smooth enough to spread between layers, on top and on sides. Decorate with extra nut meats (pecan or walnut halves).

White Icing

½ cup water
1½ cups sugar
1 tsp. Karo syrup
1 tsp. vanilla
½ cup egg whites
3 T. sugar
Pinch of salt

Cook water, sugar, and syrup until a thread is spun. Beat egg whites with pinch of salt until stiff peaks form. Pour syrup into egg whites and beat until a soft icing is formed. Add vanilla.

Pies

June is a darling month—a month when the earth tips her fruits of field and stream into our laps with lavish hand. The huckleberry bushes are full of blooms. I can just taste those fresh pies, bursting with purple goodness that is fresh berries, sweet butter, and sugar. Two a day is my quota of pies when the berries are on the bushes. Never mind that the dishes don't get washed, the cats fed, the floors swept, the chickens shooed out of the flower beds. There is good eating waiting there in the pine forest. Blackberries hang heavy and luscious in every nook and corner. It is a very easy matter to dash out and pick a pie for dinner.

Amber Pie

1 cup sugar
1 T. plain flour
1 tsp. cinnamon
½ tsp. nutmeg
½ tsp. cloves
1 T. vinegar
1 cup buttermilk
1 cup seedless raisins
4 eggs, separated
1 T. melted butter

Beat egg yolks; add sugar gradually, beating all the while. Add flour and melted butter; beat again until smooth. Add spices and buttermilk and raisins that have been plumped in hot water and well-drained. Cook in double boiler over hot water until thick. Pour into a baked pie shell and cover with meringue made with the egg whites, allowing 2 tablespooons of sugar for each white. Brown in medium oven. Let cool before cutting.

Apple Deep-Dish Pie

Pastry for 2 crust pie
¾ to 1 cup sugar
2 T. flour
⅛ tsp. salt
6 cups pared, cored tart apples, sliced
¼ tsp. cinnamon
1 tsp. lemon juice
2 tsp. butter
¼ tsp. nutmeg

People celebrate their birthdays in various ways. Many take care not to mention they will be one year older, others deny their age, while children are frank and ask, ''What are you going to give me for my birthday?'' Some will sigh and hope for visits from their children; others will bemoan that they just know they will get nothing this year, even though they were showered with gifts and visits last year. I am not above putting on the bulletin board little hints and pictures of things I hope to find when my birthday rolls around.

Dale's grandfather Stevens (we have been told this touching little story many times by Dale) simply took things in his own hands when May 2, the day of his birth, rolled around. The elder Stevenses weren't much on birthdays. Perhaps there would be a new homemade shirt for the boys and an iced cake if a birthday happened to fall on Sunday. But with Grandpa Stevens it was another story. He was as sentimental as a ruffled Valentine, and if nobody else remembered his birthday, he did the honors himself.

Well before daylight, every May 2 saw him strain up a special pan of rich Jersey milk. When daylight came he took the berry pail and went to the woods to pick enough huckleberries for a plate pie just for himself. Grandmother Stevens catered to him, turning the picked-over and washed berries into a delicious crisp crust (made with homemade lard). She buttered the berries, popped a slitted top crust over the berries, then put the whole affair in the oven of the huge wood burning stove, leaving it to cook, sputter, and ooze juice through the slits.

At dinner time this special plate pie was put before Grandpa as was the little pan of milk, now boasting a thick layer of yellow cream. The cream was skimmed directly on top of the huckleberry pie, and Grandpa ate the whole thing for dessert.

My favorite fruit pie is apple. As a rule, there are fresh apples on hand.

Heat oven to 425 degrees. Combine sugar, flour, salt, nutmeg, cinnamon, lemon juice and butter. Line 1½ quart baking dish with pastry; arrange sliced apples on pastry, sprinkle with sugar mixture. Roll other half of pastry to fit top of dish with ½ inch overhang. Cut several small slits for steam vents. Lay pastry loosely over apples, fold overhang under. Press onto rim firmly with tines of floured fork. Brush top with milk or beaten egg whites for that professional look. Bake 40 minutes or until apples are done and crust is beautifully browned. Serve to 6 hungry people with thick sweet cream, or if your family is the ice-cream-with-everything kind, have vanilla ice cream.

Apple Pie

4 large apples (use firm, tart apples
   or home-grown ones)
1 cup sugar
2 or 3 dashes nutmeg
½ tsp. flour
½ stick butter

Pare and slice apples thin and mix with sugar, nutmeg, and flour. Put in unbaked pastry shell. Chip butter over top of apples; cover with lattice top. Bake in 350-degree oven for 45 minutes. Serve with pouring cream. Some even like a thin vanilla custard to pour over. Vanilla ice cream is very tasty. Serve slightly warm if you are using ice cream.

Low Calorie Black Bottom Pie

Make ginger snap crust first:

¼ tsp. gelatin
3 T. light cream
3 T. butter
1¼ cups ginger snap crumbs
3 drops non-caloric liquid sweetener
1 tsp. cinnamon

Soften gelatin in 1 tablespoon of the cream in a small bowl. Place bowl in a pan of hot water and heat until gelatin is dissolved. Remove from heat; beat in remaining cream and soft butter until smooth and well-blended. Reheat this mixture until melted. Combine crumbs, sweetener, and cinnamon in a bowl. Pour melted mixture over and blend well. Pack crumb mixture into a 9-inch pan, pressing evenly against bottom and sides. Chill crust for 1 hour or bake 8 minutes at 375 degrees. Cool.

Black layer for pie:

1½ tsp. unflavored gelatin
1 cup skim milk
½ square unsweetened chocolate
⅛ tsp. cinnamon
¼ tsp. vanilla extract
6 crushed non-caloric sweetener tablets

Soften gelatin in milk in top of double boiler. Add chocolate and cinnamon; cook over hot water until chocolate is melted. Add vanilla and sweetener; beat to blend. Chill until mixture is slightly thickened, then whip with rotary beater until fluffy. Pour into cooled crust and chill.

Plan to visit with your family at night during the month of July. Supper eaten only a few minutes early will get you out of the kitchen in time to sit in the swing and gently push yourself back and forth. The children will gladly turn off the TV if tales of when they were little are told. Even my great big fifteen year old son enjoys hearing about the cute things he did when quite small. I have a feeling he is remembering them to pass along to his children in the not too distant future.

Dale and I enjoy these sessions with the children, and it is here we hear of their dreams and hopes for the years to come. How sweet to the soul, the heart and the mind to rest in the companionship of your family, while the whip-o-will calls with fluty voice from the pine forest. It is comforting to hear the questing, seeking voice of the tree frogs as they earnestly call upon the heavens for rain that should have come over three weeks ago.

I breathe deeply of the country smells, so dear to all

farm folk. Heady and rich is the scent of the clump of honeysuckle, growing in such rank profusion by the garden fence. Yellow and white, it furnishes a playground for countless bees early every morning. A little breeze comes slipping over the pine forest and tickles the noses with smells of brown and pine needles, freshly cut trees, and turpentine.

Even the hog pen has a smell all its own, smelling of boiled corn, roasting ear shucks and green corn stalks—a farm smell if ever there was one.

Vanilla layer:
   1 envelope unflavored gelatin
   1¾ cups skim milk
   ⅛ tsp. salt
   1 egg
   ¾ tsp. vanilla extract
   9 crushed non-caloric sweetener tablets
   Few drops yellow food coloring

Soften gelatin in milk in top of double boiler; add salt. Separate egg and beat yolk into milk mixture; cook over hot water until mixture coats a metal spoon. Add vanilla, sweetener, and coloring. Chill until slightly thickened. Beat egg white until stiff; beat chilled vanilla pudding until fluffy. Fold in beaten egg white. Pour over chocolate layer in crust. Chill until firm. Decorate top with a few crushed ginger snaps. This pie serves 6, with generous slices—only 179 calories per serving and so luscious tasting you will make it even if there is no need to lose weight.

Buttermilk Pie 1

   3¾ cup white sugar
   ½ cup plain flour
   Dash salt
   2 sticks butter
   6 whole eggs
   1 cup buttermilk
   2 tsp. vanilla

Mix sugar, flour, and salt; add unbeaten eggs, stirring only until blended. Add melted butter (not hot, though), stir a bit. Add buttermilk and vanilla, stir enough to mix. DO NOT OVER-BEAT. Pour into 2 unbaked pie crusts and bake for about 1 hour at 325 degrees.

Buttermilk Pie 2

1 pastry pie shell
⅔ cup sugar
1 cup fresh buttermilk
1 T. flour
½ T. butter
1 tsp. lemon extract
2 egg yolks

To beaten egg yolks add buttermilk, sugar, and butter. Mix well. Beat flour into a little sweet milk and add to mixture; add lemon flavoring. Pour into prepared pastry shell and bake as for custard pie. When baked, spread with meringue made of 2 egg whites and 2 tablespoons sugar. Return to oven and brown meringue. Cool before serving.

Buttermilk Pie 3

1¼ cup sugar
3 T. flour
1 T. meal
2 eggs, unbeaten
½ cup butter
1 cup buttermilk
1 tsp. lemon flavoring
2 tsp. vanilla

Beat eggs; add buttermilk, sugar, and butter, and mix well. Sift flour and meal together; add a little sweet milk to make a thin paste. Add this and the flavorings to the first mixture. Pour into raw crust. Bake at 425 degrees for 10 minute, and then at 350 until center barely sets.

Almost everybody has a sweet tooth and it often hankers for something chocolate. There are chocolate pies, puddings, cookies, layer cakes, pound cakes, custards, candies, sauces, and two favorites with young and old: hot chocolate and ice cream. Truly the saying "food for the gods" applies only to those flavored with chocolate, for chocolate comes from the seeds of a tropical tree called the "theobroma cacao," and in Latin the word "theobroma" means food for the gods.

Always I keep a jar of homemade chocolate syrup in the refrigerator for making a cup of cocoa, to flavor milk shakes or to use for a topping on vanilla ice cream or drizzled over plain cake. To my way of thinking, however, nothing can top or equal a slice of chocolate pie about three inches high—from the brown glaze meringue and beads of syrup peeping through the swirls formed with the back of a spoon right through the creamy chocolate filling and crisp tender crust—served on your best dessert sauce.

Chocolate Pie

2 cups whole sweet milk
2 squares unsweetened chocolate
½ tsp. pure vanilla
Lump of butter size of an egg
¾ cup sugar
⅛ tsp. salt
3 egg yolks plus
1 whole egg
2 T. cornstarch

Scald milk; add sugar, cornstarch, and salt that have been sifted togther. Add melted chocolate and butter. Place over boiling water, cook and stir for 10 minutes. Pour part of this over well-beaten egg yolks, beat well. Return egg mixture to double boiler and continue cooking for 2 minutes longer. Cool, add vanilla, and pour into baked crust. Cover with meringue made with 3 egg whites. Brown in slow 300 degree oven. Cool out of draft. Serve in large pieces to hungry family.

Cocoa Meringue Pie

½ cup cocoa
3 T. cornstarch
2 cups milk
3 T. butter
1 cup sugar
2 egg yolks
1 tsp. vanilla
1 baked 9-inch pie shell

Combine cocoa, sugar, cornstarch, and salt in sauce pan. Add milk slowly, stirring well. Cook and stir constantly until mixture comes to a boil and is thickened. Stir in beaten egg yolks. Cook, stirring constantly, about 3 minutes longer. Remove from heat; stir in butter and vanilla. Cool slightly and pour into baked shell. Top with meringue and garnish with grated coconut or shavings of semi-sweet chocolate. To make meringue, beat 2 egg whites stiff, add 4 tablespoons of sugar, a little at a time, beating until dissolved. Spread over filling. Bake in 325 degree oven until nicely browned.

Caramel Pie

2 cups sugar
4 egg yolks
2 T. flour
2 cups milk
1 tsp. vanilla
3 T. butter

Brown ½ cup of the sugar in small skillet. Do not let it burn, just let it turn to caramel. Mix 1½ cups sugar, flour, milk, and well beaten egg yolks. Cook over hot water; then add caramel syrup to mixture. Cook until thick; add butter and vanilla. Pour into baked pie shell. When slightly cool, cover with meringue made from 3 egg whites beaten until foamy, then beaten again with 3 tablespoons of sugar, added a little at a time, beating well after each addition. Beat until meringue is standing in peaks. Cover the pie right to the crust, making sure the meringue touches the crust and there is no gap anywhere. Bake in 350-degree oven until nicely brown; cool out of draft. Do not cut until cold and do not put under a plastic or glass cover until cold. Once you put any meringue pie under a cover and the cover fogs over, woe to the pie. These pies are delicate and should be eaten within 10 to 12 hours after baking. Don't bake them on Friday for Sunday dinner.

Rose Budd's Recipes for Country Living

Rose Budd's Varnish Remover can be used to take varnish off a bedroom floor, as well as to take off paint. The recipe calls for 1 8-ounce box of Argo lump starch and 2 cups of cold water. Work this into a paste until all lumps are gone. Stir this into two cups of boiling water and cook until thick and very heavy. Remove from fire and take outside and stir in 1 8-ounce box of soda (cooking kind). Use a paint brush to paint on mixture; let stand until varnish begins to soften. Turn hose on full force and wash off paint or varnish (scrubbing with a brush while washing helps). Remember this is not for fancy or good furniture. Before the wood dries you must wash it down with vinegar water. Use 1 cup of white vinegar in a gallon of warm water. Wipe down with old towels or soft rags. Allow to dry completely before painting or revarnishing.

Amazing Coconut Pie

2 cups milk
¾ cup sugar
½ cup biscuit mix
1½ tsp. pure vanilla
4 eggs
¼ cup butter or margarine
1 cup flaked coconut

Combine milk, sugar, biscuit mix, eggs, butter, and vanilla in electric blender. Cover and blend at low speed for 3 minutes. Pour into greased 9-inch pie pan. Let stand about 5 minutes, then sprinkle with coconut. Bake at 350 degrees for 40 minutes. This recipe makes its own crust, so don't try it with a crust or you will have too much crust.

Cherry Pie Filling

1 gallon pitted cherries, packed in water
6 cups sugar
¾ cup flour
Red food coloring

Drain cherries overnight; heat juice to boiling. Mix the sugar with flour. Gently stir this into the boiling cherry juice and cook until quite thick. Add enough food coloring to give a bright red color then pour over drained cherries. Stir and mix until every cherry is coated. Cool and put in jars; store in refrigerator or can as you would anything in water bath. When pie making time comes, add dabs of butter on the bottom crust, pour in proper amount of filling and add more butter. I also like to add 1 teaspoon of almond flavoring to my pie filling. The same method may be used with water-packed peaches, apples or apricots. Your savings comes in buying by the gallon.

Chess Pie

    4 fresh eggs
    1 cup white sugar
    ½ cup sweet cream
    ½ cup butter
    Pinch of salt

Cream butter and sugar together until silver color. Add beaten eggs and salt, cream and beat. Pour into unbaked crust and bake about 30 minutes in a 350-degree oven. This isn't a deep pie and your pie pan should be a shallow one, not over an inch.

One Delicious Pie

In 1948 the recipe below was an instant hit with my readers; the same in 1958. A new generation came along in '68 and again in '79 with many young homemakers enjoying making pies from scratch. Letters came my way saying, "When I was a little girl Mama made delicious pies using a recipe from your column. Please print this baked-in-the-crust pie so that I can have one ready when my children step off the bus," or "I am having a party and want to serve homemade pie like Mama used to make." This is exactly as was published in a 1958 column:

I love easy recipes, especially when they turn out with a real flair. In our family we lean heavily on pies for desserts; it matters not the flavor. I whip up two at one time—for supper and a snack when the school bus brings the children home.

Don't light your oven an hour before putting the pie in to bake. Light oven when you have the crust ready and begin to mix the filling. Bake in a 400-degree oven for fifteen minutes, turn heat down to 300, and bake until center is still real shaky. If you bake until center is firm, you have baked too long and your pie will be stiff. You want a slice of pie to look pretty on the plate with the point sort of melted down a little. How many readers simply cannot resist saving the pie point until the last bite of the pie?

And if I fix a lunch the next day, there is a slice of pie for the lunch box.

¾ stick butter or margarine
1 cup white sugar
2 T. flour
4 eggs
1 cup evaporated milk
1 cup sweet milk
Pinch of salt

Put butter, sugar, and flour in heavy boiler. Mix well. Add eggs one at a time, beating well after each egg. Add milk and salt. I am assuming you will make your own pie crust or if you buy crusts, get the deep-dish kind. A glass pie plate rather than an old black-as-sin pie tin really works best, but a heavy aluminum pie tin is fine. Pour into middle size pie plate. (This amount fills the plate nicely; the coconut and pineapple variations below are the fattest with the extra cup of ingredients.) Bake at 400 degrees for 15 minutes. Turn heat down to 300 and bake until center is still real shaky. In fact, if you stick a knife into the center it comes out with filling sticking to it. The pie continues to bake or set after it has been removed from the oven.

For coconut pie: Add 1 cup of canned or fresh coconut.

For lemon pie: To the juice of two lemons add one teaspoon grated lemon rind. Heat lemon juice but cool it before adding to mixture; this way mixture will not curdle.

For pineapple pie: Add 1 cup of drained crushed pineapple.

For jelly pie: Drop spoonfuls of tart red jelly on unbaked crust; pour plain filling over, adding 1 teaspoon of pure vanilla.

For chocolate pie: Add 1 square of melted chocolate

if you like it medium; for real dark pie, use 1½ square of chocolate. Do not use cocoa; it won't work. And don't mix this pie with a mixer. (This recipe was discovered or invented by Mrs. Elmer Edwards before mixers were standard kitchen equipment.)

For butterscotch pie: In place of ½ cup sweet milk add ½ cup burnt sugar syrup and a drop or so of almond flavoring.

Valerie's Sweet Potato Pie

2 eggs slightly beaten
1 cup sugar mixed with 2 teaspoons flour
1 stick oleo, softened
¾ cup evaporated milk (no substitute)
1 cup boiled and mashed yellow sweet potato
1 tsp. each of vanilla and lemon extract

Mix in order given. When well mixed, pour into 9-inch raw crust, bake at 450 degrees for 10 minutes; lower heat to 350 degrees and bake forty more minutes. Cool before cutting.

My friend Madge Mayer bakes crust in one pie plate, custard in another. Just before serving she gently slips custard into the baked crust. Eaters marvel at the crisp crust. Madge, your secret is out now!

Egg Custard Pie

6 large fresh eggs
1½ cups sugar
1 T. pure vanilla
3 cups whole milk
6 T. butter
Nutmeg (whole, to be grated if possible)

Bring milk and butter to scald point in heavy boiler; remove from heat at once. Beat eggs; add sifted sugar gradually, add vanilla. Add a bit of heated milk, stir well. Continue adding milk a little at a time until all is added to egg-sugar mixture. Line 12-inch pie pan with raw crust, brush with unbeaten egg whites. Strain custard mixture into crust. Grate nutmeg over top. Bake at 400 degrees for 10 minutes; reduce heat to 300 degrees and bake until center barely shakes.

Ripe Elderberry Plate Pie
(Two Crusts)

2 cups elderberries
1 cup sugar
2 T. plain flour
Juice from ½ large lemon

Make your favorite pie crust or like your grandmother did using hog lard, flour, salt, and hot water. Use a shallow pie plate and fit crust in plate with overhang. Take elderberries, mix with sugar (use ¾ cup sugar if you don't like too sweet a filling), flour, and lemon juice (or same amount of vinegar as they did in olden days). Mix all together and pour into bottom crust. Chip butter over top and sprinkle with a little nutmeg if desired. Fit top crust over berries, dampen bottom crust first around edges, press crusts together, and trim neatly. Use fork dampened with water to press well so juice won't bubble out. Cut slits in top crust so steam can escape. Bake in 350 degree for about 25 minutes. Due to such dry weather as we have had here in 1988, it might be necessary to soak berries in water for a few minutes.

Foolish Pie

1 baked pie crust
2 egg whites, beaten stiff
1 tsp. vinegar
½ cup sugar
Your choice of fruit

Beat egg whites with vinegar and sugar, pour in crust, and brown as for meringue. A slow oven does best. Let cool and add sliced ripe strawberries, drained crushed pineapple or, sliced peaches. Just before serving, cover with whipped cream that has been sweetened. Serve in generous slices and be prepared to give out the recipe. Keep in refrigerator; don't make too long before serving. Mrs. Cox says preachers are fond of this pie and say it is foolishly good.

Here it is folks, Foolish Pie, and as pretty as a pink—good too. Serve it to the girls. Never mind that they are pushing 40 or even 70; when women get together it is always girls, and that is as it should be. A cup of coffee or a tall glass of iced tea makes a good companion to this novel, delicious pie.

Grannie Foots

Dried apples or peaches
Sugar to taste
Pie pastry or canned biscuits
Shortening

Cook fruit until tender, following directions on package. Sweeten to taste. Roll out pie dough (or

My Grandmother Budd used home-dried apples or peaches, even pears, to make delicious Lettie Foots or Grannie Foots. We called her luscious fruit pies by these names because her nickname was Lettie, and

canned biscuits) into circles of about four inches in diameter. Place several teaspoons of fruit on one-half of each circle. Turn the other half over fruit. Dampen bottom edge and press edges together with fork to seal (do this before folding crust). Fry in heated shortening until golden brown, and sprinkle with sugar while hot. The variations you can put to Grannie Foots are endless. For a quickie dessert a pint of applesauce, a can of biscuits, and a little sugar will turn out ten of the most tempting little pies you ever saw. Chopped meats—leftovers—mixed with a thick white sauce and highly seasoned, fry up to simply mouth-watering goodness.

sometimes she made tarts as big as her foot. She would use the biggest iron skillet in the group of five given her as a wedding present. The grease would be blazing hot when the "foot" was first dropped in. Aunt Phleta and the hired lady would work as fast as they could, whomping out the dough, spooning out the fruit, and putting a fork crimp or seal to the edges. If all the biscuit dough wasn't used, Grandmother would instruct Aunt Lue to use a tablespoon of wild plum jelly—even a fig or two would be used in a pinch. This made for some interesting swaps among the children who reached in the warming oven, took a bite, then proceeded to "trade off a foot" if the insides were not to their liking.

Green Tomato Pie

1¾ cups sugar
4 to 5 tsp. all purpose flour
½ tsp. ground cinnamon
½ tsp. ground nutmeg
¼ tsp. salt
4 cups thinly sliced green tomatoes
2 T. vinegar
⅛ tsp. ground cinnamon
2 tsp. sugar

Combine first 5 ingredients in a large mixing bowl; stir well. Add tomatoes and vinegar; stir gently to coat tomatoes. Spoon mixture into a pastry-lined 9-inch pie pan. Roll out remaining pastry and carefully place over pie, leaving a 1-inch rim beyond edge of pan; seal and flute edges. Cut several slits in top to allow steam to escape. Combine remaining sugar and cinnamon and sprinkle over top of pie. Cover pastry edge with aluminum foil to prevent excessive browning. Bake at 425 degrees for 30 minutes. Remove foil and continue baking for 15 to 20 minutes. Cool.

Paradise Pie

24 to 28 marshmallows
¾ cup sweet milk
½ pint cream, whipped stiff (measure cream before whipping)
1 small can crushed pineapple, drained

Put marshmallows in milk in top of double boiler and cook stirring gently. Cool, then chill. Stir in drained pineapple, then fold in whipped cream. Now line a pie plate with graham cracker crumbs, fill pie with marshmallow mixture. Sprinkle a few crumbs on top. Place in refrigerator 4 or 5 hours before serving. This is a dessert that is fine for parties or for the ending to a very light meal of soup and crackers or sandwiches and salad. It is very rich, so don't be too generous with the size of the slices.

Molasses Pie

4 eggs, beaten separately
1 pint molasses
1 cup sugar
4 T. butter
2 T. flour
¼ tsp. nutmeg
1 cup pecans

Mix sugar, flour, and nutmeg; add half the molasses, stirring until sugar is dissolved. Add well beaten egg yolks and stir. Add rest of molasses, butter, and broken pecans, mix well. Pour in raw pie shells and bake in 325-degree oven until center barely shakes. Cool out of draft. (Pecans may be left out if desired.) This makes 2 pies. In place of

Mrs. K.M. Graves gave me this recipe for Paradise Pie. She says it is making the rounds of Roxie like the mumps. Make one, then pass the recipe on to a neighbor.

Just let spring come and the cooks of our land begin to want their spring meals. Of course, strawberries seem to take top honors along with egg custards; however, to my way of thinking nothing can beat a slice of molasses pie and a cup of hot coffee for ending a supper on a soft March evening. The recipe here is grand and so easy to make. Make two—for dinner and for the school children, and one for supper. Frankly, you won't find this too much molasses pie in one day.

To those who live in the country and try to live off the land, so to speak, opening a can of sugar cane molasses or syrup is a common thing, something done as soon as the last bit is used from a can. If there is rock sugar formed on the

butter, ham fat (from fried ham) may be used. This is really delicious, giving the pie a smoky tang. Of course, the fat must be from a real hickory smoked ham.

Peach Pie

1 cup sugar, mixed with 2 T. flour
2 egg yolks, beaten with 2 T. water
1 T. butter, cut into small pieces
1½ cups chopped frozen or fresh peaches

Mix all ingredients and put into uncooked pastry shell. Cook 1 hour at 350 degrees. Cover with meringue made of 2 egg whites and 4 tablespoons sugar. Bake 30 minutes at 250 degrees. This meringue is supposed to fall when baked properly, making a kind of crisp crust. Five times out of 10 it won't fall of its own accord, so sit it in a draft the minute you remove it from the stove and hope for the best. It is delicious either way!

Uncle Ben's Wife's Pineapple Pie

2 eggs
½ cup butter
¾ cup sugar
½ cup crushed pineapple

Beat eggs together; add butter, then sugar, adding pineapple last. Turn into raw crust and bake until firm. Make a meringue out of egg whites mixed with sugar. Spread on pie and bake to a delicate brown. Serve this pie in small pieces as it is pretty rich.

side and bottom of the can, then it is melted, a bit of hot water added, and this delicious tasting syrup is used for a super special treat—making a molasses pie.

I love to cook sweets using syrup, for the taste is so different from white sugar cooking. Among our favorites, we list molasses syrup kisses, hot water gingerbread, and potatoes cooked with molasses, making a thick rich buttery sauce to be spooned over slices of cold baked sweet potatoes. To me the growing of sugar cane, stripping, cutting, hauling to a mill for grinding and cooking the juice down to syrup is a romantic event. I still recall with a fresh wave of feeling the years when our children were small and we grew first a few rows of sugar cane in the garden for their chewing pleasure. We banked enough stalks for the next planting season. Always the opening of the seed cane bank was awaited with eagerness, for the children knew they would each be given a stalk to chew some warm spring afternoon.

Quince Pie

1 big ripe quince
1½ cups stewed apples or peaches
 (apples are much better)
Handful of raisins
2 cups brown sugar
Couple shakes cinnamon
Couple shakes allspice

Boil quince until it can be mashed like stewed apples. Mix 1½ cups quince with apples, raisins, sugar, cinnamon, and allspice. Make a very rich pie dough; add 2 tablespoons sugar just as you are ready to roll out. Line pie tin or pie plate with half of dough. Place quince mix in plate and cover with other half of rolled dough. Pinch full of holes to let steam escape; seal edges of crust with water and then crimp. Bake in medium oven until nice and brown. Note: This crust should be rather thick as it a kind of tea cake crust with the sugar. Serve warm with thick cream or cold with sharp cheese.

Lemon Pie

4 large eggs
Scoop of butter, size of large egg
6 heaping T. cornstarch
2 cups sugar
Juice of 2 lemons
½ tsp. vanilla
2¼ cups hot water

Mix cornstarch and sugar. Add well-beaten yolks of the 4 eggs, then blend in soft butter. Add lemon juice and vanilla. Add hot water, stirring all the while to keep from lumping. If you stir well and

When the children began eating lots of syrup, we then planted half an acre of cane, more than enough to "syrup us over the winter." We also planned to sell enough by the stalk to pay for the cans to put the syrup in. We depended on selling cans of the goodness to pay for the fertilizer. The man who ground and cooked the juice down took his pay in syrup, so the "sopping 'lasses" was really free, except for our labor. All we had to do was strip the cane and haul it to the mill on a frosty morning. Can anything beat a trip to the syrup mill, riding high on top of a load of cane?

We always let our sons stay home the day our syrup was cooked. How important they felt as they drove the horse or mule around and around to turn the grinders. They helped fire the roaring blaze under the cooking pan and took turns packing away the bagasse.

I kept the home fires burning and cooked food that could be eaten at the mill out of hand—meat between biscuit halves or cornbread; baked potatoes, Irish and sweet; raw carrots

for our salad; and for dessert, gingerbread or buttered biscuits, dripping with syrup so fresh it still bubbled with heat, as it was dipped directly from the cooking pan to a plate.

Beg or borrow—even buy—enough real sugar cane molasses to make a 'lassie pie. It's a real treat for children and grownups!

all the time, there is no need to cook over hot water. Cook until thick; cool. Fill a large baked pie crust, cover with the beaten whites of the 4 eggs. When the whites are very stiff, add 2 level tablespoons of sugar for each egg, or 8 tablespoons of sugar. Whip well. Spread nearly all of the whites on top of the filling and be sure to let whites touch edges of crust. Bake in medium oven (350 degrees) for about 10 minutes, remove from oven and make several large swirls with the remaining whites. Continue baking until well done and golden brown. In this way, your meringue will never fall. Please don't try to make this pie with flour, for it burns very easily with flour and the cornstarch makes a clear, jelly-looking filling.

Lemon Meringue Pie Supreme

7 T. cornstarch
1½ cups sugar
¼ tsp. salt
1½ cups hot water
3 egg yolks, beaten
2 T. butter or margarine
1 tsp. grated lemon peel
½ cup fresh lemon juice
1 9-inch pie shell, baked

Mix cornstarch, 1½ cups sugar, and salt in a sauce pan; gradually stir in water. Cook over direct heat, stirring until thick and clear, about 10 minutes. Remove from heat. Stir ½ cup hot mixture into beaten yolks a little at a time; stir this mixture into remaining hot mixture. Cook over low heat, stirring, for 2 to 3 minutes. Remove from heat; stir in butter, lemon peel, and juice. Cool. Pour mixture into a baked 9-inch shell and cover with meringue.

Meringue: Beat 3 egg whites (which are at room temperature) with ¼ teaspoon cream of tartar until soft peaks form. Gradually add 6 tablespoons sugar, beating until stiff and all grains of sugar have dissolved. Spread over lemon filling, making sure to seal to edge of pastry. Bake in a moderate oven (325 degrees) until golden brown. Be sure to let pie cool before slicing.

Muscadine Hull Pie

Take 1 full quart plus 2 handfuls of dark purple ripe muscadines, wash and drain. Pop each muscadine over bowl (set aside). Place hulls in heavy boiler and barely cover with cold water. Let boil until hulls are tender. Drain, mash with potato masher, or run through Foley food mill. You should have 2 full cups of fruit. Sift 1 tablespoon plain flour with 1 heaping cup of white sugar; stir into mashed fruit. Have pastry for 2-crust pie. Roll out half of pastry and fit into 9-inch pie plate, leaving ½ inch hanging over the edge. Add hulls and spread out evenly in bottom crust. Roll out other half of pastry, cover hulls. Press top and bottom crusts edges together, making sure they are seal-ed, or you can flute to make them pretty. Cut slits in top crust to allow steam to escape. Bake pie in 375-degree oven for 45 to 50 minutes or until pastry is brown. Juice should bubble through slits and run a bit down crust. Cool pie, serve with real cream.

There is no dish known to cooks better liked, easier to prepare, and prettier to see than Sliced Sweet Potato Pie. This recipe is ages old. Our grandmothers relied on the pie to feed large groups; it could be made, cooked, and put in the pie safe or pantry overnight without fear of becoming spoiled— almost the same as dried fruit pies.

When she was nine years old, one of my aunts, Nettie, decided to surprise her family with one of these pies. Her mother, father, older sisters and brothers were working in the field, leaving Nettie to tend the in-crib baby, the porch baby, as well as the yard baby, and to keep the fire box to the wood range filled with green stove wood, thereby continuing the simmering of pots of vegetables for the noon meal.

Armed with a short handled hoe, Nettie hied herself to the big bed where her father had bedded out sweet potato strings, so there would be plenty draws come next planting time. Of course, the vines were rank and no potatoes of any size were to be had. Nettie had plans for a great big

oversized "Mammy."
Finding none, she filled her
apron with finger-sized
knobby, ridged strings for
her pie.

  Nettie patted self-rising
biscuit dough on the bottom
and sides of a large dutch
oven and added the washed,
unpeeled potato strings.
Failing to open the lard can
where the sugar was kept,
she poured a cup of
sorghum syrup over the
potatoes.

  Knowing full-well that
under no conditions was she
allowed to draw the butter
and sweet milk from the
well, Nettie improvised to
the tune of a cup of chicken
fat (rancid, so the brothers
said years later), and two
cups of clabber milk. More
biscuit dough was patted on
for a top crust. Put into the
hot oven, the crust rose and
browned in a very few
minutes. The family said it
did look lip-smacking good.

  Soup dishes were used to
serve Nettie's sliced sweet
potato pie. Grandfather was
served first. He didn't bat
an eye at the dish of
"horror:" potatoes which
had never become warm in
their bath of sorghum,
rancid fat and clabber—all

No Milk Lemon Pie

1 cup sugar
1 T. butter
3 T. flour
2 eggs
¼ tsp. salt
3 T. lemon juice
Grated rind of 1 lemon
1 cup boiling water
1 tsp. baking powder

Mix sugar, flour, baking powder, and salt together. Add water, stirring slowly. Add butter, beaten egg yolks, lemon juice, and rind. Pour into raw crust and bake in medium oven. When pie is done, cover with beaten egg whites made into a meringue, brown lightly. Cool out of draft.

Jelly Pie

Make a nice crust, flute the edge. Spread a thick layer of tart jelly (red looks best) on the crust. Pour (easy does it) egg custard on top of the jelly, grate a bit of nutmeg on top and bake in a slow oven. Please do not put egg white on top of this pie. I make what we call Apple Cheese Pie, using apples that have been stewed in place of the jelly. Both are mighty good eating.

Oatmeal Pie

⅔ cup sugar
2 eggs, beaten
⅔ cup melted butter

⅔ cup white Karo syrup
⅔ cup uncooked oatmeal (regular or quick)
⅛ tsp. salt
1 tsp. vanilla extract
Pastry for 8- or 9-inch pie

Mix all ingredients together and pour into pie shell. Bake 1 hour at 350 degrees. This pie tastes like pecan pie, and is good for someone who cannot eat nuts. This recipe is from one of my favorite cookbooks, *Eufaula's Favorite Recipes.*

Pumpkin Pie

1½ cups cooked and strained pumpkin
½ cup plus 1 T. sugar
¼ tsp. nutmeg
½ tsp. cinnamon
½ tsp. ginger
¼ tsp. salt
2 eggs, well-beaten
1 cup whole milk

Mix cooked pumpkin with spices, salt, and milk. Heat through and add eggs. Pour in raw pie shell and bake in hot oven for 10 minutes. Lower heat to 350 and bake until firm but not stiff. Serve with whipped cream.

Sliced Sweet Potato Pie

4 medium-sized yellow sweet potatoes
1 cup white sugar
⅓ tsp. each nutmeg, cloves, and cinnamon
1 tsp. ascorbic acid mixture (important)
½ cup butter
1½ cups rich milk or thin sweet cream

raw underneath the browned biscuit dough crust.

Happily Aunt Nettie didn't let this dire failure keep her from becoming an excellent cook. In my salad days she was always urged to bring Sliced Sweet Potato Pie to all the family to-dos or get-togethers, where she was teased about her first pie. There was always a new niece or nephew, relative or visitor who had never heard the tale, which was retold with much knee slapping and laughter.

For a really special pumpkin pie, grate rind from three oranges into one pound of brown sugar. Stir well and when you go to make your pie add the required amount of sugar along with the mixed-in orange rind. The sugar seems to candy the rind if it is left to set for a few days. A few raisins added to the pie custard is delicious, and I like currants if they can be found. A meringue is delicious on this pie, that is if you only use enough pumpkin to flavor the custard.

1 tsp. lemon extract
Pinch salt

Peel and slice the potatoes. Place in enamel pot, cover with hot water, add ascorbic acid mixture (keeps potatoes bright and yellow). Bring to boil and simmer about 5 minutes. Drain and layer in a deep pastry-lined dish. As you layer potatoes sprinkle each layer with sugar and spices, dot with bits of butter. Pour milk or cream over potatoes until almost covered, top with raw pastry, cut slits for steam to escape. Bake at 450 degrees for ten minutes. Reduce heat to 325 and continue baking until potatoes are tender, about 40 minutes. Serve warm with a thin egg custard or sweet cream. Delicious plain when cold; good with tall glasses of milk.

Vinegar Pie

1 cup sugar
3 T. flour
3 large egg yolks
1 cup water
2 T. butter
4 T. cider vinegar
1 8-inch baked pie shell

Sift flour and sugar together. Add egg yolks and water, stirring briskly to mix. Drop in butter. Set over low heat and cook, stirring constantly, until smooth and quite thick, about 8 to 10 minutes. Remove from heat and add vinegar in a slow stream, beating all the while. Cool. Spoon vinegar filling into baked, cooled pie shell.

For the meringue use 3 large egg whites, beaten to stiff peaks with 6 tablespoons sugar added as you beat. Of course you will beat the whites to stiff froth before adding sugar 1 tablespoon at a

Do any of you remember the vinegar pies of your youth? People made them in the days before they could get lemons easily. My grandmother would always make a vinegar pie when she had fish, or any other bland meat. Even if she had lemons on hand, she would mix up a vinegar pie for her family. Grandmother cooked her pie in a raw crust, and I have never been able to get the knack of it. I have served some pretty sorry vinegar pies to my family trying to hit upon the exact recipe grandmother used.

time. Spread meringue on top, making sure it touches the crust all around. Swirl into peaks and valleys, using a thin-bladed knife or spatula. Bake in moderate oven for 8 to 10 minutes or just until meringue is lightly brown. Cool pie to room temperature before serving. It will taste almost like lemon pie.

Foolproof Pastry

6 cups plain flour
1 pound shortening
1 T. brown sugar
2 tsp. salt
¼ tsp. baking powder
1 egg yolk
¾ cup cold water
1 T. vinegar

Sift flour, salt, and baking powder. Cut in shortening and brown sugar. Mix egg yolk, cold water, and vinegar and add to flour mixture. Knead until the dough sticks together. You will find this dough to be very pliable and easy to handle. It keeps well in a plastic bag, up to a month in the refrigerator. Back when we raised a lard hog, I used firm white hog lard instead of the shortening, which made a much flakier crust.

Hot Water Crust

½ cup shortening
½ tsp. baking powder
½ tsp. salt
¼ cup boiling water
1¼ cups flour

Never throw away a speck of fat—chicken, turkey or duck. Cookies and pie crusts made from this fat are delicious and have a very delicate crisp air. If you have more fat than you need, melt and pour into a small tin can. Cover with waxed paper and freeze or store in a cool place. Mama and I are always pleased when someone gives us a jar of chicken fat, for then we know we can turn out something real special at our house.

Cut shortening into flour and add salt and baking powder. Add water and work up very fast. Roll out very thin and use as any other pie crust. This dough can be kept for several days in a jar by the side of the ice, or if you have a refrigerator, make up a batch and keep on hand. It improves with age and is just as flaky and tender as cold water crust. Fill with raw custard and bake or make a fruit pie for supper with this dough. I use it for apple tarts and for cheese straws—just add grated cheese and red pepper, and roll thin. Cut into strips and serve with tomato soup or salad.

Cold weather calls for fruit pies made the old-fashioned way, with two crusts. The top crust can be latticed, crossover, plain with slits or with pretty designs cut into the crust. Having a batch of ready-to-roll pastry in the refrigerator also seems to give the cook extra time to dream up other good foods for the family.

On-the-Shelf Pastry Mix

2 cups flour
1 tsp. salt
⅔ cup shortening

Sift flour and salt. Cut shortening into flour with pastry cutter, or use fingertips and rub flour into fat until it looks like coarse meal. This is enough for 3 small single crusts, or 2 10-inch double crusts. Five to 6 tablespoons of cold water will be enough to dampen this mix.

Pastry Mix

5 cups sifted all-purpose flour
1 T. salt
2⅓ cups vegetable shortening

Sift flour and salt into large mixing bowl. Cut shortening into flour with pastry blender until pieces are about the size of small peas. Store in a covered container. For 2 crusts use 2 heaping cups mix, and enough water to hold it together.

Pastry Mix

2 pounds lard
8 tsp. salt
14 cups sifted plain flour

Sift flour and salt. Cut in cold lard, using pastry blender, or let one small girl child work it well with her hands. She will enjoy the task and your mix will be crumbly and just right. I would suggest a large dishpan or stone crock for this mixture. About like small peas is the aim of this mixing. Place in a container and store in refrigerator. I find a gallon ice cream carton fine for this.

When I eat a bad crust, one that is too thick, tough or soggy, I always wonder why cooks don't get a good recipe and follow it to the letter. Nothing can take the place of pies in the homes of America, and I for one am proud of my pie crust. Either Hot Water Crust or Cold Water Crust is easy, but I use the hot water method the most. I have tried milk crusts but the little added food value isn't worth the trouble to make milk crust.

Candies, Cookies, & Other Sweet Treats

Too many wonderful old customs dear to the hearts of country folks have passed away. Now, if a smart young thing wants to have a party that will be a hit with the others in the crowd, she asks some of the older folks for ideas. Among them are square dances, box suppers for fund raising, play parties where all sorts of games are played, and, of course, the wonderful custom of making candy in the kitchen with all hands helping.

My children love to hear me tell of how we used to go to candy pullings and pull great ropes of molasses candy, a strand as big as my wrist. Your boyfriend would help you, and if the candy suddenly became a little bit soft, all that was needed was a cooling on the back porch, where it was really cold. Big platters were well-buttered, and when candy reached that glossy state, one knew it was time to begin twisting and stretching on the candy, to get those beautiful curves that would catch the light and reflect it as if it were made of satin. While several held the twisted candy, the mother or grown sister would cut the pieces about as long as your finger from the end of the long twist. These pieces then were put on the buttered platter to harden.

After the mess had been cleaned away and the failures were hidden, the candy was served along with hot cocoa, teacakes or cupcakes, pickled peaches, and often sandwiches. If enough of the candy was a success, we were filled to the brim and sick to death of the very thought of pull candy. If any was left, it was divided and we carried several pieces home wrapped in butter paper, so our folks could see what a whiz we were with candy making.

Buttermilk Fudge

2 cups granulated sugar
1 cup fresh buttermilk
½ cup butter
¾ tsp. baking soda
Few grains salt

Put soda in buttermilk and let stand 3 minutes. Mix with sugar and butter; add salt and cook to a soft ball stage. Cool and beat until creamy. Add nuts or coconut. Pour on a greased platter and cut into squares. Delicious and different is the word for this buttermilk fudge.

This recipe for Buttermilk Fudge was copied out of the **Woman's Home Companion.** *I tried it and it was wonderful. Now with sugar on sale at some of the stores at ten pounds for 46 cents, who could ask for a cheaper candy? Make up a big box for the Christmas party you are sure to have.*

*F*udge Cuts *is a recipe that is a favorite with Marguerite Piazzo, American lyric soprano who hails from Memphis. Of course, she didn't send me the recipe, but a friend of hers did and I have found it good. Try it for the children in their lunch boxes.*

Fudge Cuts

2 squares (2 ounces) unsweetened chocolate
½ cup fresh butter
1 cup granulated sugar
2 eggs, well beaten
½ cups all purpose flour
¼ tsp. salt
1 tsp. vanilla
½ cup finely chopped pecans

Melt chocolate and butter in top of double boiler. Remove top part from water, and blend in sugar; then eggs. Add flour and salt, stir well with a spoon. Add vanilla. Pour into two greased 8x8x2 baking pans. Spread smooth, sprinkle with nuts. Bake in moderately hot oven (400 degrees) for 12 minutes. Cool, cut into 2-inch squares. Makes about 32 squares. I do not advise trying to double this recipe. If you want more, mix and bake twice. It is just a little more than you can handle easily when doubled.

Chocolate Dream

1 cup plain flour
1 stick butter
1 cup chopped pecans
1 cup confectioner's sugar
1 8-ounce pkg. cream cheese
1 cup whipped topping
1 small pkg. instant vanilla pudding
1 small pkg. instant chocolate pudding
2 cups sweet milk

Mix flour, butter, and pecans. Spread in the bottom of an 8x12 pan or 10-inch skillet. Bake about

20 minutes at 350 degrees. Let cool. Mix confectioner's sugar with cream cheese, fold in whipped topping; spread this on the cooled crust. Mix puddings with milk, spread over cream cheese layer. Spread remaining whipped topping over pudding layer. Decorate with grated chocolate bar or drizzle melted sweetened chocolate over top. Chill well and serve in squares.

Coconut Strips

2 eggs
2 cups brown sugar
2 cups dry coconut
¼ cup nut meats
6 T. flour
¼ tsp. vanilla

Beat eggs, add other ingredients. Bake in moderate oven (350 degrees) in buttered and floured pan 9 inches square, or long narrow pan. Cut while warm into finger-sized strips. Use either boxed or canned coconut. Fresh grated simply won't work, so Mrs. G.L. Crawford tells me. Mrs. Crawford was kind enough to share this recipe with me, and now with you. These chewy strips are fine for company and home eating too.

Collard Candy

2 T. butter
2 cups sugar
½ cup white vinegar

Put the butter in a heavy pot and let it melt but not boil or burn. Add sugar and vinegar. Stir with a wood paddle until the sugar is dissolved, then

Not too long ago someone wrote asking for a recipe called Collard Candy. I asked, searched, and had no results. But this morning the woman who helps me three times a week brought Rose Jr. a small dish filled with green bundles. The green was pieces of collard

leaves wrapped around candy. I asked her what in the world it was and she said, "That is collard candy. My grandmother always makes a batch or two for her grandchildren when we dig peanuts." I got in my car and drove to Aunt Callie's to find out about the collard candy. Aunt Callie is very old, and this is what she told me— sounds so reasonable now that I know.

boil without stirring until a drop or so will be brittle in cold water, like sweet gum cracks. Have a big platter buttered and turn candy into it right away. As the candy cools, fold the edges into the center. When cool enough to handle, butter your fingers and thumb and pull the whole batch until it is full of little holes and light white. Make a long rope out of candy, then take shears and cut off little snips; let fall on a buttered plate or old piece of marble slab. When cold, wrap two pieces in a piece of collard leaf until all is wrapped. Seems as if the collard leaves play no part in the candy except "folks long time ago didn't have waxed paper . . . and something had to be used to keep it from sticking together."

Divinity

2 cups sugar
Few grains salt
½ cup corn syrup
½ cup water
2 egg whites
1 tsp. vanilla

Place sugar, syrup, water, and salt in saucepan and cook over slow heat. Stir until sugar is dissolved, then cook without stirring until syrup forms a very firm ball when dropped in cold water. Just before syrup reaches this point, beat egg whites stiff but not dry. Pour syrup in a fine stream over egg whites, beating constantly. Continue beating until mixture holds its shap. Beat in vanilla. Drop from tip of spoon onto wax paper. Makes about 1¼ pounds.

Irish Potato Candy

1 Irish potato (size of an egg)
Confectioner's sugar

1 tsp. pure vanilla
Pinch of salt
Peanut butter

Boil potato until tender. Mash well and start adding confectioner's sugar, a small amount at a time, until 1 pound has been added. Add vanilla and salt. Potato should be cool before adding sugar. Shape into round as for pie crust, then roll out on a board sprinkled with more confectioner's sugar. Spread with peanut butter, roll up like a jelly roll, chill several hours, and slice. By the way, if the dough is too thin, add more sugar; if too thick, a few drops of sweet cream will do the trick.

Fruit Roll

1 quart shelled pecans
1 pound graham crackers
½ pound shelled walnuts
1 small bottle red cherries
1 package dates
½ pound raisins
1 pound marshmallows
½ cup Pet milk
½ cup sweet milk

Melt marshmallows in milk in top of double boiler (over hot, but not boiling water). Crumble crackers into big crumbs, reserving 1½ cups in large flat dish. Pour hot milk-marshmallow mixture over nuts, dates, raisins, crumbs, and cherries, which have been drained. Mix well, shape in long roll. Roll in remaining crumbs until well coated. Chill several hours before slicing with a sharp knife.

Nut Oatmealies

1 cup shortening
½ cup honey

Christmas candies always seems to top the list of things given and made in the home. This Fruit Roll recipe is delicious, very easy to make, and keeps well if stored in a cool place.

I have been enjoying the little fires we have at night for the last few nights, just a small one to take the chill off the room and to give a warm glow to the living room. I take the flat iron and the hammer and sit myself down on a low stool for about an hour of nut cracking. The last of the black walnuts, the pecans, and the hickory nuts all come in for their share of cracking. I put them in separate pots to pick out when the rains come or I get time to pick out a cup for cookie baking.

I use black walnuts for the icing on a three-layer silver ribbon cake, hickory nut filling for a ten-egg yellow cake, and pecans toasted and added to a caramel pie—all good and easy to prepare, and easier still to eat. Pecans toasted and ground fine and added to the cookie dough for after-school nibbling or for gift giving or company— nothing can be nicer than a big plate of these ground pecan cookies, with coffee or cold sweet milk.

1 tsp. soda
½ cup semi-sweet chocolate pieces
¼ cup minced cherries (maraschino)
2 cups sifted all purpose flour
½ tsp. salt
1 cup quick-cooking rolled oats
½ cup chopped nuts

Cream shortening and honey, blend in nuts, chocolate, and cherries. Stir in soda, flour, salt, and oats. Mix well. Drop by teaspoonful onto ungreased cookie sheet. Bake at 400 degrees for 10 to 12 minutes.

Orange Pecans

1 cup sugar
½ cup hot water
2 T. orange juice
Pinch of salt
1 orange rind, grated
2 or 3 cups pecans

Cook sugar in hot water until syrup reaches soft ball stage or 230 degrees. Add orange juice, rind, and salt. Cool 1 minute. Add pecans and beat until creamy. Pour and spread on waxed paper. When cool, cut or break into desired-size pieces.

Penuche

3 cups light brown sugar
1 cup sweet milk
¼ tsp. salt
3 T. margarine
1½ tsp. vanilla
¾ cup nut meats

Combine sugar, milk, and salt in sauce pan over low heat. Cook until mixture forms soft ball when dropped in cold water; stir frequently to prevent curdling or sticking. Remove from heat, drop in butter, and cool to lukewarm. Add vanilla; beat until candy is creamy and loses its gloss. Add nut meats and turn into greased shallow pan. When firm cut into bars. Makes about 1½ pounds.

Lollipops

3 cups sugar
1 cup Karo syrup
2 cups water
Few drops food coloring
Few drops flavoring

Pull straws from your mama's broom; cut in short pieces, as long as your father's finger. Set aside. Mix sugar, syrup, and water, and boil until a little dropped in cold water is brittle and cracks. Add color and flavoring. Warning: Do not use a peppermint flavor if you use orange coloring, or blue coloring if you use a strawberry flavor. Beware of using nut flavorings such as coconut, walnut, and thicker nut. It's best to use known colorings and flavorings: green for mint, red for strawberry. Vanilla flavoring is good if your mama has no coloring. Put wax paper on a table, and spoon the warm mixture in puddles onto the paper. Put one end of a straw in the middle of each puddle; make sure the other end does not touch the puddle below it. When hard, tear lollipops apart and pull the wax paper off. If it won't come off, don't fret; the one who eats the most lollipops will eat the most paper.

Oatmeal Crispies

1 cup shortening
1 cup white sugar
1 cup brown sugar

Looking through my recipe file, I lucked upon this recipe for Lolly Pops (lollipops) written by Rose Jr. before she started school. She made these goodies often on days when the air was cool and crisp, the sun like liquid gold.

2 eggs, well-beaten
1 tsp. vanilla
1 tsp. soda
1 tsp. salt
1½ cups flour
3 cups 3-minute oats
1 cup chopped nuts

Cream shortening and sugars well and add eggs and vanilla. Sift together soda, salt, and flour; add to creamed mixture. Mix and add oats. Form in a roll and chill, slice very thin, and bake on ungreased cookie sheet at 350 degrees. Added hints: Nuts are grand if you have them, 1 cup chopped is about right. Chill your baking sheet before putting the cookies on. Save small tin cans, pack with the dough, slip dough out, and slice.

Syrup Kissie

10 cold biscuits
2 new-laid eggs
1 cup sweet cream
1 cup thick cane syrup
1 tsp. vanilla
⅛ tsp. salt
1 T. butter
½ cup sweet milk

I am assuming that your biscuits are about the size of a teacup and about an inch thick. Split each biscuit and place in a single layer in a large baking pan. If your heavy skillet is large enough, use it. On each biscuit put just a dot of butter. Beat eggs until foamy, add syrup, vanilla, and salt, and beat with an egg beater until well mixed; add sweet cream and milk. Mix again and pour over the biscuits. Bake in a moderate oven until it is just set. Serve either warm or cold, but be sure to save a second helping for the baby.

Give me a gallon of cane syrup and I can make desserts for three months that are good to eat, easy on the pocketbook, and wonderful to look upon. What kind of kitchen smell can beat the wonderful fragrance of hot ginger bread made with cane syrup? Here are three wonderful cane syrup desserts: Syrup Kissie, Drop Cookies, and Syrup Drink for Children.

White Pull Candy

1¼ cups sugar
¼ cup water
1 tsp. vanilla
2 T. mild vinegar
1½ tsp. butter

Oil a platter with vegetable oil or unsalted butter. Place the sugar, water, vinegar, and butter in a deep sauce pan; stir over heat until sugar is dissolved. Increase heat slightly and cook without stirring until a candy thermometer registers 268 degrees or until a small amount of the syrup forms a hard ball when dropped into cold water. Remove pan from heat and add vanilla. Stir only enough to blend mixture. Pour candy onto platter, and let cool until a dent can be made in it when pressed with a finger. Gather it into a lump and pull with fingertips until it is light and porous. Dip hands frequently in cold water to prevent candy from sticking to them. Twist into long thin strips and cut with scissors dipped in cold water, about 1-inch pieces. If you wish candy to become creamy, place in a tightly covered tin for a few days.

Easy Pralines

1 pkg. butterscotch pudding powder
1 cup white sugar
½ cup brown sugar
½ cup evaporated milk
1 T. butter
1½ cups pecans

Mix first five ingredients together; cook and stir over low heat until sugar dissolves. Add pecans.

Boil 3 to 5 minutes or until soft ball stage. Beat until shiny. Drop on waxed paper.

Peanut Brittle

1 cup white syrup
2 T. soda
1 tsp. vanilla
1½ cups water
3 cups raw peanuts
½ stick butter or margarine

Boil sugar, water, and syrup until it spins a thread; add peanuts and stir constantly until syrup turns golden brown. Remove from heat, add remaining ingredients; stir until butter melts. Pour up quickly on 2 cookie sheets with sides. As mixture begins to harden around the edges, pull until thin.

Banana Oatmeal Cookies

1½ cups sifted flour
1 cup sugar
½ tsp. baking powder
1 tsp. salt
¼ tsp. nutmeg
¾ tsp. cinnamon
1 egg, well-beaten
1 cup mashed bananas (2 to 3 bananas)
1¾ cup rolled quick oats
½ cup chopped nuts
¾ cup shortening

Make sure your bananas are fully ripe (yellow peel flecked with brown). Sift together flour, sugar, soda, salt, nutmeg and cinnamon. Cut in shortening. Add egg, bananas, rolled oats, and nuts. Beat

Mama always baked using homemade lard and grated nutmeg from a whole nutmeg. These nuts came in a small wood box. Included inside was a darling little grater. These graters are prized as collectibles.

until thoroughly blended. Drop by teaspoonfuls, about 1½ inches apart, onto greased cookie sheet. Bake in 400-degree oven for about 15 minutes, or until done.

Remove from pan at once. Cool on rack or clean cloth. Store when cool in container with tight-fitting lid. If you don't have pecans or other nuts, parched peanuts are fine. If you buy salted nuts for this recipe; use only ¼ tsp. salt.

Bourbon Balls

1 pound vanilla wafers
2 to 4 jiggers whiskey
1 cup chopped nuts (more if needed)
1 cup powdered sugar
1½ T. white Karo
2 T. cocoa

Crush wafers. Mix all ingredients and roll about a teaspoon of mixture into a ball; roll in powdered sugar.

Budd Cookies

½ cup brown sugar, firmly packed
1 large egg or 2 small ones
½ tsp. salt
¾ tsp. pure vanilla
1½ cups graham flour
1 T. dry cocoa
¾ tsp. cloves

Mama made up this recipe for Budd Cookies out of what she had back during the Depression. We ate them with such relish she decided to try to sell a few dozen to buy some things for our Christmas. She put the high price of 10 cents a dozen on them, and after the first dozen went into a home, the orders poured in. All I remember about that

Christmas was we were so busy picking pecans and beating and pounding cookie dough, Christmas came before we knew it! Ten cents was a big price, but you got a lot for your money, for the cookies were bigger than the top of a teacup. They were delicious and filling, filled with pecan pieces and tasty with spices, and there was a certain flavor you were never quite sure about. After the first one was eaten you had to try another to recall that lingering flavor.

¾ tsp. allspice
¾ tsp. nutmeg
¾ tsp. cinnamon
¾ cup cane syrup
¾ cup butter or fat
½ tsp. soda
1 cup whole grain oatmeal
3 T. strong coffee
1 cup whole raisins
Grated rind of 1 big orange
1 cup pecan halves, chopped

Sift dry ingredients together including salt and soda. Cream butter or fat with sugar, then add syrup. Add unbeaten egg, stir well. Add flour mixture, then oatmeal, and last, pecans. Mix well again. If mixture is not thick enough, add enough white flour to make medium dough. Drop a try on a tin plate that has been greased lightly. Bake 15 minutes or until medium brown in a 350-degree oven. Try it and if it is not sweet enough add 3 tablespoons of white sugar to unbaked dough, and work again. This makes cookies slightly sticky on the inside, which is their chief delight. If you have more pecans, add them. And do try to get lard or butter: the modern shortenings just won't work. You will be happier if you have real mule-ground-cooked-in-an open-pan syrup, but store bought will do, if it is real cane syrup and not man-made. If your cookie tins are dark with use, put a sheet of foil paper over and grease; drop cookies on foil. This way they won't burn so easily.

Brownies

¾ cup plain flour
1 cup white sugar
5 T. cocoa
¼ tsp. salt
½ cup shortening
2 eggs, unbeaten
1 tsp. vanilla extract

In a large bowl, sift flour, sugar, cocoa, and salt. Add shortening, eggs, and vanilla extract. Beat for 3 minutes by hand, scraping sides often. Grease bottom of a 6-inch square pan, spread dough evenly in bottom. Bake at 350 degrees for about 30 minutes. Test with finger to see if it springs back just a little. Do not overbake.

Best-Ever Brownies

¾ cup sifted plain flour
1 cup sugar
5 T. cocoa
½ tsp. salt
½ cup shortening
2 eggs, unbeaten
1 tsp. vanilla extract
½ cup nuts, chopped (optional)

Place all ingredients except nuts in large bowl and beat by hand for 3 minutes. Grease bottom of 6-inch pan (square). Spread batter evenly in bottom. Bake 30 minutes in 350-degree oven. Let cool in pan, cut in squares. Do not use mixer; it makes brownies dry.

Now that picnic and backyard eating time is here, one of the favorites for dessert is a batch of Brownies. These are never-fail goodies, rich, moist, chewy, and very fattening. Here is a helpful hint about baking brownies: If you have trouble with the bottom getting too brown before the middle and top get done, then toss out all those old dark tins and invest a few harvest dollars in a set of glass or aluminum cake pans, cookie sheets, etc. Perhaps you are tempted to remind me that cornbread and quick cakes baked in an iron skillet turn out fine. That's well and good, but that metal was black to start with and not caused from an accumulation of grease, dishwater, etc., being baked on layer by layer over a period of years.

Rose Budd's Recipes for Country Living

To make single bar of lye soap, you will need ½ cup cold water, 1 cup melted beef tallow, and 2 heaping teaspooons commercial lye. Slowly add the lye to the water, then bring both lye solution and tallow to about body temperature. Combine the two in a glass or stainless steel bowl and mix slowly and steadily with an egg beater until the mixture is the consistency of sour cream. Pour mixture into a mold that has been greased with petroleum jelly. Remove soap after 24 hours and allow to air dry for a few days.

Caution: Lye is higly caustic and should be washed off immediately with cold water if it comes in contact with the skin.

Favorite Brownies With Icing

1 cup sugar
2 eggs
1 tsp. vanilla
2 squares baking chocolate
½ cup shortening
½ cup flour
½ cup nuts

Mix as for any other cake, beating the eggs well, adding the softened shortening to the sugar and vanilla, and then combining the two mixtures, adding the flour and melted chocolate, then the chopped nuts. The mixture will be rather thick. Spread it in a greased pan—an oblong shallow one is best. Bake in 350-degree oven until straw comes out clean. Let cool in the baking pan.

Icing: 1 cup powdered sugar, 2 tablespoons cream, 2 tablespoons butter, and 3 tablespoons cocoa mixed together and placed over low heat until edges begin to bubble. Remove from heat, let cool and then beat until creamy; pile thick and swirly on top of the brownies.

Brownie Icing

Pinch salt
1 cup powdered sugar
1 T. cocoa
4 T. evaporated milk
1 T. soft oleo

Place in boiler and mix well. Place over low heat, stirring all the while. When bubbles form around boiler edges, cook for just a few seconds, remove from heat, and beat until creamy. Pour at once over the hot brownies in the pan. Let cool, cut, and serve, or store in pan until used. A half cup of chopped pecans can be added to icing before spreading over brownies, or can be sprinkled over iced brownies.

Cheese Dates

1 pkg. pitted dates
24 pecan halves
½ pound sharp cheese
2 T. margarine
1½ cups flour
½ tsp. salt
½ tsp. red pepper
Paprika

Stuff each date with pecan half; roll in granulated sugar. Work grated cheese, melted margarine, sifted flour, salt and pepper into a stiff dough. Cover each date with cheese dough. Garnish generously with paprika and bake at 300 degrees for 40 minutes. Do not brown. Makes 24 cheese dates. Better make two measures, as these call for seconds.

Date Bars

1 cup sugar
3 egg yolks, beaten
1 tsp. vanilla
¼ cup butter or margarine, melted
1 cup all purpose flour
1 tsp. baking powder
Pinch salt

The pesky crows gave us trouble with corn planted in the early spring. We put out poison, killed one or two, and hung them on fishing poles in the fields and felt we had driven the crows off to happier hunting grounds or wherever crows go when they find they are no longer wanted.

Long ago we realized the futility of making a scarecrow from one of my dresses and the most awful looking hat we could find. The crows merely came and sat in a circle on the ground and made sassy faces and laughed their harsh caw-caw. Other crows in a festivous mood would join them and make the fields ring with their gay going-on.

This year we slept on our laurels. The crows left and we never dreamed they would return—to ruin many watermelons. Strings strung this way and that over the

3 egg whites, stiffly beaten
1 cup dates, chopped
¾ cup pecans, chopped

Gradually beat sugar into beaten egg yolks. Add vanilla and melted butter, blending well. Fold in stiffly beaten egg whites. Add flour sifted with baking powder and salt. Blend well, stir in dates and nuts. Pour into 2 shallow, greased pans (6x8); bake in moderate oven (350 degrees) about 20 minutes. Makes about 4 dozen bars when cut. The shallow pans are almost a must, and two are better than one large one.

Foolproof Cookies

1½ cups white sugar
4 cups plain flour
Pinch salt
1½ tsp. cream of tartar
1 cup shortening
2 eggs
1½ tsp. soda
1 cup ground raisins
1 cup chopped nut meats

Mix as for any other cookie recipe. The dough will be stiff and you pinch off small pieces of the dough. Place on a well-greased cookie sheet. Take a fork, dip in cold water, and flatten the dough real thin. Bake in moderate oven until light brown. Serve with hot cocoa and hot biscuits with a piece of boiled ham tucked in each one after it has been buttered.

Hot Water Ginger Bread

¼ cup shortening

½ cup sugar

1 tsp. cinnamon

1 tsp. cloves

1 cup boiling water

1 scant tsp. salt

1 cup molasses (old-fashioned syrup, if possible)

1 tsp. ginger

2 tsp. soda

2½ cups plain flour

1 beaten egg

Cream shortening and sugar; add syrup and boiling water. Mix thoroughly; sift dry ingredients together twice and add to hot syrup mixture, mixing well, stirring up and over, and making sure to get all dry materials scraped from bottom and sides. Add beaten egg and stir again. Bake in medium oven (350 degrees) in well-greased skillet or muffin tins, or in two layers for a stacked cake. Serve with icy cold applesauce.

Now that the weather is getting a bit cool in the afternoon, why don't you try a measure of Hot Water Ginger Bread? If you bake layers, you can fill them with a cup of sugar, half a cup of sweet cream, pinch of salt, and one-half teaspoon vanilla, cooked to soft ball stage, then beaten until creamy. A few chopped pecans added to the filling won't be amiss.

Drop Cookies

1 cup raisins

½ cup brown sugar

2 eggs

½ tsp. soda

¾ tsp. vanilla

¾ tsp. allspice

¾ tsp. cinnamon

1½ cups graham flour

1 T. cocoa (for color)

1 cup nut meats
¾ cup cane syrup
½ tsp. salt
¾ cup fat or butter
¾ tsp. cloves
¾ tsp. nutmeg
1 teacup raw oatmeal
3 T. strong coffee
Grated rind of 1 orange

Mix dry ingredients; cream fat, sugar, and syrup, add unbeaten egg, and stir well. Add dry ingredients, mix well, then add raisins and pecans, followed by coffee last. If mixture is not stiff enough (due to different brands of flour used), add enough white flour to make dough medium. Drop on cookie sheet from end of large spoon. Bake about 15 minutes until medium brown. Try one and if sweet enough add three more tablespoons white sugar to uncooked part of dough. This makes them slightly sticky on the inside, which is their chief delight.

Ginger Bread Sauce

½ stick butter
¾ cup sugar
1 can apricot and applesauce baby food
Pinch salt
1 T. rum flavoring

Melt sugar and orange juice, but do not boil. Add other ingredients. Serve over warm ginger bread. Keeps well in refrigerator.

Skillet Ginger Bread

2 eggs
¾ cup brown sugar, packed well
¾ cup melted shortening (not butter)
2½ cups plain flour
1¾ tsp. soda
2½ tsp. ginger
½ tsp. baking powder
1 cup boiling water
¾ cup country molasses
1½ tsp. cinnamon
½ tsp. cloves
½ tsp. nutmeg

Add well-beaten eggs to the sugar, molasses, and melted shortening. Then add the flour, in which the spices, soda, and baking powder have been sifted. Beat well and lastly add the boiling water. Bake at 325 degrees for 30 to 40 minutes. This also can be baked in a heavy oblong cake pan, so they say, but I have never baked it that way.

Ginger Crackles

2 cups sifted plain flour
1 T. ginger
2 tsp. baking soda
1 tsp. cinnamon
½ tsp. salt
¾ cup shortening
1 cup sugar
¼ cup molasses
1 egg, unbeaten

Do you and yours enjoy cookies, but lean toward the same ones baking after baking? If so, do get out of your cookie rut and make a batch of Ginger Crackles. They are delicious and so pretty, very easy to make and bake. They freeze well and taste wonderful with milk, especially buttermilk.

Rose Budd's Recipes for Country Living

Many people who want to use lye soap use washing machines and therefore have no use for bar lye soap. To make soft lye soap, dissolve 1 can of lye in 11 cups of water, 11 cups of grease (grease drippings that have been strained), and ½ cup of borax. Stir mixture occasionally when you think of it. It takes about 24 hours for the soap to be done. This soap contains lots of water and is stirred frequently, so it doesn't form into cakes. It looks very much like large-curd cottage cheese. Kept in covered plastic containers, it doesn't dry out and dissolves quickly in hot water.

1 T. sifted cornmeal
Nuts may be added if chopped fine
Granulated sugar

Measure flour, ginger, soda, cinnamon, and salt into sifter; sift twice and return to sifter. Cream shortening, add sugar gradually, beat in egg and molasses; sift dry ingredients over creamed mixture, blend well. Form dough in balls about 1-inch in diameter, roll in granulated sugar and place about 2 inches apart on ungreased cookie sheet. Bake in 350-degree oven for 12 to 15 minutes or until tops are slightly rounded, crackly, and lightly browned. Makes about 4 dozen.

Dixie Molasses Wafers with Ginger

1 cup molasses
½ cup butter
3 tsp. soda
3 cups flour
3 tsp. ginger
1 tsp. salt

Bring molasses to a boil; add butter, ginger. and salt. Add soda dissolved in a little milk. Mix well; add flour, stirring in gradually. Roll mixture and add flour if necessary; knead well. Roll thin, cut, and bake in 375-degree oven on greased tins. Let cool without removing from tins.

Guess Who Cookies

1½ cups white sugar
Pinch of salt
1 cup shortening
1½ tsp. soda
1 cup ground nuts
4 cups flour
1½ tsp. cream of tartar
2 eggs
1 cup ground raisins
1 tsp. vanilla or lemon flavoring

Mix as for any other cookie, adding nuts and raisins. The dough will be stiff; you pinch off small pieces, roll between your hands, place on a greased cookie sheet, then flatten out with a fork that has been dipped in cold water—the thinner the better. Bake in a moderate oven until light brown. Served with hot tea you have a party cookie. Cold milk or hot cocoa is most welcome by the children.

Prize Winner Ice Box Cookies

½ cup butter or margarine
1 cup granulated sugar
2 tsp. vanilla
1 egg
1¾ cups sifted flour
½ tsp. baking soda
½ tsp. salt
½ cup chopped nuts

A reader sent me a recipe that was very good. I made cookies by this recipe and gave boxes of them at Christmas. The recipe was put away or lost and forgotten. Several weeks ago I went to a tea and discovered a most delicious cookie. Upon asking for the recipe I was told it was the recipe I had in my column years ago. Since the first printing many young girls have grown up, married, and now have tots of their own to make cookies for. Again I am printing this recipe—sent to me by goodness knows who.

Cream butter, add sugar gradually, continuing to cream until well mixed. Add vanilla and unbeaten egg, beat until blended. Sift dry ingredients together, add nuts. Gradually add to sugar mixture, stirring well after each addition. Shape in long rolls about 2 inches in diameter on waxed paper. Chill in ice box several hours, overnight, or even a week if you like. Slice ⅛- to ¼-inch thick; bake on ungreased pan at 400 degrees for about 7 minutes. Watch closely because they burn easily. Remove from pan while still warm; cool on clean cloth or wire rack. Store in air-tight container and be assured they will be crisp for a week.

A favorite winter dessert at our house is about three pear halves and some juice in a deep dessert dish, then sweet cream is poured over, and a sprinkle of brown sugar goes on before we sit down to eat. Thin crisp lemon cookies go with the pears nicely.

Ice Box Cookies a La La

2 ¼ cups flour
1 tsp. soda
½ cup brown sugar
2 well-beaten eggs
½ cup chopped nuts
½ tsp. cinnamon
½ tsp. salt
½ cup white sugar
¾ cup melted shortening (not butter)

Sift flour, soda, salt, and cinnamon together. Melt shortening; add sugar, then well-beaten eggs. Mix the dry ingredients into the sugar, egg, and shortening mixture; add nuts. Shape into roll on waxed paper; chill in refrigerator for several hours before slicing. Bake in a medium oven until lightly brown.

Just Cookies

1 cup shortening
1 cup brown sugar
1 cup white sugar
2 cups whole grain oatmeal
  (not the ground kind)
2 cups nuts or dry shredded coconut
1 tsp. salt
2 tsp. vanilla
2½ cups flour
2 eggs
3 tsp. baking powder
A few grains of nutmeg or cinnamon

Melt shortening, add sugar, and stir. Add beaten eggs, coconut or nuts and oatmeal. Add flour with sifted ingredients. Mix well, add a bit of sweet cream if needed to make dough stick together. Form in marble-sized balls, press out on ungreased cookie sheet with a fork dipped in cold water. Bake until light golden brown in a 350-degree oven. Remove from cookie sheet while hot. Cool on a wire rack or a nice clean cloth.

Little Nettie Cookies

5 pounds plain flour
2 cups country molasses
2 cups sugar
1 cup pure lard
2 large eggs
2 T. soda
2 T. ginger
1 tsp. allspice

In my pre-salad days whenever my sisters and I began to get on Mama's nerves or in her way, she would say, "Now, you girls take your dolls and tea set, go out, and keep Little Nettie company."

Back in those days I never thought to ask to whom Little Nettie had belonged. There was no marker at her grave, even though it was covered with seashells and had an urn for flowers. Someone had thought enough of Little Nettie to put four solid heart pine posts down and build a sharply pitched roof over the grave. The roof also was made of solid heart pine boards. In the summer the board dripped amber rosin in long strings that hardened and became brittle.

Little Nettie's grave was in the side yard—a yard in which no chicken or dog ever set foot. This side yard was used to hang special garments that had been washed in rain water. A former church bench was placed on bricks so the legs wouldn't come in contact with the ground. Here is where Grandmother Budd would take her ease in the

*morning sun. Once she
entered the yard and hung
her bonnet on the gate we
knew she was not to be
bothered—no matter what.*

*Whenever we did ill-
mannered things, Daddy
would say, "Why don't you
all be good? I know Little
Nettie would never do that."*

*We put flowers in the urn
at the head of the three-foot
grave and we always fixed
a nest of grass for the
Easter Rabbit to bring Little
Nettie a bright egg or
candy.*

*Time rocked on, and
once a storm roamed over
the country and down came
the roof over the grave.
When our sons came along
they found the shells over
Little Nettie's grave and
asked about them. I asked
my father who Little Nettie
was and he said, "I have
no idea. The grave was
there when I first remember
anything." I asked my Pa
about the grave and Little
Nettie. He said he had no
idea who was buried there.
He said that he asked his
grandmother, who said the
grave was there when she
came to Shady Rest as a
bride, and that was before
the Civil War.*

Our sons were so

1 tsp. cloves
1 tsp. cinnamon
¼ tsp. salt

Sift flour into dough tray or container small enough to press flour down firmly and make a deep well in the center. Mix soda with molasses and stir well. Beat eggs slightly; add sugar, sifted with spices and salt. Add molasses, mix well; add lard and beat. Pour this mixture into well with flour. Using your hand or heavy spoon, stir gently around and around gathering up a little flour at a time. (Do this the same way biscuits are made when lots of flour is sifted into dough tray or pan used for making biscuits. Leave flour in container to be used in another biscuit-making spree.)

Make a rather hard dough. Remove from container. Have pastry cloth or waxed paper on counter. Roll out thin as if you were making dumplings. Cut into strips. Place on lightly greased cookie sheet and bake at 350 degrees about 15 minutes. Remove at once, even though they may be a bit limp. Once they are cold they are crisp and delicious.

Store in air-tight container. They are grand tasting with buttermilk or skim milk.

Crisp Molasses Cookies

1¼ cup unsifted flour
1 tsp. baking soda
¼ tsp. salt
¼ tsp. ginger
6 T. butter or margarine
⅔ cup sugar
⅓ cup light molasses
1 large egg

On wax paper, thoroughly stir together the flour, baking soda, salt, and ginger. In a medium mixing bowl cream the butter and sugar; beat in the molasses, then the egg; gradually stir in the flour mixture. (Batter will be very soft.) Using level tablespoons of the batter, drop several inches apart onto greased and floured cookie sheets. Bake in a preheated 350-degree oven until lightly browned around edges, 8 to 10 minutes. Let stand out a minute to become firm enough to remove with a wide metal spatula. Cool on wire racks. Store in a tightly covered tin box. Makes about 3 dozen.

Molasses Oatmeal Cookies

1½ cup syrup
2 cups whole oats
1 tsp. cinnamon
1 tsp. nutmeg
1 tsp. cloves
1 tsp. allspice
½ cup sugar
3 eggs
¾ cup butter
¼ cup milk

interested in Little Nettie they wanted to do something to remember her, so they came up with the idea of baking a batch of cookies in her memory. We did, and to this very day, I bake a sort of sugar-molasses cookie and call it Little Nettie Cookies.

1 tsp. soda
1 cup nut meats
1 cup raisins
Enough flour to make a very soft dough

Combine all ingredients. If not soft enough, add another egg. Dough should be soft enough to run a little bit when you drop it on the cookie sheet. They are wonderful warm from the oven when served with cold milk or cold peaches.

Peanut Butter Cookies

1 cup butter
1 cup brown sugar
1 cup white sugar
2 eggs, well-beaten
1 cup peanut butter
1 tsp. vanilla
1 tsp. soda
2½ cups flour

Cream butter and sugar. Add beaten eggs, peanut butter, and vanilla. Sift flour and soda together and add to mixture. Mix well. Roll into balls and press with fork. Bake in pre-heated oven at 375 degrees for about 10 minutes, on a greased cookie sheet.

Raisin Oatmeal Cookies

1 cup flour
1 tsp. baking powder
½ tsp. salt
¼ tsp. nutmeg
⅓ cup sweet milk
3 cups quick oats

1 tsp. cinnamon
Grated rind of 1 orange
¾ cup butter
1 cup brown sugar
2 eggs
1 cup raisins
1 cup nut meats

Sift dry ingredients into bowl. Add shortening, brown sugar, eggs, and half of the milk. Beat until smooth, about 2 minutes. Fold in remaining milk, nuts, raisins, and oats. Spread mixture in well-greased pan and bake in moderate oven for 15 minutes. Let cool in pan and cut into squares.

Sugar Cookies

3 ⅓ cups flour
1 tsp. baking powder
½ tsp. salt
1 cup butter or butter substitute
1½ cups sugar
2 eggs
Few grates nutmeg

Cream butter and sugar. Add eggs, one at a time, beating well after one egg is added. Sift together flour, baking powder, and salt; add to butter, sugar, and egg mixture. Add nutmeg. Chill well, roll on floured board, and cut into squares (saves rolling scraps of dough). Decorate with nuts or colored sugar. Bake in a moderate oven or 300 degrees if you use gas or electricity.

If Mother Nature continues to shower us with warm days, sunshine and cool nights, there will be flowers to spare for Valentine decorating. Some years in the past I have had to scratch pretty hard to find enough purple violets to fill our ages-old "Valentine violet dish." Often I have crawled under the edge of the porch, turned back drifted leaves to pick a few brave violets blooming under the blanket of leaves—just enough to look pretty and perky in grandmother's silver thimble, about five or six blooms with a green leaf for accent. Dale wonders if there isn't something just a wee bit the matter with a person who sets a store by violets for

Valentine, and pussy willow limbs for St. Patrick's Day in March.

Grandmother Budd made a little party for Valentine, using her best dishes and always a few purple violets for a center piece. We would have hot cocoa, homemade ''light'' bread spread with fresh churned butter, which was then fried in a black iron skillet, heart-shaped tea cakes iced with pink frosting, and a dish of peppermint stick candy (part of a ten-pound sack given to her at Christmas).

I remember I would go directly to Grandmother's from school. It was a delightful thrill going into the dining room where a fire took the late afternoon February chill from the air. Aunt Phleta, our unmarried aunt, would pour the cocoa from a real chocolate pot into small cups said to be hand painted. The cups were so small we often drank six or seven cups of the rich sweet brown brew, relishing the click of the little feet on the cup as they met saucer. The pitcher was eight sided; a different flower, very tall and elegant, was painted on

Tea Cookies

1½ tsp. baking powder
1½ cups plain flour
1 tsp. salt
½ cup margarine
1 cup sugar
1 egg
1 tsp. vanilla extract
1 T. milk

Sift flour, baking powder, and salt together. Soften margarine (almost to melt stage), then cream into flour mixture. Beat in sugar, then egg, vanilla, and milk; cream well. Gradually add flour from an extra ½ cup until dough is stiff enough to roll. Chill well. Place on lightly floured board and roll to ⅛-inch thick. Cut with lightly floured cookie cutter and place on lightly greased cookie sheet. Sprinkle with sugar. Bake at 400 degrees for 8 to 10 minutes.

Eggless Tea Cakes

1½ cups sugar
½ cup water
1 tsp. vanilla
½ cup lard
1 tsp. salt
1 tsp. baking powder

Mix all ingredients well and add enough flour to make a dough easy to handle. Roll out on floured cloth or board, cut in squares, and bake in moderate oven until lightly browned around edges.

Tea Cakes

⅓ cup butter
1 cup sugar
2 whole eggs
½ cup buttermilk or clabber
½ tsp. soda
1 tsp. baking powder
3 cups flour
½ tsp. vanilla
½ tsp. lemon extract

Cream butter and sugar well; add eggs that have been beaten together. Add flavorings. Mix well and beat for 2 minutes. Sift flour and baking powder and add half of it to above mixture. Dissolve soda in sour milk and stir it in. Add remaining flour, and mix well. Roll on lightly floured board about ¼-inch thick; cut in squares or in rounds the size your family likes them. Bake on well-greased baking sheet for about 15 minutes at 375 degrees. Watch the first batch to see just how long it takes your oven to get them to the right degree of brown your family likes. Store in an air-tight container after they have cooled. I like to spread a clean towel on the table and turn the whole sheet out at one pop.

Old-Fashioned Tea Cakes

3 cups plain flour
2 tsp. baking powder
1 cup sugar
½ cup butter
2 eggs
1 tsp. vanilla or your choice of extract

each side. There were eight cups and each one had a flower to match one on the pot. The cups not having height, the flower was painted around the cup. One cup also had a flower painted on the inside—the oldest grandchild was honored with this cup.

What have you planned, party-wise, at your house this Valentine Day? Bake a batch of sugar cookies, make cocoa, and don't forget the marshmallows. The recipe below is quick and has a good crunch.

These Old-Fashioned Tea Cakes were made by mothers 50 or 60 years ago—no fuss, frills, very little bother. Only the rolling out and cutting in squares took extra time. But when there were small children in the house playing in the kitchen, napping under the big table on a folded quilt, mothers weren't always in a rush and seemed to get pleasure keeping the stone churn filled with tea cakes.

Sift together flour and baking powder. Cream butter and sugar well; add well beaten eggs and mix well. Add flour mixture and flavoring; mix. Roll dough thin, cut in squares, and bake 8 minutes. Watch carefully and do not let them get too brown. Eat some while hot with a glass of buttermilk. If you want to be fancy and fix a surprise for schoolchildren, make a little chocolate icing, spread it on a tea cake and top with another tea cake for a cookie sandwich.

200 Cookies

1½ cups butter
3 cups sugar
6 tsp. vanilla
3 eggs
1½ tsp. soda
1½ tsp. salt
5¼ cups flour
1½ cups finely chopped nuts

Cream butter and sugar until light and fluffy. Add vanilla and eggs and work until well-blended. Sift dry ingredients together and gradually add to sugar mixture, stirring well after each addition. Add nuts. Shape into long rolls, chill for an hour or so and roll on floured cloth. Cut in fancy shapes and bake on ungreased pan in 400-degree oven. Cool on wire racks or clean cloth. Decorate with icings, colored sugars, colored coconut, nuts, chocolate bits, raisins, little silver balls, etc.

John Ransom's Favorite Thumbprint Cookies

¼ cup sugar
½ cup butter
1 cup flour
1 tsp. vanilla
Granulated sugar
Tart jelly

Cream butter and sugar, add flour, then vanilla. Chill thoroughly. Shape in 1½ -inch balls. Roll in granulated sugar. Indent with thumb and fill with tart jelly. Bake slowly, on greased cookie sheet, for 15 to 20 minutes at 350 degrees, until jelly bubbles. Makes 2 dozen.

Dried Apple Pudding

1 cup dried apples
2½ cups plain flour
½ cup molasses
¼ cup brown sugar
½ cup buttermilk
1 tsp. soda
½ tsp. cinnamon
¼ tsp. cloves
2 T. butter
2 eggs

Soak dried apples overnight; squeeze some of the water from the apples and chop fine. Beat eggs; stir in buttermilk, brown sugar to which butter and soda have been added, and molasses. Sift and measure flour; add spices and sift again. Gradually add and mix flour into first mixture. Pour into

My Grandmother Budd dried apples in season when apples were heavy on the trees at Shady Rest. She made tarts or fruit pies, two-crust pies, and stewed up a batch of the dark, leather-appearing apples for sauce. We even ate the sweet sticky slices when hunger pangs came. A recipe enjoyed hot or cold was rich, dark Dried Apple Pudding.

greased baking pan; bake in 325-degree oven for about 1 hour. Serve with roast pork, hot corn bread muffins and snap beans. This is delicious with pork gravy dipped over.

Bread Pudding

½ stick butter
1 quart milk
4 eggs
2½ cups sugar
½ loaf stale poor boy bread
¾ cup raisins
1 T. pure vanilla
¼ tsp. mace

Spread soft butter over 12-inch round baking pan. Mix eggs, sugar, milk, vanilla, and mace well; stir in raisins. Add pieces of bread and allow to soak 10 minutes. Pour gently into the pan. Bake in a 375-degree oven until pudding is firm; remove from oven. Increase oven to 425 degrees. Carefully pour ½ cup of liquid whipping cream over top of pudding; then sprinkle ⅓ cup of sugar over the top; add chipped pieces of ½ stick of butter over the sugar. Bake 10 to 15 minutes. This is said to serve 6 to 8 people, but it is so delicious and rich that 10 people can be served from this pudding pan.

Evelyn Bain's Baked Fudge Pudding

2 eggs
½ cup butter
⅛ cup flour

A delicious bread pudding recipe is a treasure to keep right inside the cover of your favorite cookbook. The one given here is such. What I like about this bread pudding is that there is no saving biscuits, loaf bread ends, or stale crackers. Read and make bread pudding for supper later on in the next week. You see, you will need to buy a loaf of po' boy bread (French bread) and let it become slightly stale for best results.

When I bake a bread pudding, I remember one woman who always saved a slab of her last bread pudding to put in her weekly pudding, made each wash day, which was Wednesday, come rain or shine. When she was ready to make her pudding, she went to the pie safe (on her long back porch) and took down a stone crock where she had stashed away anything in the bread line. One child would be sent to the hen house to get eggs, and if none were there all the children were sent to

½ tsp. vanilla
1 cup sugar
1 heaping T. cocoa
1 cup nuts
Pinch of salt

Beat eggs well; add sugar and continue beating until well mixed; fold in cocoa, flour, salt, vanilla, melted butter, and nuts. Pour in greased pan. Set in hot water and bake 45 minutes. Cool and serve with whipped cream or ice cream.

Cornstarch Pudding

3 cups whole milk
5 T. corn starch
4 T. sugar
1 egg
¼ tsp. salt
½ tsp. vanilla extract

Scald 2¼ cups milk. Combine and stir in corn-starch, 3 tablespoons sugar, ¾ cup milk, and salt. Add mixture to scalded milk, stirring all the while. Continue to stir and cook over low heat until it thickens. Beat egg, add 2 tablespoons sugar, pour in some of the hot mixture, heat, and return all to boiler. Stir over low heat until mixture thickens slightly. Remove from heat and cool at room temperature, add vanilla, and chill. Serve with stewed fruit or fruit sauce. Makes 6 servings.

Lemon Pudding

2 T. butter or margarine
⅔ cup sugar

look for hidden nests. In fact, once when we were visiting this home, I was given the honor of going to the pasture with a daughter to help milk a cow for the pudding milk.

I remember our aunt sending Cornstarch Pudding to Shady Rest by the mail rider when Brother and I were housebound with chicken pox.

Monday morning is a commanding sort of morning, isn't it? So many things needing to be done—the house is usually tumbled after a nice, long lazy Sunday afternoon (most of us leave the Sunday night dishes until morning). The children getting off to school after two mornings free can play havoc with the nerves of an iron woman.

*Let's give just a bit of
thought to late Sunday night
after the children are in
bed, fresh from a bath and
well filled from a bedtime
snack, and prayers have
been said. The dishes are
stacked with care. Now pick
up books, magazines, and
papers and put them in
their right places. Any
clothes left out should be
put away, school clothes
placed handy, and your
husband's work clothes
placed on a chair. Of
course, you will start the
day in fresh, clean
garments—not a long,
droopy housecoat or
robe—so place your cotton
house dress and a clean
apron close by. Brush up
the living room and, the last
thing before you go to bed,
fix the breakfast table.
(Many women sort their
wash on Sunday night, but
to me that smacks too much
of actual labor on Sunday.)
Monday is all-too-often a
day given over to house
cleaning and washing, with
little thought for food. Just
take the Sunday leftovers
and put them with this
Lemon Pudding for dessert,
and your Monday night
supper is a hit!*

2 tsp. grated lemon rind
Pinch salt
2 eggs
2 T. lemon juice
2 T. flour
1 cup milk

Cream butter or margarine in a 2-quart bowl. Add sugar, ⅓ cup at a time; cream until fluffy. Beat egg yolks till thick, add with lemon juice and rind to butter sugar mixture; mix well. Fold in flour, pour in milk, and stir gently until mixed. Beat egg whites until just stiff enough to form peaks (should be still moist). Fold into first mixture until just blended. Pour pudding into a greased 1-quart baking dish. Set dish in a pan a little larger. Pour boiling water into pan to a depth of 1 inch; place on middle shelf of moderate oven (375 degrees). Bake until lightly browned on top.

You will be delighted with the top layer firm and the soft creamy custard underneath. This will serve four well. If the servings appear small, remember this is very rich and a little goes a long way.

Dessert Pancake

1 cup lukewarm milk
1 tsp. lemon rind
1¼ cups flour
2 well-beaten eggs
1 cake yeast
1 tsp. salt
1 T. sugar

Soften yeast in a little warm water; add to the beaten eggs and milk. Stir in remaining ingredients. Beat until well-blended. Cover and let rise in warm place for about 1½ hours. Do not stir, but very carefully lift by tablespoon and fry on a well greased hot griddle. Serve spread with butter and your favorite jelly or cinnamon and sugar mixed.

Persimmon Pudding

2 cups persimmon pulp
3 eggs
1¾ cups milk
2 cups flour
½ tsp. soda
½ tsp. cinnamon
½ tsp. nutmeg
1 tsp. salt
1½ cups sugar
3 tsp. melted butter

Mix pulp, beaten eggs; add milk and dry ingredients alternately; stir in melted butter. Pour into greased pan about 2 inches deep. Bake 1 hour at 300 degrees.

Orange Sauce

1 tsp. grated lemon rind
1½ tsp. lemon juice
½ cup orange juice
1 tsp. vanilla
2 egg yolks, slightly beaten
⅛ tsp. salt
2 egg whites

To my way of thinking good living can cover many things, such as making a big batch of cookies for the cookie jar or an extra measure for freezing or giving away. Good living can mean saving odd bits and pieces of money from selling eggs and butter, then storing in the sugar jar to use later to treat the whole family. It also can mean walking by the heavy-fruited persimmon tree and gathering enough persimmons to make Persimmon Pudding.

Our middle child, Tim, was always happy when Persimmon Pudding was on hand for an after-school snack. He claimed this pudding didn't break, bend, run, sag, or get messy. He could put a nice piece on a big tea cake and take off for the woods, barnyard, or just the yard to play.

Persimmon time is as near as the first hard frost. Many of us have our mouths primed for a good bite of these delicious fruits of field and yard. True, there are those who simply cannot wait and stash persimmons in the freezer, hoping for the same effect as a frost. Others pour scalding water over the just-pulled 'simmons. I have tried both ways and the results were not to my liking. I like to wait until the frost has turned the persimmons into sugar before making Persimmon Pudding, which can be eaten warm, frozen, and thawed. Or serve it with pouring cream, ice cream, or even the whipped topping bought in the frozen food sections of stores.

If you want to start eating persimmons before first frost, wash and drain persimmons and put in the freezer for about two hours. They will be almost the same as those eaten after a sharp frost. After you have frozen your persimmons, run them through a sieve or Foley food mill to get the two cups of pulp you need for this recipe.

When my boys were little fellows and even into their teens, Woodford Pudding was their favorite "something that is real good, can be eaten out of hand, and doesn't crumble when you bite it—also something that won't break

Combine first five ingredients; place over low heat. Stir constantly until smooth and thick. Remove from fire. Add salt to egg whites, beat until stiff, fold into sauce, cool, then add vanilla. This will make about 1¼ cupfuls.

Lemon Sauce

⅓ cup butter
1 cup sugar
3 egg yolks
⅓ cup boiling water
3 T. lemon juice
Few gratings lemon rind

Cream butter and sugar gradually. Add egg yolks, slightly beaten, then add water and cook over boiling water until mixture thickens. Remove from heat; add lemon juice and rind.

Woodford Pudding

3 eggs
Scant cup plain flour
1 tsp. soda
½ tsp. cloves
1 cup blackberry jam
1 cup sugar
Scoop of butter size of large egg
3 T. buttermilk
¼ tsp. allspice
¾ cup finely chopped nuts

Beat eggs and add sugar while beating. Add soft butter; sift spices with flour, mix, then dissolve soda into buttermilk and add. Stir in jam and nuts, bake in pudding pan (I use biscuit pan) that has 2-inch sides. In fact, a 13 by-9-by-2 pan holds this recipe just right. The corners of this pudding cake are muchly desired by my boys. Each corner usually sort of turns over on itself. It's crispy on two sides, and soft yet not crumbly on two sides.

Thin Egg Custard

4 T. sugar
2 tsp. cornstarch
1 cup thin cream
½ tsp. vanilla
3 egg yolks
Few grains salt
½ cup milk
Sprinkle of nutmeg

Mix sugar, cornstarch, and salt. Stir in thin cream. Heat over boiling (not too rapid) water, pour in slightly beaten egg yolks, stirring constantly. Add milk, vanilla, and nutmeg. Continue to cook over water until mixture coats a spoon. Remove at once and pour into a cool bowl. Cover so a skim will not form. When cool, chill well.

Ramon's Old-Fashioned Freezer Ice Cream

6 whole eggs
2 cups sugar
2 T. flour
2 quarts sweet milk (whole)
½ pint whipping cream
Pinch salt
1 tsp. pure vanilla extract

out faces fast." The pudding cake recipe fills the bill in every way. You can bake it and leave it in the pan, or cut and remove it as soon as it comes from the oven—suit yourself.

Thin Egg Custard sauce will dress up the most simple dessert of chilled fresh fruit. I make this recipe tripled and pour into custard cups, add a spoon of tart jelly and serve with slices of pound cake. For sick folks this custard is just right, as it gives a hint of sweet, and isn't too heavy.

This is fine for large bunches of children. Take six slices of store bread, break in small pieces, and place in well-buttered baking dish. Over this pour a very rich egg custard, flavored with just a hint of chocolate. Bake in slow oven. Serve with plenty of sweet cream. cream. It is truly grand, as each piece of bread swells to twice or three times its normal size, and what a mouthful of sweet custard a piece makes. Sometimes I use maple, lemon or just vanilla in the custard.

Put milk in large boiler to heat slowly. Beat eggs until light yellow. Sift together sugar and flour; add to mixture. After egg and sugar mixture is thoroughly mixed, add small amounts of hot milk until about half the milk has been added. Then return egg, sugar, and milk mixture to the large container holding rest of the hot milk, which has been removed from the fire. Place over low fire and heat thoroughly, stirring with a wooden spoon or paddle. Do not allow mixture to boil as it will curdle. Do not use spoon that has been used to stir tomato relishes or other spiced dishes. Remove from heat, allow to cool at room temperature; add salt and vanilla. Place mixture in ice cream freezer; pour the pint of cream, which has been lightly whipped, on top of mixture. Freeze and stand by with bowl and spoon for some smacking good eating.

Caramel Ice Cream

2 quarts sweet milk
1 tall can evaporated milk
2 cups sugar
6 eggs, well-beaten
½ cup sugar, caramelized, to which ¾ cup hot water is added to make syrup
2 tsp. vanilla
Few grains salt

Scald sweet milk, evaporated milk, and sugar. Burn sugar (the ½ cup) in a heavy skillet, add hot water, and cook and stir until a syrup is made. Stir caramelized syrup into scalded milk and egg mixture. Beat eggs and then add other hot mixture a little at a time, beating as you add. Cool and add vanilla and salt. Freeze in a dasher-type freezer.

Refrigerator Ice Cream

6 eggs
4 T. cornstarch
1 quart whole milk
1 quart thin sweet cream
¾ cup sugar
Vanilla to taste

Mix sugar and cornstarch, then well-beaten eggs, then whole milk. Cook over hot water until thick; add sweet cream and cool. Turn into large tray of freezing unit of the refrigerator. When frozen 1 inch from sides, beat well, add vanilla, and return to tray. Stir 3 times before serving. It is just as tasty as the cranked-in-the-freezer kind. It doesn't keep too well overnight for it gets too icy. I never have any left over anyway. When I make cream custard, I make enough for a gallon and freeze half for dinner and half for supper.

Peach Melba

4 scoops vanilla ice cream
4 canned peach halves
½ cup heavy cream, whipped stiff
1 ounce brandy
4 maraschino cherries
2 T. minced pistachio nuts

Put a peach half on each dessert plate with a scoop of ice cream on top. Sprinkle with brandy and pile on whipped cream. Top with a cherry and sprinkle with nuts. If you have no brandy, raspberry may be substituted, or for a different dish, mint sauce.

The figs are here! Don't you just love to pick them and when they are chilled in the ice chest, call the children and everyone sits down on the porch and eats figs, cheese, and crackers until you can touch them. I make crisp tart shells and store in a tin box. Then I make a clear Lemon Sauce, pile half the frozen figs in tart shells, pour Lemon Sauce on, and serve at once. This is wonderful served with real mint tea.

Uncooked, Hand-Cranked Ice Cream

1 tall can Pet milk
1 quart sweet cream
2 tsp. vanilla flavoring
5 eggs
1 quart whole sweet milk
1¼ cups sugar

Beat eggs well; add sugar gradually, beating well after each sifting of sugar. Add vanilla, then Pet milk that has been mixed with whole milk. Pour this mixture over the whipped cream, mix, and immediately pour into freezer. I like to add a pinch of salt to my ice cream. Makes it taste more creamy, if you know what I mean. Crushed strawberries are good added to this mixture. Mashed bananas are fine if you plan to eat and not store this recipe. Crushed peppermint stick candy makes a pleasing flavor, and if you want something extra special, caramelize ½ of the sugar, toast a cup of pecans (without butter and salt), and when crisp, crush with rolling pin. Add just before freezing. This ice cream is something to make you lick your chops about, and ask for seconds.

Index